Christmas
2003

John —

Merry Christmas —

Enjoy this
informational
book —

Love
Mary Beth

ANTI-CATHOLICISM
IN AMERICA

ANTI-CATHOLICISM IN AMERICA

The Last Acceptable Prejudice

MARK S. MASSA, S.J.

A *Crossroad Book*
The Crossroad Publishing Company
New York

The Crossroad Publishing Company
481 Eighth Avenue, New York, NY 10001

Library of Congress Cataloging-in-Publication Data

Massa, Mark Stephen.
    Anti-Catholicism in America : the last acceptable prejudice / Mark S. Massa.
      p. cm.
    Includes bibliographical references and index.
    ISBN 0-8245-2129-3
    1. Anti-Catholicism – United States. I. Title.
  BX1770.M28 2003
  305.6′2073 – dc21

                                              2003005351

To Ned Mattimoe, S.J.,
and Jerry Reedy, S.J.

Optimi Magistri

Any archeological account involves the creation of a past in a present and its understanding. Archeology in this sense is a performative and transformative endeavor, a transformation of the past in terms of the present. This process is not free or creative in a fictional sense, but involves the translation of the past in a delimited and specific manner. The *facts* of the case become facts only in relation to convictions, ideas, and values. However, archeology would amount to an exercise in narcissistic infatuation if it *only* amounted to a deliberate projection of present concerns onto the past. The archeological record itself may challenge what we say as being inadequate in one manner or another. In other words, *data* represents a network of resistances to theoretical appropriation. We are involved in a discourse mediating past and present, and this is a two-way affair.

—Michael Shanks and Christopher Tilley
Re-Constructing Archeology

Contents

Part Two
CRISIS IN
AMERICAN CATHOLICISM

Introduction

To be called "prejudiced" in the United States today constitutes one of our culture's most damning accusations. For as that word is most commonly understood, prejudice refers to an irrational or unfair bias against particular racial, ethnic, religious, or gender groups based simply on characteristics of affiliation — for instance, distrusting people of Scottish descent simply because they are Scottish, or suspecting all New Yorkers of dishonesty only because they are New Yorkers. In its most common usage, then, prejudice has the connotation of both immorality and illegality. Such biases against certain groups of people — or against their beliefs and customs — are widely understood to be based on immoral bases of judgment, irrational or self-interested fear, ignorance, or willful hatred; and result in illegal bases of action, biased behavior that discriminates on the basis of characteristics that have little or nothing to do with job qualifications or the right to live in certain neighborhoods. As such, prejudice is always — quite correctly — decried and condemned as morally demeaning both to the person who is prejudiced, and to the person against whom such bias is directed. It is, in any case, against the law of the land when it is used to deny people their rights on the basis of skin color, belief, ethnic background, or gender.

But the literal meaning of prejudice refers to neither immoral discrimination nor illegal bias. Indeed, the word's Latin roots have a far more neutral meaning. The two Latin words from which our English word derives, *pre* and *judicio*, mean simply "pre-judgment" and refer simply to pre-rational and unexamined beliefs and standards that everyone — including morally good and law-abiding people — carries around all the time. In this *literal* sense of the word, everyone has "prejudices" or "prejudgments" about a vast array of things that navigate them through daily life. Among other things, these pre-judgments save people time every morning by freeing them from having to decide anew whether to put on their socks or their shirt first. They form the screen through which the

1

world is seen, understood, and lived in. Prejudices in this sense of the word are neither morally good or bad, nor legal or illegal, but simply constitute part of the apparatus by which human beings interpret their world.

For instance, all parents (hopefully) share the "prejudice" or "pre-judgment" that their children should not play soccer in the middle of an interstate highway. This prejudice needs no revisiting each day to convince parents of its utility, but is accepted as unworthy of explanation. Such a pre-judgment is held by all parents as part of the *seemingly* self-evident (and therefore unexamined) set of beliefs about how children should be raised. And it remains unexamined, by and large, precisely because it appears so self-evidently *true.* Indeed, the very need to present arguments to parents about the wisdom of such a pre-judgment would raise questions about the parents demanding the explanation. But, in fact, this pre-judgment about children and interstate highways *is* a "prejudice" in the etymological sense of the word, *precisely* because it almost always remains an unexamined and pre-rational judgment. It is, we might allow, a very good prejudice.

An even more obvious example of such a prejudice is the belief about prejudice itself — at least as such a belief is held by the vast majority of North Americans. Most people in the United States at the beginning of the twenty-first century would be scandalized, amused, or fearful of anyone demanding a carefully constructed extended argument as to why bias against other persons based on age, gender, race, or ethnicity was not a good thing. For most North Americans in mainstream culture (apart from members of the Ku Klux Klan and certain white supremacy groups), such a "pre-judgment" about "prejudice" is self-evidently true, and even to raise the question of defending such a position would raise questions about the morality or sanity of the person requiring the explanation. Members of the Ku Klux Klan and other white supremacy groups are widely perceived as deviant and non-mainstream precisely because they appear to be unconvinced by the (self-evident) immorality of holding such prejudice.

The following work is a study of prejudice in which both senses of the word will be utilized to explain why certain persons in the United States view Catholic Christians as culturally suspect, religiously corrupt, or at least as espousing non-mainstream values compared to their fellow citizens. It is both fruitful and necessary to understand these two meanings of *prejudice* as intimately related to each other in accounting for the animus against Catholics in the United States. Anti-Catholic prejudice is both an irrational nativist bias and a pre-rational (and often deeply religious) pre-judgment about both Christianity and democracy.

At least some prejudice against Catholics was, among other things, a manifestation of a congeries of sociological, economic, and historical fears about "outsiders" that many citizens of the United States from the mid-seventeenth to the mid-twentieth centuries shared. These fears (usually termed "nativism" by social and cultural historians) often reflected the British/North Atlantic, reformed Protestant, and/or Enlightenment rationalist loyalties of the majority of the population during that long (three-century) period during which the Protestant Establishment in the United States constituted the real but unofficial civil religion of the Republic. This civil religion made others — Catholics, Jews, Mormons, etc. — somehow "un-American" precisely to the extent that they did not share the Reformation/Enlightenment principles on which Mr. Jefferson's "lively experiment" was ostensibly founded.

Such nativist scholarly explanations for anti-Catholic prejudice are obviously true (in part), but they fail to account for the full range of the prejudice, especially in its most recent form at the end of the twentieth century. The "new" anti-Catholicism is focused in secular, and often militantly libertarian, quarters. Not all criticism of Catholicism and its adherents in the course of the last half century proceeded from unfair stereotyping, or from servile, nativist distrust of others. Indeed, while Catholic Christians in the United States have quite correctly (and often brilliantly) countered biased attacks against them in the most forceful ways available to them under the law, they have also not helped their cause by automatically labeling all criticism of their tradition as rooted in bias and ignorance.

It is possible that Catholics were perceived to be outside the public consensus of mainstream U.S. culture on a number of ethical, social, and political issues because they were, in fact, outside the broad public consensus. From a Catholic theological point of view, such a possibility is not necessarily a bad thing; on the contrary, it might be a very good thing indeed. Prejudice directed against Catholics might proceed from unbiased cultural or even profoundly religious principles, and actually be based on something in Catholic Christianity that does make Catholics different from other citizens in the Puritan-founded "City on a Hill."

It is my sense that both Catholics who perceive any criticism of their religious tradition as ineluctably based in hostile bias and hatred, and critics of that tradition who dismiss any talk of prejudice as whining nonsense, will be equally frustrated by the argument in the pages that follow.

Part One

THE ANTI-CATHOLIC IMPULSE

Chapter One

Catholic Otherness

Three Explanations

The perception of Roman Catholic faith, practice, and polity as superstitious, corrupt, undemocratic, and "un-American" is culturally ubiquitous. It was labeled the "deepest bias in the history of the American people" by political and cultural historian Arthur Schlesinger Jr.; others have termed it the "anti-Semitism of the intellectuals" and "the last acceptable prejudice in the United States." The history of the animus against Roman Catholics in the United States, no less than the labels and historical precedents used to explain it, has generated a small cottage industry among scholars that offers lively and informative reading, not least for Catholics.

In the welter of interpretive voices attempting to explain the anomalous but virulent presence of the anti-Catholic impulse in a country resolutely dedicated to separation of church and state, however, one can discern three essential groups of explanations for this deepest bias. Compelling if sometimes competing cultural, intellectual, and sociological explanations have been offered to account for the anti-Catholic impulse in the United States.[1]

Perhaps the oldest and most revered set of explanations can be categorized as cultural, although there is a fair amount of dissension within this set about the dating and location of the roots of fear and distrust of Catholicism. What unites this set is an understanding of North American public culture — the concrete political processes of democracy, the materialistic protocols of capitalism and its particular work ethic, the social traditions of public education — as rooted in a profoundly Protestant ordering of human society. Scholars pressing this cultural explanation, perhaps most famously exemplified by Ray Billington over half a century ago, locate the deepest roots of anti-Catholic prejudice in the settling of North

7

culture / ethos

America. Distrust of the Roman faith was transported from the Old World to the New by English Puritans whose nationalistic memories of the bitter Catholic persecutions of their sixteenth-century Protestant forebears by Bloody Mary Tudor, the treasons of the Gunpowder Plot, and the Spanish Armada, were regularly refreshed through reading works like *Foxe's Book of Martyrs*.[2]

The cultural loyalties nourished in such works gave rise to what would become the "American character" after the Puritans themselves had disappeared. This cultural interpretation of the Protestant origins sees in the American national identity itself evanescent traces of its Puritan founding, and thus of its anti-Catholicism: a fear of unlimited government and a commitment to political democracy based on the Puritan belief in original sin; a pragmatic and experimental understanding of both physical science and political reality based on the English Reformed tradition of personal conversion as the basis for church membership; a Protestant work ethic arising from what Perry Miller once termed Puritanism's "Augustinian strain of piety," which bade believers to devote themselves soberly and diligently to their "worldly pursuits" — which led to a material prosperity that scholars like Max Weber have argued provided the rich soil from which modern capitalism grew; a revered tradition of literacy and public education, in which all citizens were expected to encounter the Word of God for themselves in Holy Scripture; the suspicion of Catholic nations like Spain and France, both of which represented absolute monarchies that were the avowed political enemies of Protestant England, and whose corrupt state churches produced carnal Christians marked by superstition and ignorance of the Bible.[3]

For the (white) Protestant descendants of the New England Puritans, these essentially Protestant traditions defined what the American cultural experiment was about and provided a handy scorecard for distinguishing "ours" from "others." The Roman Catholic Church provided the single largest pool of others, particularly in the nineteenth century, with so many illiterate, hard-drinking immigrants arriving from nondemocratic nations like Ireland, Italy, and the Rhineland.[4]

A slight variation on this myth of Protestant cultural origins has been pressed by scholars of evangelical revivalism like William McLoughlin and Donald Mathews, who date the emergence of the American character to the nineteenth century. In this version, the successive waves of "great awakenings" that shaped U.S. political and social history gave rise to a resolutely evangelical understanding of religion and culture that found in the Catholicism of nineteenth-century Irish and Italian immigrants a rhetorical and institutional foil against which revivalist preachers could rail.[5]

Scholars like McLoughlin and Mathews have brilliantly reconstructed a nineteenth-century evangelical Protestantism that offered the young republic small-scale congregations whose leaders were chosen, paid, and personally solicitous to every person in a local congregation, set against an Old World ecclesiastical hierarchy that offended the deepest sentiments of second-generation republican Americans. In contrast to what most American evangelicals considered an ignorant Catholic piety and a hierarchical (even monarchical) institution that citizens of the Early Republic found foreign in a number of ways, they offered an intensely immediate, egalitarian piety that made the blinding experience of conversion available to everyone — women, slaves, children. "Just do it!" revivalist preachers like Charles Grandison Finney shouted with thoroughly democratic energy at the nineteenth-century American forebears of sneaker-wearers, and many of them, in good early Republican Era–fashion, did.[6]

Mathews has argued that the messy camp meetings of the frontier gave both form and substance not only to their small congregations, but to the western frontier. In setting up, financing, and running the many voluntary societies through which converts shaped their local communities (societies for Sunday and public schools, slavery and temperance, foreign and domestic missions) the citizens of the fledgling republic quite literally learned what the American democratic experiment was about. In that sense, Mathews has argued, the revivalist religion of the Second Great Awakening "organized" Republican America itself.[7]

This myth of Protestant cultural origins and of the "otherness" of Catholics continued to produce adherents in the twentieth century, although many of its exponents were now avowedly secular or even antireligious in terms of personal values. Harvard sociologist Talcott Parsons (the brilliant translator of Max Weber's *The Protestant Ethic and the Spirit of Capitalism*) wrote in a 1940 "Memorandum" to the Council on Democracy that "Anglo-Saxon Protestant traditions" in the United States — and by these cultural "traditions" Parsons meant everything from the Protestant work ethic and the separation of powers of the federal government to the devotion to experimental science — provided the most reliable barriers to the threat of American fascism, just then embodied in vibrant form in the person of Detroit Catholic priest Charles Coughlin. Parsons feared an "authoritarian element in the basic structure of the Catholic church itself which may weaken individual self-reliance and valuation of freedom." Likewise the widely acclaimed social scientist Robert Merton confirmed Weber's argument that the Protestant ethic supported not only capitalism, but also the emergence of a modern science based on experiment. Merton argued in a famous essay that Calvinist Protestants replaced "cloistered contemplation" with an "active experiment" that reflected their own "experiential piety" of conversion and personal accountability. Counting the numbers of Catholic and Protestant scientists in seventeenth-century Europe, Merton argued that even in Catholic France, Protestant scientists were more likely to achieve distinction.[8]

The second set of explanations for the anti-Catholic impulse can be labeled "intellectual." In place of embodied cultural traditions like the work ethic and a commitment to public education, this explanation posits a group of epistemological or philosophical ideas that undergird and define what Thomas Jefferson termed the "lively experiment," a set of ideas against which Catholic theology and piety posed a profound ideational threat. These ideas have been presented as arising variously from the Reformation, the English (Lockean) or Scottish ("Common Sense Realist") Enlightenments, the Whig tradition of political thought, or a combination of all of them. The specific intellectual content of this course of American democratic thought varies considerably, depending on the interpreter, although the ideas of religious liberty and the inviolability of individual conscience, the free expression of personal opinion in both speech and print, the separation of religion from a secular state, and a profound belief in America's mission as the universal beacon of democracy (presented as either "manifest destiny" or "millennialism") invariably show up as core ideas. Perhaps the single most important and influential scholarly voice behind this intellectual interpretation of America's cultural roots — at least from the standpoint of the role of Protestantism as the source for distinctively "American" ideas — was Yale scholar Ralph Henry Gabriel.[9]

Gabriel's *The Course of American Democratic Thought*, published in 1940, influenced several generations of intellectual and religious historians, political scientists, and cultural commentators, and came close to being considered the authorized version of American intellectual history. The history of "defining ideas" was organized around what Gabriel termed three "doctrines." The foundation of this democratic faith (Gabriel's word) and the first of his doctrines was a "frank supernaturalism derived from Christianity" that by the mid-nineteenth century was conceived of as a "fundamental law" that transcended and judged all historical personages (including divine right kings and infallible popes) and laws (like the recognition of slavery by the U.S. Constitution).[10]

Gabriel's second doctrine of democratic faith was the belief in the "free individual . . . derived from the moral order." In this article of the common faith, individual rights always took precedence over communal constraints and governmental regulation; indeed, it made civil disobedience against an immoral state or dissent from a moribund church a moral duty. The third doctrine was the belief in the "mission of America [because of] its unique origin and its unique destiny" to lead the world to freedom, decency, and economic affluence.[11]

The intellectual legitimacy accorded to evangelical Protestantism's role in shaping U.S. values and ideas by Gabriel's work produced in its wake both a triumphal genre of monographs at mid-century with titles like *The Great Tradition of the American Churches* and *The Triumph of Faith: Contributions of the Church to American Life, 1865–1900*, as well as brilliant studies like Ernest Lee Tuveson's history of the "idea of America's millennial role" in international politics. The former genre valorized evangelical Protestantism as the "established faith" of the United States, and called evangelical Americans to be true to the great intellectual tradition they inherited — an inheritance that sometimes proved harrowing for the small but growing minority of nonevangelical Americans. The latter tradition produced (and still produces) superb studies of the Protestant ideas that most assuredly shape even today's ostensibly secular American polity.[12]

The scholar who inherited Gabriel's mantle as the premier student of the role of religious ideas in shaping U.S. culture was Sidney Mead, a religious historian who sought to apply to the American religious experience American philosopher Alfred North Whitehead's "history of ideas" approach to culture. In a series of brilliant collections of essays with titles like *The Lively Experiment* and *Nation with the Soul of a Church* (a phrase borrowed from G. K. Chesterton), Mead outlined the seminal role of Protestant ideology in shaping North American civilization, in the process contextualizing North American thought within the much broader history of ideas of Western civilization. In an essay entitled "From Coercion to Persuasion," Mead explained with breathtaking intellectual clarity how the American church-state separation "represented one of the two most profound revolutions which have occurred in the entire history of the church on the administrative side." Mead showed that far from simply being European baggage "brought over" on the *Mayflower* and applied to an outpost of the real show on the other side of the Atlantic, American Protestant ideas represented profoundly unique and protean creations that

shaped not only the United States but Western civilization itself.[13]

The secular version of this intellectual set of interpretations for America's "common faith" offers the various phases of the Enlightenment (and religious belief, most especially not evangelical Protestantism) as the basis for the profound distrust of Catholicism in the United States. In this account of America's intellectual life, it was the bracing air of reason, pressed by figures like Tom Paine, Thomas Jefferson, Ben Franklin, and John Adams, that bequeathed to the Republic its distrust of hierarchical institutions and the argument from authority. Scholars like Daniel Boorstin, Henry May, Bernard Bailyn, and Gordon Wood have presented the real American intellectual tradition as intimately tied to the Enlightenment's distrust of both revealed truths and nondemocratic sources of authority in every form. This approach was most elegantly presented in May's great study of four enlightenments that hit British North American culture in successive waves of influence: the real key for understanding U.S. culture was not the relation of Enlightenment *and* religion, but rather Enlightenment *as* religion for the founders of the American republic. This version of the intellectualist reading of American cultural roots argued that the common cultural faith was rooted in profoundly egalitarian, rationalist presuppositions about the world, and anti-authoritarian impulses against which the Catholic tradition appeared to many as an easy target.[14]

This set of explanations positing the dominance of Protestant ideas and principles in shaping the democratic experiment in the United States has been even more successful than cultural explanations in producing twentieth-century intellectual distrust of Catholicism among academics and public intellectuals. John McGreevy has brilliantly reconstructed the herculean effort of "secular" public intellectuals between the 1930s and 1950s to "demonstrate the nonhierarchical sources of American culture" versus the threatening ideological propaganda of communist and fascist intellectuals. According to McGreevy, these American "public thinkers" sought to construct a resolutely democratic national vision in which a hierarchical, monolithic, and authoritarian Catholicism played an antithetical role. McGreevy notes that John Dewey asserted that America's "common faith" was a pragmatic belief that the "continued disclosing of truth through directed cooperative human endeavor is more religious in quality than is any faith in a completed revelation"; that Harold Laski identified the Roman Catholic Church in the United States as the source of "a good deal of what is most reactionary in the political and social life of [postwar] America"; that Yale University's A. K. Rodgers averred that (Catholic) Thomists seemed incapable of taking part in the "open-ended search for truth"; and that Walter Lippmann observed (without objection from fellow intellectuals) that "of course [Catholicism] was hostile to democracy and to every force that tended to make people self-sufficient."[15]

In the late twentieth century one of most sturdy and vociferous bastions of this intellectual strain of disdain for Catholicism was the academy; many scholars denounced the very idea of any university's dedication to religious "first principles," of teaching as character formation, or of denominational "tests" for faculty as a direct assault on "academic freedom." This somewhat amorphous term was originally used by academics to guarantee the integrity and independence of published scholarship, although in the course of the twentieth century it came to include classroom discussion topics, assigned reading for undergraduates, and the removal of the topic of religion to chaplaincies or semi-separate divinity schools within the university. Increasing numbers of American academics took as axiomatic Walter Lippmann's famous assertion that "there is no compromise possible between authority and the scientific spirit," as well as Abraham Maslow's well-known 1954 social scientific study which found

" 'self-actualizing' people unlikely to accept 'supernatural' religion and 'institutional orthodoxy.' "[16]

As George Marsden has shown in a number of very smart historical studies, the indifference to, even active disdain for, religious issues and the study of religion shown by many American academics is, in part, the result of the long establishment of religion (especially liberal mainstream Protestantism) in the American academy, in which "so many of America's pace-setting universities were products of liberal Protestant culture." In the 1960s, when so many establishments came under attack by the counterculture, so did the white Protestant establishment that had founded, funded, and directed these institutions.[17]

Although all religiously affiliated institutions in the United States came to be seen as suspect by university intellectuals, Catholic colleges and universities were especially targeted for criticism and questioning, not least because of their insistence on making both theology and ecclesial identity central components of their university mission. While this story of twentieth-century academic anti-Catholicism in some respects represents a nasty turn in the road for the religion that claimed to have invented the concept of the university itself, as well as the tradition of *disputatio* as the core academic discussion, it was not exactly surprising. Social scientists, an increasingly prestigious and numerous presence in the American academy in the first third of the twentieth century, had learned from Sigmund Freud that Catholicism had "resolutely opposed any idea of this world being governed by advance toward recognition of truth." The founding document of the American Association of University Professors asserted that claims to religious truth were both unscientific and potentially dangerous to rational modes of inquiry. In fact, it claimed that the duty of the university professor was to enable students to "think creatively about heresies."[18]

The third set of explanations for the anti-Catholic impulse in U.S. culture and thought is rooted in the social sciences. It is usually offered as either "nativism" or "secularization."

Nativism is a fear and distrust of "outsiders" by cultural "insiders." It is a reaction to alterity, or "otherness."[19] This view rests on the argument of social theorist Emile Durkheim that social deviance in all its forms (the persecution of religious heretics, the hunt for political subversives, the oppression of ethnic and racial outcasts) actually performs an essential service in human societies by establishing the boundaries that define the group. Deviance supplies a focus for group identity by drawing attention to those values and beliefs that constitute the collective conscience of the community. Thus, Durkheim argued — in one of the founding documents of the modern discipline of sociology — that all societies might be said to invent deviance, a property that is conferred on certain kinds of political, racial, or religious behavior by the community to demonstrate where the line is drawn between behavior and values that belong to the group and behavior that defines the outsiders. Durkheim posited that such boundaries are never fixed in any group, but always shift as the group itself discovers new outer limits to its universe. Whenever a community confronts a significant relocation of its social boundaries, either through a realignment of power, the appearance of new groups of aliens in its midst, or the propagation of a new set of ultimate — religious, philosophical, political — beliefs, the emergence of a new deviant cause célèbre is almost essential.[20]

Social historians applied these insights to the North American tradition of anti-Catholicism to read the animus not as a cultural or intellectual inheritance, but as a function of boundary maintenance. John Higham, in what was regarded for a number of decades as the most thorough and reliable historical study of nativism in the United States, wrote in 1963 that

> whether the nativist was a workingman or a Protestant evangelist, a southern conservative or a northern reformer, he stood for a certain kind of nationalism. He believed — whether he was trembling at a Catholic menace to American liberty, fearing an invasion of pauper labor, or simply rioting against the great English actor William Macready — that some influence originating abroad threatened the very life of the nation from within.[21]

Higham allowed that the distrust and persecution of the Roman Church was "by far the oldest and — in early America — the most powerful of the anti-foreign traditions" in the United States. This nativist approach to explaining anti-Catholicism enjoyed a long life as the preferred explanation for the riots and convent burnings of the mid-nineteenth century, the rise of the Native American Party, the reappearance of the Ku Klux Klan after World War I, and the political opposition to Al Smith in his run for the presidency in 1928. Catholic historians like John Tracy Ellis, Thomas McAvoy, and James Hennessey, as well as more recent popular narrators like Charles Morris, have interpreted the Catholic threat to white Anglo-Saxon natives as an economic fear of recent immigrants stealing jobs at the bottom of the pay scale as well as the status strain experienced by old cultural elites in the new, culturally pluralistic world of Gilded Age America. Like the adherents of both the cultural and intellectual sets of interpretations, they do explain part of the anti-Catholic tradition in U.S. culture.[22]

The other sociological category used to explain the fear and distrust of Catholics in the United States is secularization, which has a revered intellectual pedigree and, from the standpoint of theology at least, a greater possibility of providing a satisfactory answer. One of the most sophisticated interpretations of secularization as a social and religious process has been advanced by renowned American social theorist Peter Berger, whose approach posits the close relationship between social pluralism and religious secularization.[23]

In Berger's thesis, the modernization of western European culture since the seventeenth century was a sociological process that inevitably included the secularization or privatization of religious belief. In modern cultures like the United States, religious claims and loyalties are removed from the public to the private sphere in order to gain political peace, social comity, and civilized public discourse in cultures where citizens no longer share first principles. However,

> Private religiosity, however "real" it may be to the individuals who adopt it, cannot any longer fulfill the classical task of religion — that of constructing a common world within which all of social life receives ultimate meaning binding on everybody. Instead, this religiosity is limited to specific enclaves of social life that may be effectively segregated from the secularized sectors of modern society. ... The world-building potency of religion is thus restricted to the construction of sub-worlds, of fragmented universes of meaning, the plausibility structure of which may in some cases be no larger than the nuclear family.[24]

The plausibility structures of any single religious tradition lose social status because of all those others in the same society who deny their reality. All religious traditions thus, of necessity, become subjectivized in a double sense: their reality becomes a private affair of individuals, and is apprehended as rooted within the individual consciousness rather than in the external (and presumably more real) world. Berger has pointed out that all modern industrial societies have made religion voluntary (and therefore by definition private) for the sake of social peace; in such pluralistic environments, religion ineluctably tends to become more concerned with the therapeutic needs of its adherents, and less concerned with offering a comprehensive worldview for the whole of culture.[25]

In this view, it is easy to understand why Catholicism presents a special problem to the American circumstance: Catholicism as a magisterial religious tradition has resolutely refused to play by the rules of the privatized religious game. Even though Catholicism's legal status, like every other religious body in the culture, is that of a denomination and not of a church (in the sense that it has no social or legal status as the single or preferred faith of the culture), it refuses to claim authority only in the private realm. Indeed, on a wide spectrum of very public issues that divide the culture — including abortion, school vouchers, sexual education for school children — it has continued to make very loud and very public claims to morally authoritative teaching in ways that outrage significant segments of the culture, not least journalists and academics who fear authoritative teaching as the death blow to the democratic and free life. To those who accept Berger's interpretation, distrust of and disdain for Catholicism in twentieth-century America makes perfect sense.

Chapter Two

The Varieties of Anti-Catholicism in the United States

A Brief (Unpleasant) History of Incidents Aimed at Catholic Otherness

These cultural, intellectual, and sociological interpretations — brilliant in many cases and for the most part compellingly argued — in fact do explain a great deal about the attitudes, fears, and specific historical incidents targeted at Catholics that stretch from the earliest years of European settlement in North America to World War II. The very ubiquity of these cultural manifestations makes it difficult to offer anything like a complete history in a short compass, but a brief historical overview will serve to show that it is reasonable to believe that there is something in all this talk about anti-Catholic prejudice that needs to be interpreted by students of American culture.

In its earliest manifestations in colonial America, anti-Catholicism was well grounded, Ray Billington argued, long before the first English settlers arrived in the United States, as both the Puritans of New England and the cavalier Anglicans of Virginia, "despite their many differences, shared the fear and hatred of Rome.... The settlers themselves had been cradled in an England more bitter against Catholicism then than at any other time."[1] Billington posited that the hatred with which average seventeenth- and eighteenth-century English citizens and colonial settlers looked on "popery" was owed in large part to Catholicism's "anti-national character," making the Church of Rome feared not only as a theology antagonistic to the reformed faith embodied in the Church of England's Thirty-nine Articles and the Puritans' Westminster Confession, but also as a political and military force that consistently sought to overthrow the English government itself. The detection and foiling of treasonous Catholic attempts at overthrowing the Elizabethan Settlement in church and state, most famously embodied in the Gunpowder Plot, were concerns brought from old to New England, and celebrated annually in Boston and throughout the colonies on Guy Fawkes Day on November 5. Also called "Pope Day," this yearly public holiday was celebrated by burning the effigy of the pope on town commons up and down the eastern seaboard while children sang anti-Catholic ditties and adults drank rounds of toasts to the overthrow of the pope, more popularly known on these occasions as "The Beast" described in the Book of Revelation. Guy Fawkes Day was celebrated in northern and southern colonies until 1775, when General George Washington issued an intercolonial order forbidding its observance, fearful of its effect on securing the aid of French Catholic Canada in what was emerging as a revolutionary war against the mother country.[2]

The annual celebrations for over a century and a half served as an emblematic public ritual testifying to a much broader series of political and social constraints on Catholics in colonial America: "papists" were forbidden from holding public office, carrying firearms, or serving on juries in both Virginia by a 1641 act of the House of Burgesses, and in Maryland after 1654 by a law that stated that "none who profess to exercise the Popish religion can be protected in this province." The Maryland law was especially surprising, as the colony of Maryland's Catholic founder, Lord Baltimore, had sponsored what many scholars date as the earliest act of religious toleration in British North America.[3]

Far more famous for the virulence of its anti-Catholic animus was the Puritan colony of Massachusetts, whose General Court decreed in 1647 that "any Jesuit or priest coming within the colony was to be banished," and if he return, executed. That same body enacted laws forbidding celebration of the "popish festival of Christmas" and the importation of any "Irish persons whatsoever" into the colony, and instituted oaths of allegiance for all public office holders and militia marshals that specifically included denunciations of the pope. "Break the Pope's Neck" was a popular fireside game for New England children, while the *New England Primer* — the "hornbook" on which children learned their ABCs with little phrases for memorizing the alphabet — offered as its phrase for the letter A, "Abhor that abhorrent Whore of Rome."[4]

The American Revolution is often presented as the cultural moment when colonial anti-Catholicism was finally put to rest, especially after the entry of Catholic France into the conflict in 1778 on the side of the colonies. This dampening of prejudice against the Roman Church is often presented as one of the healthy by-products of the triumph of Enlightenment reason among colonial leaders and its enshrinement in the founding documents of the new republic, which announced the commitment of the new nation to the proposition that all people (including, presumably, Catholics) are created equal. This supposed salutary displacement of older Puritan biases by the egalitarian premises of the English and Scottish Enlightenments sees the Revolutionary Era itself as that moment when Puritans and Cavaliers became Americans, free of the tired prejudices of the Old World. But much like the rumors of Mark Twain's death, this is a premature conclusion about anti-Catholic bias during the Revolution and the Republican era that followed it.

Scholars like Carl Bridenbaugh, Nathan Hatch, and Alan Heimert have documented with compelling evidence the continuing importance of evangelical Protestant loyalties.[5] Several historical incidents illustrate the continuing Protestant ideological force moving the ostensibly enlightened colonies toward revolution against the mother country, most famously the Quebec Act of 1774. This British bill sought to pacify the ever-fractious North American colonists by granting religious toleration to Catholics in the British province of Quebec, the vast majority of whose citizens were in fact Catholics and previously forbidden by British law from publicly practicing their religion. But revolutionary propagandist Samuel Adams refused to see in the parliamentary gesture a reasonable granting of religious freedom to a colony denied one of their most basic liberties. To the contrary, Adams claimed to see in the act an unholy alliance between an autocratic king and an equally autocratic pope, and in response drafted the Suffolk Resolves — perhaps the single most violent and inflammatory colonial petition against the British produced in the years before 1776. Bridenbaugh and other colonial historians claim that the Resolves, which denounced both king and Parliament as "papist tools," played a crucial role in mobilizing the colonies against the mother country.[6]

More arresting and revealing than the bitterness of the Suffolk Resolves in showing the genesis of attitudes toward Catholics that grew out of the

Revolutionary era was the close association between the Revolutionary cause and the ideology of evangelical Protestantism, which was uncovered in the work of Alan Heimert and James Davidson. Heimert's *Religion and the American Mind from the Great Awakening to the Revolution* presented compelling historical evidence that the left wing of the evangelical Protestant tradition that had supported the revivals of Jonathan Edwards in New England and the Tennent brothers in New Jersey played a far more important intellectual role in sponsoring the American Revolution as an ideological event than the deistic and rationalist ideas of Locke, Montesquieu, and Tom Paine. The warm and immediate "heart religion" of the Great Awakening, which denounced the "carnal Christianity" of a Catholic-Anglican hierarchical tradition, was far more crucial in galvanizing the colonial Americans to fight the most powerful standing army in Europe than Enlightenment ideas about natural rights and representative government.[7]

In this evangelical interpretation of the American Revolution, while the Constitution that defined the new republic at the end of the war separated the institutions of church and state, the religious impulses driving the great majority of its Protestant citizens were left free to effect what Robert Handy termed the "voluntary establishment" of evangelical Christianity for the next 150 years. In Handy's reading of the years between 1790 and 1930, most Protestants accepted their vocation to provide the soul and ethos of the new nation as both self-evident and providential. The means to effect this vision "were to be voluntary and persuasive, but the goal of a Christian society was as clear as it had been in the days of legal establishment — even clearer." As Handy has also pointed out, those who opposed this evangelical vision of America — Catholics especially — soon became the brunt of nationalistic, theological, and political fears:

> Believing that by the separation of church and state they had separated religious from secular concerns, [evangelicals] seem to have been largely unaware of how much specifically Protestant content they had in fact invested in their understanding of state and society. Groups which did not share their basic premises could become only too painfully aware of it.[8]

Handy's thesis accounts thoroughly for the rise of anti-Catholic activity in the first half of the nineteenth century, after the ostensible triumph of

Enlightenment ideas in the Revolution, and just as Irish Catholics began appearing in steady but hardly overwhelming numbers in the ports of Boston and New York. Perhaps the single most famous artifact in American popular culture that witnesses to the animus was the publication in 1836 of Maria Monk's *Awful Disclosures of the Hotel Dieu Monastery in Montreal*, a deliciously salacious (and almost completely fictitious) escape account of a poor Protestant girl held captive against her will in a convent full of secret doors to priests' bedrooms, buried bodies of nuns' illegitimate children, and dark rituals in the chapel. Equal parts pornographic depiction of priest and nun couplings and purple prose, Monk's account was published by a dummy press in New York City funded by several Protestant clergymen, the manuscript having been prudently rejected by the Harper publishing house. It was, nonetheless, one of the best sellers of antebellum culture, along with *Uncle Tom's Cabin,* if aimed at a somewhat less discriminating readership.[9]

Applying the deconstruction theories of contemporary cultural or gender studies to Monk's shocking "exposé" makes for provocative and amusing reflection, although a simple narration of the prurient story line helps to account for its dozen or so reprintings. It is still in print today. The heroine had made her vows with a confused sense of religious vocation, but was immediately initiated into the sinful ways of nunneries. Chief among these were the instructions given to her by Mother Superior that she must "obey the priests in all things." Readers learned, along with poor Maria, that she "to her utter astonishment and horror, was to live in the practice of criminal intercourse with them." The children born from these unholy unions were immediately baptized and strangled.

> "This secured their everlasting happiness," the Mother Superior explained, "for the baptism purified them from all sinfulness, and being sent out of this world before they had time to do anything wrong, they were at once admitted into heaven. How happy, she exclaimed, are those who secure immortal happiness in such little beings! Their little souls would thank those who kill their bodies, if they had it in their power."[10]

Monk's account led to convent investigating committees in several cities made up of outraged citizens concerned about the unholy doings going on in their neighborhoods under the guise of religion, which in turn led to a number of official convent exposés. Monk's best seller was just the most famous of a flourishing literary genre with titles like *Six Months in a Convent, The Testimony of an Escaped Novice,* and, perhaps the most intriguing of all, *Rosamond,* a sort of nineteenth-century predecessor of off-Broadway skits of dubious taste like *Late Night Catechism,* in which a self-professed mistress to a Cuban priest confessed to her knowledge of a Roman clerical plot to capture Negro boys, kill them, and grind them into sausage meat to raise money for their penurious Catholic mission. *Rosamond's* story line represented a delightful mixture of hilarious ignorance about the details of Catholic religious life, a disturbing fixation on eating flesh that might very well represent a perverted (if unconscious) trope on the Catholic doctrine of the Eucharist, and a salacious interest in how priests and nuns really remained pure. It sold like hotcakes at a communion breakfast.[11]

This popular genre of convent tales simply represented the low culture version of a vast anti-Catholic publishing tradition that flourished in the first half of the nineteenth century at every level of U.S. society. Both the American Home Missionary Society and the American Tract Society — pillars of the evangelical empire that provided literally hundreds of pamphlets to be read both at home and at Sunday school — produced numerous works "exposing" the crimes of Jesuits and assorted other clerics against the liberties of freedom-loving American citizens. The title of one of the most famous of these works — written by Samuel F. B. Morse (the inventor of the Code) — encapsulated the theme of most of them: *A Foreign Conspiracy against the Liberties of the United States.* It was serialized in the pages of the New York *Observer* throughout the fall of 1834 to sensational popularity and was immediately picked up and reprinted by various religious newspapers before appearing in monograph form in December. Morse's foreign conspiracy posited a labyrinthine plot between the pope and the crumbling monarchies of a tired Old World: in order for the European monarchies to survive, they had enlisted the aid of "the other great foe of liberty, the Catholic Church," to inundate the United States with Catholic immigrants hatching unspeakable plots against the democratic liberties of Protestants under the evil guidance of the recently restored Jesuit order. Morse urged his fellow Protestants to rise above their denominational differences and unite against Catholic parochial schools and Catholic officeholders. Morse's reception was so favorable that he returned to the theme of the Catholic plot the next year, publishing a series entitled *Imminent Dangers to the Free Institutions of the United States* in the New York *Journal of Commerce* throughout 1835.[12]

The same year, Lyman Beecher, president of the Protestant western outpost of Lane Seminary in Cincinnati, Ohio, and patriarch of America's most revered evangelical clan, produced *A Plea for the West*. Beecher (father of Harriet Beecher Stowe and Henry Ward Beecher) amplified the Catholic plot sketched by Morse, "uncovering" the central role that Catholic schools were intended to play in this looming cultural threat. Through a vast school system just then being constructed, against the tradition of the free public schools that had spread from New England, Catholic converts were to be won until that dreadful day when converts and recent immigrants would win control of the entire nation.[13]

In several hundred overwrought pages Beecher proceeded to lay out the evil designs of Catholic teachers on the free souls of Protestant children in the dark recesses of schools putatively dedicated to civilizing the West. Works like those of Morse and Beecher witnessed to a widespread sense of unease with the Roman Church among the educated middle classes, analogous to the coarser concerns of the working class readers of Maria Monk and *Rosamond*.

But both of these streams had already cooperated in the kind of anti-Catholic violence possible beyond literary assaults, in what has been termed "the most important political event in [nineteenth-century] Massachusetts prior to the agitation surrounding the passage of the 1850 Fugitive Slave Law": the burning of the Ursuline Convent in Charlestown, Massachusetts, on August 11, 1834.[14]

On the extraordinarily hot evening of August 10, 1834, Lyman Beecher delivered the last of three virulently anti-Catholic sermons in as many churches in the city of Boston, a preaching example matched in vitriol by other Protestant pastors in the city that Sunday. A number of the city's evangelical pulpits had been given over to denunciations of Catholicism that stifling Boston Sabbath, some of them directed specifically against the Ursuline Convent across the Charles River. Beecher declared that "the principles of this corrupt church are adverse to our free institutions, from the contempt and hostility which they feel towards all Protestants." The mesmerizing preacher announced to a sweltering but rapt audience that if the Catholics had their way, especially through their crafty ruse of running schools like the one in Charlestown, they would "subvert our free institutions and bring into disgrace all ideas of an effective government."[15]

The Ursuline Convent was an exclusive finishing school run by the sisters and had been the target of evangelical outrage in Boston long before that Sunday, for a number of social, theological, and economic reasons. A significant number of the convent school's students were the wealthy daughters of Boston's liberal Unitarian aristocracy — a mercantile class that had become increasingly disdainful of the kind of emotional ravings offered at the resolutely evangelical Park Street Church (known as "Brimstone Corner"), where Beecher had delivered the last, and most virulent, of his sermons on August 10. The fact that the working-class mob that attacked the convent less than twenty-four hours after Beecher's sermon was composed largely of Scots-Irish Calvinist bricklayers is relevant for understanding the event; they were workingmen envious of, and outraged at, Unitarian bankers and merchants who had delivered their own daughters into the hands of Catholic nuns for their education. Furthermore, the expensive education offered these daughters of fellow Protestant Bostonians was well beyond what the rioters could afford to offer their own daughters. The misogynist fear and suspicion of nuns as self-sufficient women living on their own (a fear that would fuel the publishing careers of both Maria Monk and Rebecca Teresa Reed in a few years) likewise informed the attack. One rioter, interviewed a few days after the attack, defended his own part in burning down the convent by averring that "bishops and priests pretended to live without wives; but that nuns were kept to supply the deficiency in this particular. He said this in vulgar language." Theological, sociological, and economic impulses were so hopelessly entangled in the motivations of the rioters that any number of explanations could be offered to explain the real reasons for torching the convent and all be historically accurate and supported by the conflicted evidence.[16]

Harrison Gray Otis presided over a meeting of fellow Brahmins in Faneuil Hall shortly after the destruction of the convent to "call loudly on all good citizens to express individually and collectively the abhorrence they feel of this high-handed violation of the laws." The principal defense attorney stated in his opening address to the court that the defendants at the bar "cannot be convicted without Catholic testimony, [and] we will endeavor to show what that testimony is worth." In the estimation of the jury, it counted for very little. All of the rioters save one were acquitted in the trial that followed. The animus would flare again a decade later in Philadelphia, where two Catholic churches were destroyed by an angry mob on May 8, 1844.[17]

The local "No Popery" impulses became organized on a national level in May 1848 with the formation of the American and Foreign Christian Union, whose constitution announced a dedication to "diffuse and promote the principles of Religious Liberty, and a pure and Evangelical Christianity, both at home and abroad, wherever a corrupted Christianity exists." The new Union, however, actually represented the merging of three distinct evangelical Protestant voluntary societies that had been operating for some time: the American Protestant Society, which had dedicated itself to converting to Christianity both unchurched Americans and recently arrived Irish and German Catholic immigrants; the Foreign Evangelical Society, which had been formed in 1839 to convert French Catholics to solid Bible Christianity; and the erstwhile Christian Alliance in Italy, an American-founded and operated group sending very frustrated Protestant missionaries to convert resolutely anti-clerical and unchurched Catholics in southern Italy, who turned out to be even more hostile to the poor *Inglese* missionaries sent to deliver the good news than they were to the clergy of their mother church. By all accounts, the Union enjoyed remarkable success during the first decade of its existence: by 1854, it had raised $80,000 — a princely sum at the time — to fund missionaries and lecturing agents both abroad and, more importantly, at home. The home missionary agents roamed the country "working zealously to save Catholic souls wherever they were to be found," especially at ports of entry like New York and New Orleans, where Irish and German Catholic immigrants could be found in large numbers.[18]

The Union also ran an anti-Catholic library in New York City that proudly claimed to be the largest of its kind in the world, and sponsored free lectures about Catholicism so inflammatory that crowds thronged them. A riot broke out at a lecture in Newark, New Jersey, when certain (presumably Catholic) members of the audience attempted to silence

temptation of beautiful Catholic Churches

the speaker. The Union's publication, *The American and Foreign Christian Union*, proclaimed its mission in its first issue to be "enlightening its readers about the nature and position of Romanism." The successful career of the *Union* embodied an animus that was the impetus that drove a host of religious papers in the 1850s to spread the "No Popery" gospel, including Pittsburgh's *Protestant Union*, Louisville, Kentucky's *True Catholic*, Boston's *Christian Alliance*, and the Milwaukee *Banner*. New Yorkers — then as today — were offered a much broader range of choices, including the *Protestant Advocate*, the *True Freeman's Journal*, the *Protestant Standard*, and the *New York Crusader*. All of these papers warned about the special temptation that Catholic worship posed for unprepared American Protestants: "the pale light entering softly through the painted windows, the paintings on the walls . . . are all eminently fitted, as they were designed, to take hold of the imagination of all classes. Such excitement is pleasant; it is grateful to the feelings of men who are naturally superstitious."[19]

These journalistic manifestations of a vibrant anti-Catholic impulse found political form and power in the meteoric career of the American Party, more generally known among students of American history as the Know Nothings (about which most U.S. Catholics — then and now — know nothing). While the Know Nothings later claimed George Washington himself as their founder and first member, the party in fact grew out of a secret society gathered in 1849 by Charles B. Allen of New York with the fervently patriotic name of the Order of the Star Spangled Banner. The Order was to avoid direct political organizing in favor of behind-the-scenes support for nativist anti-Catholic candidates in the existing political parties. For several years it languished as a local society, largely unknown on the national scene; but in 1852 Allen handed leadership of his group over to James W. Barker, whose organizational skills were such that within four months a thousand new members were enrolled, and the New York municipal elections of 1852 saw several candidates sponsored by the Order elected to city office. The Order's candidates in the 1852 elections were popularly labeled Know Nothings after being questioned about the political goals of their new party; each and every one responded that he knew nothing.[20]

With the marked success of the Order in local elections, a State Wigwam was created to encourage the formation of branch lodges throughout

New York State. Lodges were eventually formed in New Jersey, Maryland, Connecticut, Massachusetts, and Ohio. By June of 1854, a national convention with delegates from thirteen state lodges was convened in New York City to create a national network of Local, Grand, and National councils, and to formally designate the rituals proper to each level: "grips, pass-words, phrases of recognition, signals of distress, were successfully used by the order . . . and probably lured many curious Americans into its ranks." The ritual of the Order likewise provided for two distinct degrees of membership: the First Degree, in which the initiate had to prove he was born in the United States, that both his parents were Protestant, and that he was not married to a Roman Catholic, and then swear to use his influence and vote for "native-born American citizens for all offices of honor" and "the exclusion of all foreigners, and Roman Catholics in particular." Second Degree initiates were called to bring the Order's loyalties into the public sphere by running for political office, in which they pledged "when elected or appointed to any official station . . . [to] remove all foreigners, aliens, and Catholics from office." Notwithstanding all this talk of aliens and foreigners in its rhetoric, the Order was "really a No Popery party, despite all the gloss and fine phrases in its pronouncements. This fact alone accounts for its unity."[21]

Indeed, its unifying ideological bond of anti-Catholicism was something that the major political parties lacked in the tense decade before the Civil War, when sectional disputes split party loyalty along the Mason-Dixon Line. It sponsored a series of candidates who swept into political office in a series of triumphs in the elections of 1854 and 1855 that startled the nation: whole tickets of the Order's candidates in Massachusetts, Delaware, and Pennsylvania, not even listed on official voting ballots, won election; candidates running unopposed found themselves defeated by write-ins whose party affiliation was not known. About seventy-five newly elected members of the Order were sent to the federal Congress in 1854, pledged to oppose the pope and his minions. State politics also witnessed the triumph of Know Nothing efforts: the Massachusetts State Senate was composed entirely of the Order's candidates, while its House of Representatives was composed of one Whig, one Free Soiler, and 376 Know Nothings.[22]

The Know Nothing political *blitzkrieg,* however, was stopped after the elections of 1855 by an even larger political and economic storm: the debates over states' rights, slavery, and the tariff that ended in the Civil War. That holocaust buried the deep anti-Catholic feelings that had swept the Know Nothings into office just five years before.

As Reconstruction's reformist agenda following the war was abating, a new crop of secret, anti-Catholic societies sprang up at the end of the 1870s and throughout the 1880s in reaction to the mushrooming numbers of parochial schools, the massive tides of Irish immigrants, and the American Catholic Church's newfound organizational maturity following the Third Plenary Council of Baltimore in 1884. Josiah Strong, the progressive Congregational minister who oversaw the Evangelical Alliance (the grandfather of the National Council of Churches) published *Our Country* in 1885, which warned of the deleterious effects of recent Catholic immigration on America's democratic institutions. In 1889 an eminently respectable group of influential New Yorkers founded the National League for the Protection of American Institutions with the sole aim of protecting schools from the Catholic aggression posed by parochial education. The United Order of Native Americans, the American Patriotic League, the Loyal Men of American Liberty, and a super-secret group with the name of the Red, White, and Blue all attracted loyal followers. The most influential of these postwar groups was the American Protective Association, founded in Clinton, Iowa, in 1887.[23]

The A.P.A.'s founder, Henry F. Bowers, has been described as a deeply pious, slightly paranoid widower who saw Catholic conspiracies everywhere. Bowers blamed the deficiencies in his own education on a "subversive Jesuit conspiracy against the public schools of Baltimore." He traveled widely in the Midwest, lecturing publicly on the Roman peril and secretly founding A.P.A. councils modeled on the Masons; its members swore a solemn oath never to vote for a Catholic, never to join one on strike, and to avoid hiring one if a Protestant was available. By 1893 A.P.A. membership stood at around seventy thousand, most in the larger towns and cities of the upper Midwest from Nebraska to Michigan, where Catholics were rising in political and social power. That year leadership of the Association passed into the hands of former saloon-keeper "Whiskey Bill" Traynor, who oversaw the group's explosion into national prominence: by

the summer of 1894, the Association claimed half a million members nationwide, with ten thousand members in Columbus, Ohio, and sixteen
thousand in Buffalo, New York. Riding on the coattails of the economic
depression then at full tide, A.P.A. speakers preached to crowds of un-
employed Protestant workers that their jobs had been stolen from them
by the flood of Catholic immigrants washing up on American shores; to
prove their accusation the agitators distributed the fictitious "Instruction
to Catholics" supposedly sent by the pope to his followers in the New
World:

> In order to find employment for the many thousands of the faith-
> ful who are coming daily to swell the ranks of our catholic army,
> which will in time possess this land, we must secure control of every
> enterprise requiring labor. This will render it necessary to remove or
> crowd out the American heretics who are now employed.[24]

For several years in the mid-1890s, A.P.A. membership boycotted
Catholic merchants, discriminated against Catholic labor, and played a
major role in two anti-Catholic riots; but by the end of the decade its
political and social influence had dissipated, owing in part to its very success in mobilizing working-class anger, to the ambivalent discomfiture of
middle-class Protestants, as well as to the improved economic circumstances of the country, which robbed it of much of its rhetorical appeal
to displaced workers. Its role as animator of No Popery impulses, however, was filled with even greater energy several decades later by the most
famous nativist organization in American history, the Ku Klux Klan.[25]

The modern Klan was revived in Atlanta, on October 16, 1915, by
William J. Simmons, who proclaimed himself Imperial Wizard. "Colonel"
Simmons (a rank earned not in military service but through membership
in a Masonic-like order known as the Woodmen of the World) modeled his
twentieth-century group on the defunct Reconstruction era Klan, which
had been made up of ex-Confederate soldiers dedicated to intimidating
Yankee Carpetbaggers and uppity African Americans running for political
office. But the good colonel envisioned a broader range of targets than
just Yankees and the descendants of freed slaves: the Klan's improbable-
sounding ranks of Kleagles, Cyclops, Geniis, and Goblins (all ordered
according to the ritual of the Kloran) attracted hundreds of small-town

patriots concerned with a growing list of foreigners threatening American ways, a list that now included Jews, socialist radicals, and Catholics. D. W. Griffith's immensely successful film *The Birth of a Nation* — the first blockbuster movie hit in American popular culture — valorized the bravery of white-hooded ex-Confederate soldiers riding in the night to protect their womenfolk and children from the brutal designs of assorted others and contributed significantly to the romantic mythology of the Klan's heroic past. But while the old Klan had championed racial superiority as its chief agenda, Simmons's group championed a more complex mix of nationalist, racial, and religious loyalties that played on the fears of native Americans.[26]

For several years after its founding, Simmons's Klan achieved a modest success with perhaps five thousand members; but in the summer of 1920 a rapid expansion began in terms of numbers and activities. Both were a result of new social conditions at the end of World War I, as well as the hiring of a pair of hard-boiled publicity agents, Edward Clarke and Mrs. Elizabeth Tyler. In return for $8 on every $10 taken in initiation fees, Clarke and Tyler launched a mammoth membership campaign in Masonic lodges throughout the land, bringing in ninety thousand new Klan members in sixteen months. They had defined the Klan's mission as "protecting the interests of those whose forebears established the nation," a mission in which racial, economic, political, and religious impulses would mix freely. Fear of the New Negro (which had played such a central role in Simmons's original vision) declined as American blacks either "accepted their place" or moved to northern industrial cities. By the beginning of 1921, anti-Catholicism had emerged as the most effective rallying cry. Clarke and Tyler's propaganda refreshed the old stories about stores of arms stockpiled in the basements of Catholic churches, which now reverberated in preachers dedicated to a new form of militant evangelical anti-modernism called Fundamentalism. This resolutely new form of the old time religion had caught fire in the Year of the Great Reversal, 1919, which saw the demobilization of military troops, significant economic disruptions, the disquieting discovery that others were now in positions of cultural, economic, and literary authority and that Protestant leaders responsible for America's culture had betrayed their trust — even the Methodists now allowed dancing! Many cultural conservatives felt like strangers in their own culture in the decade after World War I. The Klan's denunciatory finger pointed at the growing ranks of Catholics.[27]

By 1921 the Klan had crossed the Mason-Dixon line into the north and claimed to be operating in forty-five states and enrolling a thousand members a day; the following year witnessed massive initiation rituals at which a thousand new Klansmen were sworn in simultaneously, and hundreds of candidates to political office publicly acknowledged the debt they owed for their successful elections to Klan support, including the governors of Georgia and Oregon, and the junior senator from Texas. The invisible empire reached its zenith in 1923, claiming a membership of three million followers dedicated to legislation against Catholic schools and Papist-owned saloons, and the intimidation of individuals with too much power. Catholic city councilmen, state legislators, and newspaper editors were the special objects of a repertoire that ranged from crosses burned on front lawns at midnight to personal physical violence.[28]

But by 1924 disputes and tensions within the Klan itself (over access to admission fees, among other issues) led to murder and nasty newspaper headlines, which in turn led to denunciations of the hooded patriots by northern urban intellectuals, outraged evangelical pastors, and small-town mayors embarrassed by the glimpse behind the white sheet. The governor of Kansas (a state that boasted flourishing chapters of Kleagles and Goblins) brought suit to forbid all public appearances and activities of the Klan within his resolutely Protestant state, while a mob of six thousand anti-Klan protesters in Perth Amboy, New Jersey, led by Catholics and Jews, broke through a police barricade and fell on five hundred hapless Klansmen, kicking and beating them as they fled. New York State's Catholic governor, Al Smith, sponsored a series of typically canny and quite successful legislative riders that effectively closed down Klan operations in the Empire State, while Minnesota, Iowa, and Michigan passed laws forbidding the wearing of masks in public. By 1925, the once ineluctable invisible empire of the Klan fell on hard times, all but disappearing as a serious presence on the national scene. Save for its role in the Al Smith campaign.[29]

The much-weakened Klan had one last hurrah in the presidential election of 1928, which saw the Catholic "wet" governor of New York running as the Democratic candidate against the Republicans' "dry" Herbert Hoover. Smith lost by a landslide, a defeat that fueled a cottage industry about what really happened in the most acrimonious political campaign of the twentieth century. Certainly Smith's anti-prohibition stance worried southern and midwestern Americans as dedicated to the campaign against alcohol as to a religious crusade; his urban ethnic style of leadership and campaigning likewise concerned small-town voters uncomfortable with big city politics. But it was Smith's religion that generated the most controversy, both at the time and since, and is usually credited with his crushing defeat. Even before the campaign began in earnest, there were seismic warnings that large sections of the culture were uncomfortable with the idea of a Catholic president: in the April issue of the *Atlantic Monthly* New York lawyer Charles Marshall, a respected member of the Brahmin class and himself an Episcopalian, published an open letter to Smith, explaining what he believed was an "irreconcilable opposition" between the egalitarian principles of the U.S. Constitution and the hierarchical loyalties demanded by the Roman Catholic Church. While Smith offered a coached but compelling response in the May issue of the *Atlantic*, prescient pundits knew that the gloves would be taken off in what was going to be a bitter fight.[30]

For both Republicans and Democrats looking for organizational networks to oppose Smith, the Klan now appeared as a godsend. Alabama senator J. Thomas Heflin, a southern Democrat himself, addressed ten thousand Klansmen gathered on an open field outside Jamesville, New York, on the night of June 14, having been introduced by the mayor of Syracuse as the man "who will lead the forces of Protestant Americanism at the coming Democratic Convention." His two-hour harangue against the duplicities of the Catholic Church was interrupted by the collapse of the wooden platform on which he and the other speakers were standing—which he immediately announced was a Roman Catholic attempt on his life.[31]

Governor Smith would probably have been defeated with or without the help of a moribund Klan. Reformation Sunday, the Sunday nearest October 31, on which Protestants celebrate Martin Luther's great reform of the medieval church, was the day on which many Protestant pastors, regardless of personal party affiliation, preached against Smith's candidacy. The *American Lutheran* observed in September 1928 that "the mere mention of a Roman Catholic as President of the United States has aroused Lutherans all over the country." Likewise, the *Baptist Progress* of Dallas predicted on October 4 that "if Al Smith is elected President, the Catholics will not rest until they have succeeded in stealing the garments of the Goddess of Liberty and given them to some nun to cut up for dish rags for a Catholic convent." And in its leading editorial on October 9, the *Christian Leader* of Cincinnati observed that "a Roman Catholic assassinated President Lincoln. A Roman Catholic assassinated President Garfield. A Roman Catholic assassinated President McKinley. Al Smith for President?" On November 3, 1928, Herbert Hoover was elected president by a majority of almost six million votes, including five states of the Democratic Solid South.

The anti-Catholic impulse, despite some signs of quieting down or being brushed aside by embarrassed political and cultural leaders after World War I, made an impressive showing in the fall of 1928. After the 1928 episode, according to some both inside and outside the Catholic Church, the culture's oldest prejudice just disappeared.[32]

The Disappearance of Catholic Otherness?

By the outbreak of World War II, anti-Catholicism had apparently been so far pushed to the backwater local culture of small southern and midwestern towns as to be considered almost irrelevant to the larger national story. Several explanations are offered for the surprisingly evanescent fate of a once quite sturdy and respected prejudice. The most famous is Will Herberg's spin on the secularization thesis in his classic 1955 essay in religious sociology, *Protestant, Catholic, Jew.* In Herberg's estimation, the labels identifying one as Protestant, Catholic, or Jewish had, by the mid-1950s, become largely irrelevant in explaining the real religion of the United States, a belief system that Herberg termed "the American Way of Life." Catholicism and Judaism, religious traditions once used quite effectively as boundary markers by the Protestant mainstream, now represented culturally safe manifestations of America's true creed:

Just as sociologically we may describe the emerging social structure of America as one great community divided into three big
sub-communities religiously defined, all equally American, so from
another angle we may describe Protestantism, Catholicism, and Judaism as three great branches or divisions of the "American religion."
The assumption underlying [this] view is... that they are three diverse representatives of the same "spiritual values," the "spiritual
values" American democracy is presumed to stand for (the father-
hood of God and brotherhood of man, the dignity of the individual
human being, etc.).[33]

The true creed informing most American culture in the 1950s was
a sociological construct less concerned with creed and belief than with
social identification and location. An idolatrous kind of secularism had
inverted means and ends in American culture for Herberg, an inversion
classically embodied in the Religious Revival of the 1950s about which he
was both suspicious and, finally, dismissive. Impressively high numbers of
Americans were indeed joining churches and synagogues, buying religious
books like Fulton Sheen's *Peace of Soul* and Norman Vincent Peale's *The
Power of Positive Thinking*, and flocking to see *The Ten Commandments* and
The Robe. In Herberg's estimation, though, they were doing so less for
theological reasons than for therapeutic ones, or as a way of identifying
themselves as dedicated to American cultural values and beliefs — an
identification especially important in the early years of the Cold War.
Under the large umbrella of the true common faith, then, Catholicism
was now a safely recognized expression of the "underlying unity [that]
not only supplies the common content of the three communions, [but]
also sets the limits within which their conflicts and tensions may operate,
and beyond which they cannot go." In other words, the actual theological
content of Catholicism had been safely eviscerated in the service of a
culture religion. As Herberg pointed out, however, this victory for being
included was won at the high price of cultural irrelevance and doctrinal
domestication, although it did assure a somewhat hypnotic religious peace
since Protestants, Catholics, and Jews now all believed the same thing
about what really mattered: the equality and dignity of every person, fair

play in social relations, and the sanctity and effectiveness of education as the cure for individual and social evil. Herberg argued that compared to these real beliefs, denominational differences over church governance and worship appeared to most Americans as minor indeed.[34]

Another explanation for the disappearance of Catholic otherness might be described as the assimilationist account and argues that by sheer dint of numbers, educational level, per capita income, political party affiliation, and self-described values, Catholics (along with other outsider groups like Jews and Mormons) had become so successfully embedded into the fabric of American life by the late twentieth century — helped in no small part by the G.I. Bill — that their perceived threat to the American Way of Life had disappeared.

Roger Finke and Rodney Stark, in their 1992 study of America's religious economy, *The Churching of America, 1776–1990,* have provided a masterful set of graphs, charts, and tables illustrating the quantitative "givenness" and "ecological success" of Catholicism in the religious economy of the United States. The inexorable demographic growth of Catholics as a percentage of the total population (14 percent in 1850; 26 percent in 1890; 28 percent in 1926) is set against the two largest Protestant denominations: Methodists (30 percent in 1850; 18 percent in 1890; 12 percent in 1926) and Baptists (15 percent in 1850; 9 percent in 1890; 6 percent in 1926). Building on these statistics as well as on the work of sociologists like Andrew Greeley and Seymour Martin Lipset, Finke and Stark argued that while in the 1940s Catholics had been economically poorer and less educated than their Protestant neighbors, the data had changed dramatically by the 1960s:

> Reanalyzing data collected by Stouffer in 1955, Seymour Lipset and Reinhard Bendix (1959) found that the difference between the occupational status of Protestants and Catholics disappeared when first- and second-generation immigrants were excluded. Moreover, by the mid-1960s there was little doubt that Catholics had achieved economic and educational parity with Protestants. Today, because the Catholic population is so urban and non-southern, the average Catholic earns slightly more and has a job of slightly higher status than does the average Protestant.[35]

In the estimation of Finke and Stark it was an open question in 1992 whether American Catholics were "going the way of the Congregationalists, Presbyterians, Episcopalians, and Methodists" in terms of cohesion and numbers, to become in time "just another mainline body specializing in comfortable pews, while slowly sliding downhill." Whatever the answer to that last question, it seemed clear to them that, at the end of the twentieth century, Catholics were indistinguishable from their one-time mainstream Protestant opponents on a spectrum of economic, political, ethical, and educational indicators. Because of assimilationist demographic indicators like these, which rested on hard statistics, most social scientists took it as axiomatic that the anti-Catholic animus had all but disappeared by the late twentieth century. Why would anyone bother to single out Catholics for any kind of animus if they were indistinguishable as a demographic group from everyone else?[36]

The third explanation for the disappearance of Catholic otherness is theological (or at least ecclesiastical), and tends to focus on the momentous Americanizing changes in U.S. Catholicism sponsored by the Second Vatican Council. Vatican II formally ended its sessions in 1965, but its decrees set off a Catholic version of the Sixties that could be dated as occurring between 1965 and 1975. During that Catholic decade, the older theological and liturgical traditions of Tridentine Catholicism — traditions that had emphasized the institutional, hierarchical, and otherwordliness of the Catholic tradition — came under frontal attack by Catholics claiming conciliar blessing and emphasizing personal, democratic, and socially activistic virtues.[37]

Theologically speaking, the weightiest of the Council's documents — *Lumen Gentium*, the magisterial Dogmatic Constitution on the Church — appeared to sponsor just such a theological revolution in ecclesiology by foregrounding the democratic metaphor of church as "People of God" against the older preferred metaphor of church as a "perfect institution." This biblical way of speaking about the church as a people on a pilgrimage in which hierarchy mattered much less than what Christians shared in common appeared to fit in perfectly with the egalitarianism of North American culture. Vatican II's biblical metaphor was taken by many to be Rome's blessing on accommodationists who had been pressing for some time to tear down the walls between American egalitarian values and Catholic authoritarian ways.[38]

But far more important to the faithful was the decree *Sacrosanctum Concilium,* the Council's document on divine worship, which set off the liturgy wars of organs versus guitars, altar rails versus banners, Latin versus English. Habits and taboos that had acquired the authority and sanctity of revelation (never touching the consecrated bread, not speaking in church, an all-male presence in the sanctuary) were suddenly and traumatically overturned as Catholics were invited to receive communion in the hand from female eucharistic ministers. No longer was mass the divine drama played out safely on the other side of the altar rail by ordained professionals as lay people silently read their missals or prayed to their favorite household saints: now everyone was expected to participate, and even introduce themselves to the people sitting around them during an exchange of peace that appeared to many to be undignified or even protestant in its fervent devotion to fellowship and informality.[39]

Catholics at worship, and even Catholic belief, now appeared to be safe for American consumption: the foreignness of Catholic worship was now replaced with the tentative sounds of congregational singing, invitations to join the parish liturgy committee, and calls to married fathers to consider becoming lay deacons.[40]

The Dogmatic Constitution on the Church, by far the premier theological product of the Council, seemed to open Catholics up to fellow Christians, who were no longer schismatics or heretics, but rather separated brethren. Suddenly American Catholics were establishing or joining ecumenical discussions from which they had previously held themselves aloof; likewise, Protestants discovered to their surprise and delight that Catholics were voting at the end of Sunday mass for representatives to parish councils and diocesan boards. Much of the foreignness of Catholic piety, belief, and institutional organization seemed to disappear or was at least challenged by official Catholicism itself— to the joy of many and the consternation of not a few within the American branch of Holy Mother Church. But on a number of levels — liturgical, ecclesiological, theological — U.S. Catholics were evolving in directions that made non-Catholic Americans both comfortable and pleased: many of the liturgical trappings and much of the theological substance of a hierarchical, authoritarian, and Eurocentric immigrant religion appeared to be in the process of incultura-tion into a society established and presided over by Protestants. The older fears of Romanism as the Mother of Harlots now appeared unfounded, or even embarrassing.

Or so it seemed.

Chapter Three

A "New" Anti-Catholic Bias

An Ugly Little Secret

In 1977, sociologist Andrew Greeley, with his usual habit of having a finger on the pulse of things Catholic in American culture, published *An Ugly Little Secret*. This study traced the history of anti-Catholicism in North America from its Puritan inception to the twentieth century — a history well known and well documented by students of religion and immigration in the United States. Greeley also argued in his study that the old cultural bias against Catholicism was very much alive and well and flourishing in the United States in the final quarter of the twentieth century. Given the talk among public commentators at the time about the disappearance of the Protestant establishment, as well as the emergence of the celebration of the virtues of diversity and multiculturalism, Greeley's argument seemed remarkably anachronistic, or perhaps just cranky. Surely after the presidency of John Kennedy, the reforms of the Second Vatican Council, and the much-commented-upon rise of Catholic ethnics (Irish, Italians, and Poles among them) into middle class affluence, the old nativist fears had been long-since buried and forgotten.[1]

But Greeley's work represented the first of a number of works published in the decades after its appearance, produced by Catholics of various ideological stripes and commenting on what they perceived to be the resurgence of what Arthur Schlesinger had termed "the deepest bias in the history of the American people." Neoconservative public intellectual George Weigel christened this late twentieth-century appearance of the old bias "the new anti-Catholicism." Weigel likewise drew attention to the fact that the kinds of people now perceived as anti-Catholic were certainly more difficult to characterize than the older variety. Catholics as ideologically diverse as Greeley, journalist James Martin, George Weigel, and William Donohue of the pugnacious Catholic League for Religious and Civil Rights, have reached the surprising consensus that the supposedly secular culture of the contemporary United States — a culture labeled by one non-Catholic pundit as "the culture of disbelief" — is itself a quite vibrant engine of anti-Catholic impulses.[2]

Greeley argued that the new anti-Catholicism that he saw growing in the last quarter of the twentieth century wasn't all that new. He observed that the old animus never really went away. George Weigel, on the other hand, offered a smart application of the secularization theories of Peter Berger and Martin Marty in his interpretation. Weigel said that secularity in the United States does not mean the disappearance of religion — as in European countries like France and Germany, where church attendance and membership has plummeted since World War II — but rather the privatization of religion — its removal from the public sphere into domestic quarters, so that belief becomes one's private affair. Thus a resolutely public religion like Catholicism inevitably opens itself to cultural criticism and derision. The interpretations of both Greeley and Weigel undoubtedly explain at least some of the impulses that watchdog groups like Donohue's Catholic League label as anti-Catholic in contemporary U.S. culture. Catholicism is the largest and most hierarchically organized denominational presence in the United States, with what have come to be considered controversial positions on sexuality, gender, and education. And in certain areas of the United States — Bob Jones University comes to mind immediately — the fear of the Roman Church never really subsided. (When George Bush appeared at Bob Jones during his presidential campaign in 2000, even secular media pundits remarked on his embarrassing choice of hustings, as the leaders of Bob Jones quite regularly refer to the pope as the "Anti-Christ," and the Catholic Church as the "Mother of Harlots.") Likewise, the United States Catholic Conference (the official voice of the national church located in Washington, D.C.) has published very public, and very unpopular, critiques of pure capitalism, the death penalty, and the U.S. nuclear defense policy, which irk many Americans who want their churches to sit down and behave in public.[3]

But what Catholic observers as diverse as Greeley, Weigel, Martin, and Donohue have noted in common is that official Catholic positions on abortion, homosexuality, and the role of women in the community are so targeted for cultural ridicule, media carping, and political litmus-testing so often, and so nastily — in comparison with other religious groups who espouse analogous or identical nonmainstream beliefs (say evangelical African Americans, Orthodox Jews, devout Muslims, and white Fundamentalist Christians) — that a palpable but indefinable something else can reasonably be argued to be going on.[4]

The evidence supporting the fear of such a something else is impressive when presented in summary form. Sexually rapacious and physically abusive nuns and priests now appear as stock characters in TV soap operas like *Ally McBeal*, as well as in off-Broadway shows like *Late Night Catechism*. Greenwich Village tourist shops sell an amusing but disturbing Boxing Nun wind-up toy (presumably to bring back pugilistic memories of parochial school days), while Hollywood-made movies like *Dogma* and *Stigmata*, probably more irreverent than anti-Catholic, nonetheless consistently present religion in ways quite consciously targeted to highlight and undoubtedly offend Catholic sensibilities. The Easter cover of the *New Yorker* several years ago featured a crucifixion scene on its cover, with a figure of the Easter Bunny in the place of Christ. The San Francisco Board of Supervisors granted permission to the "Sisters of Perpetual Indulgence" — a Bay Area–based group of gay men parading in nun customs with names like Sister Homo Fellatio and Sister Joyous Reserectum — to hold a "Condom Savior Mass" on the streets of the city, during which the "celebrant" held up the Latex "host" before the assembled worshipers to pronounce "this is the flesh for the life of the world."[5]

David Bolt, editorial page director of the *Philadelphia Inquirer*, opined in an op-ed piece in July 1990 that the National Catholic Bishops Conference, in taking a range of culturally unpopular stands on gender, sexual, and educational issues, risked reawakening old religious prejudices by giving them substance. Indeed, he reminded his Philadelphia readers that

the Roman Catholic Church, it needs to be remembered, is quite literally an *un-American* institution. It is not democratic. The Church's views on due process and on the status of women, to name just a couple of key issues, are sharply at odds with those that inform the laws of American secular society. And its principal policies are established by the Vatican in Rome.[6]

The debate in the U.S. House of Representatives over the proposed appointment of a Roman Catholic chaplain raised a subtle but nonetheless disturbing unease with the idea of outsiders offering prayers in the inner sanctum of the republic's temple, while the furor over a dung-covered picture of the Virgin Mary at the 1999 Sensation exhibit at the Brooklyn Museum of Art merited articles in the religion column of the *New York Times*, in which the mayor of New York charged the museum with anti-Catholicism. Virginia governor L. Douglas Wilder, commenting on Clarence Thomas's nomination to the Supreme Court in 1991, noted that the nominee "has indicated that he is a very devout Catholic. ... How much allegiance is there to the Pope?" In the ensuing controversy over Wilder's remark, *Washington Post* columnist Judy Mann weighed in on Wilder's side by observing that "Thomas makes much of his education at the hands of Catholic nuns, and much should be made of it during his Supreme Court confirmation hearing."

An "expert" on PBS's *Newshour with Jim Lehrer,* discussing mandatory DNA testing for criminals, identified Catholic priests, along with homeless people and teenagers, as being at risk for criminal behavior, while Tony Kushner, author of the Broadway hit *Angels in America,* referred to the pope in an article in *The Nation* as a "homicidal liar" who "endorses murder." During an especially nasty act of political theater in St. Patrick's Cathedral in 1989, sponsored by the New York chapter of ACTUP against the church's repeated condemnation of the use of condoms despite the latter's efficacy in slowing the spread of the AIDS virus, a consecrated host was desecrated in an act so religiously repugnant that it provoked Catholic outrage across the ideological spectrum. Catholics agreed with the response of a furious Mayor Ed Koch, himself Jewish: "If you don't like the Church, go out and find one you like, or start your own."[7]

Journalist Jimmy Breslin wrote in a 1993 *Newsday* column entitled "Old Men in Rome Don't Get It" that "unless the Catholic Church quickly changes its mind about abortion, celibacy, women in the priesthood, and the like, it will die." As several commentators observed at the time and since, whatever one's opinion about an all-male clergy, women priests, or abortion, it is difficult to imagine analogous articles appearing with titles like "The Old Rabbis in Jerusalem Don't Get It," or "Harlem Pastors Should Keep Silent on Controversial Topics." In a 1989 exhibition of paintings about AIDS funded by the National Endowment for the Humanities, the show's catalogue described New York's John Cardinal O'Connor as a "fat cannibal" and a "creep in black skirts" whose St. Patrick's Cathedral was "that house of walking swastikas on Fifth Avenue." The *New York Times* coverage of the controversy opined that these characterizations were simply matters of "critical opinion."[8]

Perhaps the journalist most famous for offensive anti-Catholic commentary is British commentator Christopher Hitchens, self-described atheist and hater of Mother Teresa. In articles like "The Devil and Mother Teresa" and in his scurrilous monograph about her entitled *The Missionary Position*, Hitchens seemed to delight in debunking what he called "the ghoul of Calcutta" in language especially targeted to provoke Catholic offense. He calls the founder of the Missionaries of Charity a "presumable virgin" with a "face like a cake left out in the rain," whose "lifestyle was butch." In a 1995 article in Tina Brown's gleefully irreverent *Vanity Fair* entitled "Mother Teresa and Me," Hitchens observed that while the image of the winner of the Nobel Peace Prize was "sweet, unworldly, and selfless, in fact Mother Teresa's a tough-minded ideologue who has cozied up to the likes of Baby Doc Duvalier and Robert Maxwell." Indeed, Hitchens more than implied a violation of honesty in advertising in the nun's taking money intended for the poor and using it to proselytize for what he termed the religious fundamentalism of the Catholic Church's position on birth control and abortion. In Hitchens's estimation, Mother Teresa was a dangerous, sinister person, whose putative holiness was actually based on spewing "propaganda for the Vatican's heinous policy of compelling the faithful to breed."[9]

Planned Parenthood International, dedicated to providing reproductive choices to women and families in developing countries around the world, argued in a letter to Pope John Paul II in June of 2000 that "the opinions and actions of the Holy See ... are seen by many as a kind of war" against the Third World poor; indeed, the organization listed the U.S. National Conference of Catholic Bishops (NCCB) among its "Political and Social Organizations Dedicated to Anti-Choice Extremism." On their website, Planned Parenthood accused both the NCCB and the Christian Coalition of quite purposefully breaching the constitutional wall of separation between church and state in the United States in order to press a reactionary social agenda (traditional "Christian" society) in the name of religion.[10]

The very randomness of these examples of what some have termed Catholic bashing — spanning the cultural spectrum from up-scale magazines of cultural comment and mass-market newspapers on the east coast to street theater in the Bay Area on the west coast — form a disturbing web of evidence. Some Catholic observers have argued that it is as though Catholic iconography, leadership, and sensibilities are somehow perceived by large sections of U.S. culture as fair game for attack, in ways that the beliefs and practices of other religious groups are not. Other Catholic commentators argue that this prejudice has been created by the problematic positions of the church itself on a number of social, sexual, and political issues. But what both groups would agree on is that Catholicism somehow doesn't fit into North American cultural values and presuppositions. But why?

Insider Explanations for the New Anti-Catholicism in the United States

A number of Catholic observers have offered compelling and cogent explanations for the resilience of anti-Catholicism in the United States since World War II. An intriguing example can be found in a "theological reflection" published by Jesuit scholar Avery Dulles in *America* magazine in 1994.[11]

Dulles noted that at least some of the hostile perception of Catholicism in contemporary U.S. culture is a result of its negative portrayal in the press and media. He posed seven tensions that help to account for the beating that many Catholics accuse the press of inflicting on their faith. Opposing the reverence needed to understand the church's mystery of faith, Dulles argued that the "press is by nature iconoclastic," dedicated to exposing what is pretentious, hypocritical, or hidden from public view by secret elites. He suggested that the eternal Gospel that constitutes Catholicism's core message seeks continuity with the past, while the media lives off novelty and thrives on the ephemeral; that Catholicism sought unity among Christ's followers by minimizing dissent and discord in its ranks while the news media specialize in disagreement and conflict. Dulles argues that the church is, according to its own self-understanding, a hierarchical society passing the authority it receives from its divine founder from the top down, while the press in a democratic society "tends to import democratic criteria into its assessment of any organization," being especially critical of large organizations that don't seem to share power with the folks who pay the bills. Indeed, Dulles noted that any effort by the church to assure normative teaching for its own members is regarded by many journalists as equivalent to censorship of the press by the state: disobedient clergy and dissident theologians are celebrated as champions of freedom fighting against an oppressive social system. Dulles also argued that church teaching on such issues as sexuality and doctrine is frequently complex and subtle, dealing with "fine points that cannot be expressed without technical terms," while the press and the electronic media, on the other hand, are "hungry for stories that are short, simple, and striking." They "slur over nuances and qualifications that may be crucial."[12]

Another explanation was offered by George Weigel in the *Commentary* article that named it the "new anti-Catholicism" in U.S. Catholic circles. But Weigel argued that the new anti-Catholicism was best understood as a "crucial component in a more radical and comprehensive campaign to establish secularism" — the outlawing of religion from public areas of culture like politics and education — as the official doctrine of the United States. This secularism "resolutely sets its face against all notions of transcendence," and particularly against religiously informed notions of transcendence. The real reason for this banishing of religious language and categories of meaning from public debate was

> not a concern for the maintenance of democratic civility amid social and religious pluralism, but the secularizers' contempt for religious conviction as something inherently repressive and authoritarian. The claim of the new secularists, like that of the old nativists, is that Catholicism is not safe for democracy.[13]

To Weigel, the new anti-Catholicism represents a North American version of Bismarck's *Kulturkampf* in nineteenth-century Germany — a culture war for the very soul of U.S. civilization between those who affirm classic Jewish and Christian notions of an objective moral order and

Weigel

those who on ideological grounds deny that there is any such thing as an objective moral norm. The Catholic Church has been targeted for special attack in that war, precisely because of its consistent and very public support for the idea of objective moral norms on a number of culturally disputed issues. In the real cultural struggle underway, says Weigel, Catholicism — which would surely survive in any case — was but a collateral (if nonetheless real) target in the siege on the American democratic tradition itself, which would suffer a fatal transformation if the new secularists win the battle. Thus, "the real threat to American pluralism is not Cardinal O'Connor, but the forces of political correctness, imposing their own radical deconstruction of reality through the public purse and public institutions."[14]

Other Catholic commentators point the finger of blame squarely at institutional Catholicism itself for its perceived woes. These internal critics of the church argue that Rome's hierarchical, Euro-centric, and clerical culture has pitted it against a number of basic values that post-Enlightenment and post-colonial societies accept as simply and obviously true. These values, whatever Rome's wishes on the matter, represent what most Americans accept as the real world. These inside commentators argue that it is past time that church leadership get with the democratic program. These Catholic critics have also argued that the values Rome so fears — women accepted as equal partners with men in the priesthood, the validity and healthiness of sexual relations for other than procreative purposes, the validity of nonhierarchical, democratic sources of church authority — far from being foreign or hostile to either the Gospel or the church's life, represent a creative working-out of Christian principles that the church itself proclaims.

Catholic theologian Elizabeth Johnson has written extensively and lucidly about the disappointment and anger among women (perhaps especially among faithful Catholic women) by the Vatican's consistent refusal to incorporate inclusive language about God in its worship and theological statements. She has argued that the Catholic Church's refusal to pluralize its god-talk — referring to God in the pronoun "she" as well as "he" in worship and theology — both reduces the divine mystery to a "single, reified metaphor of a ruling male" (which becomes an idol eclipsing the true

Mystery of God), and justifies the social dominance of "one group over those who by sex, race, or class are not part of their privileged group."

> Exclusive use of male language is both religiously idolatrous and socially oppressive. It does damage to the truth of the living God and to the dignity of women made in her image. Given the lodestar quality of a community's image of God, it results in a community bent out of shape by the relations of patriarchy. What is at stake in this question is not only the truth about God but the identity and mission of the Christian faith community itself.[15]

Andrew Sullivan, the Catholic (and gay) one-time editor of the *New Republic*, offered a similar explanation as to why so many gay Catholics felt both betrayed and angry at their own church in *Virtually Normal: An Argument about Homosexuality*, published in 1995. In Sullivan's estimation, the Vatican's 1975 document *Declaration on Certain Questions Concerning Sexual Ethics* complicated things. Before the publication of the *Declaration*, Sullivan argued that the church had offered a more coherent (and arguably more believable) natural law view of homosexual acts. The older (pre-1975) Vatican position

> held the view that homosexuals as such did not exist; it believed that everyone was a heterosexual, and that homosexual acts were acts chosen by heterosexuals, out of depravity, curiosity, lust, or bad moral guidance. They were an abuse of the essential heterosexual orientation of all humanity. Such acts were condemned because they failed to link sexual activity with a binding commitment by a man and woman in a marriage — and [were] therefore condemned in exactly the same way and for exactly the same reasons as premarital heterosexual sex, adultery, masturbation, or contracepted sex. [Homosexual acts] failed to provide for the essential conjugal and procreative context for sexual expression.[16]

The document, as Sullivan read it, appeared to allow that there might in fact be an innate instinct in a group of people that made them "predisposed to a violation of this 'natural law.'" Sullivan's question was thus simply this: if one accepted the *Declaration's* own argument that certain individuals were born with an instinct that was not a result of their choices or formation (thus rendering the homosexual predisposition morally neutral "since anything unchosen could not be moral or immoral; it simply *was*"), how could the pursuit of the ends of those instincts be intrinsically disordered if they were there by nature?[17]

Sullivan's book outlined the position of many Catholics in the United States who have said "no" to Vatican positions on certain sexual teachings, not necessarily because they are what some conservatives term "cafeteria Catholics" — picking and choosing which teachings to follow based on their personal choices — but because of what they perceived to be the intellectual thinness of the church's teaching.

Catholic writer and cultural commentator Garry Wills has likewise weighed in on this internal reflection on the anti-Catholic animus of the last quarter century, perhaps most famously in his 2000 book *Papal Sin: The Structures of Deceit*. Wills argued that the distrust that many Catholic lay people evince toward their own institution is the fruit of the institutional church's own intellectual dishonesties.[18] Pope John Paul II and influential figures around him like Cardinal Ratzinger have "ratcheted up the degrees of obligation on favorite points of doctrine, calling them 'definitive' and 'irreversible.' Yet there is still a gap, a widening lacuna, between the teaching organs in Rome and the laity in the pews."[19]

At least part of the answer, Wills asserts, is because the priests charged with passing on Rome's official teaching cannot "keep a straight face or an honest heart if they echo what Rome is saying about women or the priesthood, marriage or the natural law." Indeed, Wills observed that

> the arguments for what passes as current church doctrine are so intellectually contemptible that mere self-respect forbids a man to voice them as his own. The very fact that the intellectual level of the church has been raised makes it harder for a priest to swallow the scriptural fundamentalism reverted to by Rome when it claims that priests must be celibate or that women cannot be priests. The cartoon version of natural law used to argue against contraception, or artificial insemination, or masturbation, would make a sophomore blush.[20]

When church officials attempt to account for reassigning priests repeatedly charged with molesting children, for removing Catholic theologians from their teaching positions for doctrinal regularities, or for publicly condemning efforts at passing out condoms to drug users and HIV sufferers because such efforts violate natural law, Wills argues, a number of Catholics in the United States join others in describing their own the church as arbitrary and closed to democratic dialogue.

What is very revealing, and from the standpoint of both cultural study and theology very important, is the perception shared by loyal Catholic defenders of the faith denouncing critics, by devout but critical practitioners of the faith, and by overtly hostile external critics of the church at both *Vanity Fair* and Bob Jones University, that Catholicism somehow doesn't fit in to modern American culture. The new Catholic apologists like Greeley and Weigel — on the one hand positing the new anti-Catholicism as related in essential ways to the old anti-Catholicism, and on the other positing it as a unique recent form of American secularity — seem to share a perception with self-identified critics of an oppressive institutional hierarchy, that certain aspects of the Catholic mind-set somehow embody a worldview that is different from and threatening to the concerns and values of popular culture in the United States. Catholic apologists, strangely enough, would appear to agree with Catholic and non-Catholic critics that somehow Catholicism seems to actually see a different world than the one many Americans accept as real.

It is this shared sense of non-fit, of Catholic otherness, that is so arresting for both understanding Catholics' perceptions of themselves and others' perceptions of them.[21]

This sense of Catholic differentness in U.S. culture since World War II — a sense of outsiderhood shared by both apologists for and critics of the Roman Catholic Church — is actually quite important for understanding the position of Catholicism in the culture of the United States, and needs to be examined from theological as well as from cultural perspectives.

Chapter Four

Do Catholics and Protestants See the World Differently?

Two Ways of Imagining God and the World

In *The Analogical Imagination*, one of the most important works of theology written in the United States in the twentieth century, David Tracy says that underneath statements of religious belief, forms of worship, and codes of religious ethics (all of which Tracy would label secondary manifestations of religion) there exists a more basic level of religious understanding. This more fundamental understanding of who God is, and how God works, operates through conceptual languages. Long before people learn the language of their catechism, read the letters of Luther or the pope, or turn to ethical guides like *Why Bad Things Happen to Good People* to understand how they should act, they learn a far more basic language that shapes their concepts of the Holy. In the history of Western Christianity, there have been two distinctive (and to some extent, opposing) conceptual languages that have shaped how Christians understand God and themselves.

The conceptual language of Roman Catholic theology, worship, and ethics is what Tracy calls analogical language. This language uses analogy, that is, it utilizes things we know to understand things we don't know, including and especially God. In the analogical tradition that has shaped Catholicism in Western culture, God is made present to the community in concrete, material ways—through water and oil, bread and wine, rings and words, church statues and church officers. Further, the Catholic tradition has come to recognize that the vehicles for its sacraments (water, bread, oil) not only represent God, but actually cause God to be really present to us. These sacraments are thus not only signs pointing beyond themselves to the thing represented (like stop signs representing to us that we should stop); they are real symbols in that they also share in what

51

they point to. For example, the body and blood of Christ is actually made present in the bread and wine of the eucharist. Thus, by analogy, something we can understand (bread and wine nourishing us) reveals something we can't understand (God's nourishing us in the bread and wine that the community shares in the eucharist). And precisely because God encounters us in humble created forms like bread and wine, creation itself comes to be understood as good, as revelatory of the Holy.[1]

As Tracy applies the term to Catholicism, "analogical" has profound communal implications as well. Because God comes to us in an act celebrated by the entire community, that community, the church, is central in the story of human salvation. St. Paul's famous metaphor of the church as the body of Christ in his First Letter to the Corinthians is understood by Catholics as not only metaphorically true. For Catholic Christians, the statement that the church is Christ's body is sacramentally true in an analogical way: the church is the incarnational embodiment of Jesus in the same organic way in which the developed tree is the embodiment of the acorn seed. While they are not exactly the same thing, they are more similar than different, more related than opposed. They are constituted of the same stuff.

The language shaping the Catholic tradition focuses so centrally on both community and sacrament because "the Incarnation of Christ represents the primary analogue for the interpretation of the whole of reality": in other words, Catholics see God's taking on flesh in the historical person of Jesus as God's own chosen way of coming to us in history — through physical and material reality. To Catholics, the entire world is sacrament, as the enfleshing of God.[2]

But Tracy reminds his readers that while the rich and ancient Catholic tradition has always allowed for and taught the importance of the distinctions between God and the world, nonetheless the emphasis remains on similarities in difference, on connections linking humans to each other and to the Holy. With this emphasis on God's presence in history, a fundamental trust and confidence in the goodness of persons and human institutions ultimately emerges, even in the face of absurdity and chaos.[3]

Against this sacramentally based Catholic language of analogy, Tracy posits another: dialectical language. Theologians using this language — Protestant thinkers like Martin Luther, Søren Kierkegaard, Karl Barth,

Reinhold Niebuhr, and Paul Tillich — insist on the radical difference separating the Holy from human culture. Dialectical language focuses on the gulf between salvation and the human condition: knowing about this "rupture at the heart of human pretension, guilt and sin," is, in fact, the basis for knowing God's purposes in history. This approach to Christianity is dialectical in that it asserts that the divine revelation of salvation and grace comes only after divine judgment and rejection. God's saving us is much like the three-stage progress of any dialectic: thesis = we sin; antithesis = God says "no" to our efforts to save ourselves as full of pride; synthesis = God saves us when we confess the truth and justice of God's "no" to our sin. Against what it sees as the pretension and pride of the confidence that God and human beings are essentially alike, dialectical language focuses on the fact of human estrangement and distance from God. In such a conception of the Good News, Jesus came to us not because we were so much like God, but rather to proclaim by the "Word" a judgment on just how far we are in fact from grace and redemption. And the word that is so important to this religious language refers both to the person of Jesus (the *Logos,* or Word, of God), and to the primary means of disclosing God. In contrast to the sacramental and communal emphases of the Catholic system, dialectical language focuses on the preached word as the real presence of God's coming to us: the word of judgment and of grace that first convicts us, and then prepares us for an internal conversion that makes us true children of God. This word emphasizes what Kierkegaard called the "infinite qualitative difference" between this world and God's Kingdom, between the human and the divine, between the historical church and Christ's disciples.

Christian traditions using this conceptual language, Tracy observes, tend not to emphasize the sacramental presence of God in worship or in the institutional church; on the contrary, they fear that such an institutional, material understanding of the Holy is always potentially an idolatrous source of overweening pride and oppressive power that must be resisted by true Christians. As Tracy himself notes, not all Protestant traditions within Christianity claim this dialectical language to the exclusion of the analogical: Anglican and Lutheran Christians, for instance, have maintained rich sacramental and liturgical ("analogical") traditions of piety from the time of their reformations. But the most radical strains of Protestantism — like that brand of British Calvinism known as Puritanism that settled New England in the seventeenth century — have explored the implications of the dialectical understanding of Christianity to its extreme.[4]

The most polar forms of dialectical Christianity — like British Puritanism — warned against the all-too-easy confidence in God's presence in history and the human community that they accuse Catholicism of abetting: against Catholicism's celebration of God's advent in the sacraments, this strain of Christianity witnesses to a prophetic judgment on "all poisonous dreams of establishing any easy continuities between Christianity and culture." It emphasizes the negation of all liturgical and ethical efforts that would lessen or bridge the fearsome divide between the world and its institutions and God. This form of conceptual language produced Karl Barth's memorable observation in his *Commentary on the Epistle to the Romans*, "God's 'Yes' is the 'No' to all human institutions."[5]

Now, while David Tracy's distinction between these two conceptual languages may appear far too disembodied and theoretical for the practical business of interpreting specific historical phenomena like the perception of anti-Catholicism in the United States, just the opposite is the case.

Sociologist of religion Andrew Greeley has argued, using the definitions of culture of anthropologist Clifford Geertz, that all human religions operate, on one level at least, as culture systems. Greeley accepts Geertz's assertion that all human religions inspire certain moods and feelings among their faithful that seek to offer explanations to ultimate questions that all human cultures ask: What is the good person? What is the good society? Where did the world come from, and where is it going? All religions, in this sense, offer worldviews that answer these ultimate questions. In order to allow people to live out the implications of these worldviews in human history, all successful religions (those that endure beyond one generation) take on certain cultural features that allow them to be practiced and passed on — rules to live by and raise children; communal expressions of grief, forgiveness, and joy; ethical guidelines for knowing right from wrong in complex situations. For Greeley, the worldviews that give rise to these cultural systems represent something like the hardware on which the software of creeds and liturgies operate. Greeley observes that religion, both in the life of the individual and in the great historical traditions, was experience, symbol, story (most symbols were inherently narrative) and community before it became creed, rite, and institution. The latter were essential, but derivative.[6]

Greeley argues that the symbols and stories of the great religious traditions inspire quite distinctive religious imaginations that actually see the world through the lens of those stories and symbols. Onto the primary template of the religious imagination, institutions built their theologies, liturgies, and laws.

> Therefore, the fundamental differences between Catholicism and Protestantism are not doctrinal or ethical. The different propositional codes of the two heritages are but manifestations, tips of the iceberg, of more fundamentally differing sets of symbols. The Catholic ethic is "communitarian," and the Protestant "individualistic" because the preconscious "organizing" pictures of the two traditions that shape meaning and response to life for members of the respective heritages are different. Catholics and Protestants "*see*" the world differently.[7]

Greeley has argued that the Catholic imagination tends to see human societies, including the institutional church, as sacramentally embodying God: in this worldview, human institutions are historical embodiments of the communal virtues of justice and love, embodiments that reveal — however imperfectly — the goodness and presence of God. As Catholics see the world, human communities are both natural and good, sacramentally revealing the divine blessing on human effort. For this very reason, threats to communities must be resisted both by an assertion of communitarian/institutional values, and by strong support for the beliefs and doctrine on which the community is based. Greeley therefore predicts that Catholics are more likely than Protestants to value social over individual relations because of their optimistic view of communal relations; they are more likely than Protestants to value equality over freedom, because equality makes for smoother social relationships. And because of the sacramental/analogical nature of community itself, Catholicism emphasizes institutional, communal expressions of religious belief and organized, public piety.[8]

Greeley further argues that groups who utilize the dialectical imagination — by no means all Protestants today, but certainly groups like those Calvinists who settled New England — see human institutions as necessary to ensure public peace, but as being both unnatural and oppressive to the individual, who must struggle for autonomy. Societies organized around this set of impulses see the individual as struggling for personal freedom against the sinful oppression of social networks; these societies stress values and behaviors that contribute to personal freedom and independence from group control. Such societies deplore vices that diminish personal integrity and individual rights, and celebrate contracts and laws that protect individuals from one another. Cultures shaped by the dialectical imagination, Greeley argues, always fear that "power corrupts, and absolute power corrupts absolutely" precisely because human institutions represent massed groupings of individual selfishness and pride. While the Catholic imagination emphasizes the sanctity of communal relationships, the Protestant imagination emphasizes respect for the individual and concerns about social oppression. Institutions must be monitored for violations of individual rights, and held to account to those individuals who give them legitimacy in the first place.[9]

Biases as Theological Commitments

Both David Tracy's understanding of conceptual languages and Andrew Greeley's sociological application of that understanding to worldviews and specific cultures offer students of American religion valuable resources for interpreting the perception of Catholic difference in contemporary American culture.

The very diffuseness of the dialectical impulses of Protestantism in U.S. culture often hides the very real religious forces that shape our ostensibly secular society. But because those impulses are not readily apparent in no way makes them less real or powerful; on the contrary, precisely the opposite may be the case. The United States was, and to some extent still is, a culture powerfully shaped by the Puritan and evangelical Protestant values, which posited that the individual must be protected from the encroaching oppressions of the community and its demands. Both the Declaration of Independence and the Bill of Rights were built on firm

Calvinist foundations in warning that the individual was always to be protected from the inevitable oppressions of the group.

In this reading of American culture, the Catholic imagination is indeed foreign. The perception shared by those in and outside the Catholic Church that Catholics somehow see the world differently might not be as far-fetched as some older and newer Catholic apologists claimed. The analogical, or Catholic, impulse — which emphasizes mediation, community, sacrament, and respect for tradition — really does represent a different set of cultural emphases than the dialectical, or Protestant, one of unmediated experience, individualism, and communal restraint.

The very secularity of the new anti-Catholicism in the culture at large offers a valuable clue to its lineage and energies. Many Americans in the media, academia, and popular culture perceive Catholicism to be different from what has emerged as the American way of life. For growing numbers of Catholic intellectuals (like Tracy and Greeley), that perception is probably a good thing. Historian R. Laurence Moore has compellingly argued that being a religious outsider represents the canonical stance for being American. In his provocative study of how religious outsiders contributed in crucial ways to the making of Americans, he says that "outsiderhood is a characteristic way of inventing one's Americanness":

> Most people who lived in this country did not gain a sense of what it meant to be an American by going to the frontier. Far more of them gained that sense by turning aspects of a carefully nurtured sense of *separate identity* against a vaguely defined concept of mainstream or dominant culture.[10]

Of course many individuals and groups outside the mainstream stand in a revered line of cultural heroes — the Puritans themselves, Roger Williams, Emerson and Thoreau, Frederick Douglass — who witnessed prophetically to truths that transcended the mores of their time and place. Catholics being other or on the outside in the twenty-first century is nothing to apologize for or explain away.

Sometimes Catholic bashing arises from an unbalanced devotion to the dialectical principle that highly organized, hierarchical communities with large constituencies are presumed to be unjust, oppressive, and sinful. At least some of the new anti-Catholicism — including Christopher

Hitchens's attacks on Mother Teresa come to mind — exemplify prejudice in an almost naked way, and must be answered from the Catholic "side" forcefully, clearly, and without apology for the Catholic faith. The right to difference of opinion does not include permission for scurrilous derision and public mockery.

The sense of Catholic differentness might very well turn out to be what saves the Catholic tradition from being swallowed up by contemporary North American culture.

Tracy's recognition of the complementary nature of the two imaginations, that is, that they balance and enrich each other, might help American Catholics to hear critiques of their church without automatically hanging all of them on the anti-Catholic hook. Honest critics of what *does*, in some cases, look very much like a problematic collapsing of the tension between God's purposes and the church's laws in the name of protecting the community might offer a salutary caution to Catholics who are, perhaps, too sanguine in trusting the leaders of the community. Catholics in the United States — like all other citizens — have been profoundly shaped by the Protestant imagination in the very process of growing up in the culture and accepting its values: suspicion of communal oppression of the individual is part and parcel of being a citizen in our culture (for good and for ill).

Chapter Five

Catholic-Protestant Tensions in Postwar America

American Freedom and the Catholic Problem

On June 7, 1949, public philosopher and educational theorist John Dewey, revered by secular intellectuals as the closest thing to a saint that a non-theistic universe allows, felt compelled to write to Melvin Arnold, the young publisher of Boston's stalwart liberal publishing house Beacon Press. Dewey praised Arnold's courageous decision to publish Paul Blanshard's exposé of Catholic attempts to breach the wall of separation between church and state in the United States in the years after World War II. Dewey also praised Blanshard's book, which he praised for its "exemplary scholarship, great judgment, and tact."[1]

The book that elicited Dewey's praise had first seen the light of day as a series of twelve articles published in the staunchly libertarian journal *The Nation* beginning in November 1947. Those articles had already raised a storm of Catholic protest against their anti-Catholic rhetoric before being published by Beacon Press in 1949 as *American Freedom and Catholic Power*. Dewey's esteem for Blanshard's work was shared by a broad range of academics and public intellectuals across the United States. Bertrand Russell, Professor Robert Hutchins of the University of Chicago, Union Theological Seminary's Reinhold Niebuhr, New York State Governor Herbert Lehman, and Eleanor Roosevelt had already weighed in on Blanshard's timely call to protect the First Amendment of the Constitution against the encroachments of a Catholic hierarchy living within the very fortress of the free world but hostile to American democratic and political values. Blanshard's call clearly struck a nerve well below the level of elite culture as well; the book went through eleven printings in as many months, and remained on the *New York Times* best-seller list for seven months.[2]

On the opening page of what is the most famous twentieth-century work about liberal fears of Catholic authoritarianism, Blanshard announced that "probably no phase of our life is in greater need of candid discussion than the relationship of the Roman Catholic Church to American institutions." Especially noticeable, in his estimation, was the rise of lobbying on the part of Catholic bishops to secure public tax monies for such obviously religious purposes as the running of parochial schools and the banning of birth control literature in the public mail. An alarmed Blanshard announced that the "Catholic problem" (a phrase used by him and others in subsequent books) was "not primarily a religious problem; it is an institutional and political problem."

> The policy of mutual silence about religious differences is a reasonable policy in matters of personal faith; but when it comes to matters of political, medical, and educational principle, silence may be directly contrary to public welfare. When a church enters the arena of controversial social policy and attempts to control the judgment of its own people (and of other people) on foreign affairs, social hygiene, public education and modern science, it must be reckoned with as an organ of political and cultural power.[3]

Blanshard thus claimed not to focus on theology and piety at all, but rather on what he termed "the philosophy of church and state espoused by the Vatican," which constituted the "most important thing in the whole Catholic system" in terms of recognizing the totalitarian threat posed by the Roman faith to democracy in the United States. "Underneath all its ponderous verbiage the Catholic theory of church and state is quite simple. It is essentially a variation of the doctrine of the divine right of rulers" and represented a looming moral and cultural threat, especially to a United States that was leading the forces of light against authoritarian forces of darkness in the years immediately after World War II. It was, at best, a naive and uninformed understatement "to say that the Roman Catholic Church is in politics":

> It *is* political. "Separation of church and state" is described by Father John Courtney Murray, the leading current writer on this theme in

the American hierarchy, as "that negative, ill-defined, basically un-American formula." In making such a statement Father Murray is simply echoing the official teachings of many popes. Pius X in his *Syllabus [of Errors]* denounced as one of the "principal errors of our time": "The Church ought to be separated from the State, and the State from the Church."[4]

Catholics in the United States were outraged by Blanshard's liberal questioning of both their constitutional loyalty and their religious faith, and a number published pointed rejoinders. Dale Francis published *American Freedom and Paul Blanshard* a year after Blanshard's work; James O'Neill, a professor at Brooklyn College and a Catholic layman, offered his own response as *Catholicism and American Freedom* in 1952. But viewed from the standpoint of later events in North American Catholic history, it is now clear that Blanshard's most important Catholic conversation partner was theologian and political theorist John Courtney Murray, who undoubtedly received some good-natured ribbing from his Jesuit confreres at having been identified in Blanshard's book as the leading scholar on these issues "in the American hierarchy."[5]

In the mid-1940s Murray had already fashioned a Catholic interpretation of the American constitutional circumstance in the pages of *America* and *Theological Studies*, two influential American Jesuit publications, the latter of which Murray edited.[6] By the time of the Second Vatican Council in the mid-1960s, Murray's would be the most significant American voice in crafting conciliar documents that would shape world Catholicism in the last third of the twentieth century — a voice especially influential in the council's epochal "Declaration on Religious Freedom." Likewise, Murray's magisterial "Catholic Reflection on the American Proposition," published in the year of Kennedy's presidential election as *We Hold These Truths*, was received at the time (and is still considered by many scholars) as the most compelling Catholic natural law interpretation of the U.S. Constitution.

When *American Freedom and Catholic Power* appeared in 1949, Murray was already widely perceived as the most thoughtful Catholic voice in the public conversation over what many pundits saw as the widening gulf between Catholics and Protestants on church/state issues in the United States. He had an exchange of views in the pages of the *American Mercury* with Protestant W. Russell Bowie, founder of the public interest group Protestants and Others United for the Separation of Church and State, at the same time he was penning his review of Blanshard's book for the June 1949 issue of the *Catholic World.*

> Mr. Blanshard has about done it, I think. That is, he has given what is to date the most complete statement of the New Nativism. In the cold, cultured manner of its utterance it is unlike the ranting, red-faced nineteenth-century Nativism. Its inspiration is not Protestant bigotry, but the secularist positivism that deplores bigotry, at the same time that it achieves a closure of mind and an edge of antagonism that would be the envy of a Bible-belt circuit rider. At all events, despite the intellectualization, it is pretty much the same old article.[7]

The core of Blanshard's critique was the tired old accusation that the Catholic Church was essentially a "great power-organization, a state within a state and a state above a state." Indeed, in Murray's opinion, the only interesting thing in the entire, sadly predictable, effort was the book's potential as grist for the mill of studying this New Nativist phenomenon.[8]

But it was in an article entitled "Paul Blanshard and the New Nativism," published in the Catholic periodical *The Month* over a year later, that Murray built on his insight that Blanshard's position was part of a broader drift toward cultural monism and offered what would become the most compelling intellectual response to Protestant and secular fears of the kind voiced in *American Freedom and Catholic Power.*[9]

Murray labeled Blanshard's fears of Catholic designs on the democratic institutions of the United States as simply the most recent incarnation of the nativist impulse and argued that he had presented the categories of "American" and "un-American" as "ultimate categories of value, supplanting the usual categories of true or false, right or wrong." Murray asserted that Blanshard's primary accusation was that Catholicism was un-American (or, more to the point, anti-American) because America was a democracy, and democracy is necessarily based on a secularist or "naturalist" philosophy, and Catholicism is, at its core, anti-naturalist:

Not that Mr. Blanshard is a philosophical naturalist; he is no philosopher at all, in any discernibly conscious sense. . . . He is, to give him a name, a social monist, who wears his social monism with the twentieth century difference. It is not so much a monism of the political *order*, as a monism of the political *process*. Mr. Blanshard's idol is not so much the democratic state as the democratic process. But in his worship of this idol he is a thoroughgoing monolatrist.[10]

From Murray's standpoint, Blanshard's error was based much more in a misplaced worship of the democratic process itself as real religion than in any theological or philosophical loyalty, and rested on four untenable presuppositions about the place of religious belief in modern democracies. Murray identified them as, first, the belief that the sole area of religion's competence was private religious devotional life; secondly, the belief that the democratic state appropriately wielded sole and supreme power over all aspects of the remaining secular areas of existence, including education, family welfare, sexual mores, and marriage and divorce; thirdly, the belief that the democratic process itself possessed universal validity for resolving all issues in the secular sphere; and finally, the belief that scientific method (which came closer to the worship of than the practice of science) represented the only valid guide for forming social and political opinions about individuals and culture. On this democratic creed ostensibly under attack by plots within the Catholic Church, Murray said, "as indictments of the Church go, Mr. Blanshard's is not very substantial."[11]

Paul Blanshard and John Courtney Murray asserted that the real issue between Protestants and Catholics actually had nothing to do with religious belief or theology. This seems, in retrospect at least, highly unlikely. Blanshard and Murray underestimated the quite substantial religious impulses that informed these tensions, and as a result failed to offer compelling models of legitimate differences on church-state relations that both sides in the debate could accept or understand.

The model of Catholic analogical and Protestant dialectical imaginations are a useful lens for viewing the substantial religious impulses informing the supposedly nontheological debate between Paul Blanshard and John Courtney Murray and the religious passion informing it.

A Common Faith?

Paul Blanshard claimed that his decision to follow his father into the Protestant ministry represented "the worst blunder of my life." He was one of twins born in 1892 to the pastor of the Congregational church in the small town of Fredericksburg, Ohio. Blanshard's childhood as a "P.K." (preacher's kid) followed the standard line, including the requisite adolescent conversion under the fervent preaching of a "large-bellied evangelist who came to the First Methodist Church." Inspired by the religiously informed socialism of Walter Rauschenbusch and Edward Bellamy, Blanshard joined the Socialist Party in 1912 and enrolled at the Harvard Divinity School two years later. Far more important than Harvard in shaping his spiritual journey during these years, however, was his service as a seminary intern at the Maverick Church, "a big socialist Congregational Church in east Boston." It was this pastoral internship, during which he met birth control advocate Margaret Sanger and clerical radical Albert Rhys Williams, rather than his distaste for the academic theology he found at Harvard, that shaped the trajectory of his true vocation. After reading Leslie Stephen's *An Agnostic's Apology* while serving as pastor of a Congregational church in Tampa, Florida, Blanshard left his pulpit to enroll in a graduate sociology program at Columbia University/Union Theological Seminary. His somewhat apologetic autobiography tells us that his arrival in New York in 1917 marked the end of any kind of formal theism in his life. He found the teachings of John Dewey and Bertrand Russell far more to his liking than those of the New Testament.[12]

Between 1924 and 1933 Blanshard served intermittently as associate editor of *The Nation*, while also working at the League for Industrial Democracy. Blanshard emphasized that he had been unfairly accused of bringing an anti-Catholic bias onto the editorial page of that staunchly libertarian publication, when in fact

> the editors had taken a specifically anti-Catholic line on many aspects on church policy long before I arrived on the scene. It was more than an anti-Catholic line; it was an anti-Christian line, almost an anti-religious line. We Young Turks at *The Nation* thrived on free thought, sexual liberalism, and Fabian socialism, a blend that might be described as the spiritual wine of the period. . . . In a 1929 review

that Mencken wrote of the *Twilight of Christianity*, he said: "I believe that, on the whole, religion is a curse to the human race, even when it is relatively mild and decent." I had not yet gone that far in my iconoclasm.[13]

But the event that would reveal the path that brought Blanshard fame (or infamy) for several decades occurred while he was browsing in the Dartmouth College library. He came upon a four-volume work by the English Jesuit Henry Davis entitled *Moral and Pastoral Theology*. His eyes "bulged with astonishment" at the hypocrisy of sexually repressed celibate priests who "dared to prescribe the most detailed and viciously reactionary formulas" on sexuality, childbirth, and birth control. As Blanshard would later describe this accidental encounter, he stood dumbstruck in the Baker Library:

> Did the public really know about this amazing stuff? Why should I not take this volume and other documents of the Catholic under-world and do a deliberate muckraking job, using the techniques that Lincoln Steffens and other American muckrakers had used in expos-ing corporate and public graft in the United States? Why not? This was apparently one field not yet preempted by the muckrakers.[14]

After a "short dip into the lower reaches of Catholic medical dogma," Blanshard went to Washington, D.C., and began "long research into Catholic documents which was to occupy much of my time and energy for several years." Blanshard's course on Catholic "dogma" took him to carrels in the Library of Congress and even into the belly of the Beast itself, the library of the Catholic University of America.[15]

The fruits of this intensive study were the articles in the pages of *The Nation*. Blanshard never discovered anything in the complex webs of intellectual traditions that comprise Catholic theology, canon law, and philosophy that even nuanced the blinding insight he claimed to have had that fateful afternoon at Dartmouth College. Like the faith delivered to the saints of old, his original sense that the "viciously reactionary for-mulas" of the Roman Church represented a looming threat to democratic culture in general and to the political traditions of the United States in particular never wavered.

The dish that Blanshard presented to his readers as the "Roman Catholic Church" was a mash in which anything published under a bishop's *Nihil obstat* (disparate works on theological nominalism and realism, neo-Thomistic scholasticism, the *Code of Canon Law*, and confessional manuals) all became "Catholic dogma." The resulting confusion for Catholics attempting to read the work and discern Blanshard's polemical intent rested in part on the fact that many of these works of "dogma" pressed mutually exclusive interpretations of Catholic belief. One of several results of this confusion was that Protestant uneasiness — during a tense Cold War — about a seemingly authoritarian institution that had never formally repudiated the Holy Inquisition and the ideal of establishment status for Catholicism in civil states, was dismissed by many U.S. Catholics as so much nativist nonsense resting on shallow scholarship. This in turn led to even more uneasiness.[16]

But quite apart from questions of intellectual comprehension and interpretive sophistication in Blanshard's "scholarly" treatment of Catholic belief and practice, there lurked just below the surface of his work what David Tracy would term a distinctly religious conceptual language that did lend intellectual coherence to Blanshard's often-problematic presentation of Catholic belief. The religious imagination informing this conceptual language presupposed a network of specific beliefs about the nature of churches and their relation to human culture and the political process that might not unfairly be termed theological.

American Freedom and Catholic Power took as axiomatic a model of church identity and authority that emerged among the English Reformed churches in the late sixteenth century, but that had been hammered out in the New England Standing Order in the next century. In this Puritan ecclesiology, all legitimate ecclesiastical authority rested in a gathered congregation of converted individuals who freely joined together to elect church officials, decide church policy, and collectively manage and hold church property.[17]

The Puritan theology grounding the democratic congregationalism of these New England churches did *not* offer Greek philosophical or Enlightenment beliefs about the basic reasonableness or goodness of human beings as the reason for democratic practices in the church; on the contrary, it offered St. Augustine's interpretation of original sin, retrieved by

John Calvin in the sixteenth century but greatly elaborated on by English Protestant disciples like William Perkins in the seventeenth century. In this Augustinian interpretation of what constitutes human nature, power and authority in both the church and the civil state needed to be spread among as many people as possible, precisely because of the fallen state of a humanity deeply tainted by original sin. Trust no individual or institution from monarch to deacon with too much power, William Ames and William Perkins had warned their Reformed followers, as all power corrupts. As a Boston Puritan preacher grimly reminded his seventeenth-century congregation during an Election Sermon before voting for a new governor, "if you chain a dog at night, it will know the length of its tether by morning."[18]

The unintended irony in this remote but quite real theological basis for Blanshard's critique of Catholic authoritarianism consists in part in his self-professed intellectual disdain for all theological systems (including the Calvinism of his own family's tradition). Likewise, the remote and unconscious biblical foundation for Blanshard's commitment to democracy in the church no less than in the state — which rested on a literalistic reading of the Acts of the Apostles in the New Testament which saw democratic congregational churches as the only legitimate ones — remained opaque to Blanshard. Much like similar intellectual raids made on a disparaged Puritan theology by Thomas Jefferson and John Adams, Blanshard simply presupposed, as self-evidently obvious to all right-thinking rational persons, an entire religious worldview.[19]

Utilizing a perfectly legitimate dialectical distinction between church officers and the church proper drawn from this tradition, Blanshard drew a distinction between hierarchy and church that was almost literally incomprehensible to most pre–Vatican II Catholics reading his book:

> It is important, therefore, to distinguish between the American Catholic people and their Roman-controlled priests. If they controlled their own church, the Catholic problem would soon disappear because, in an atmosphere of American freedom, they would adjust their Church's policies to American realities. . . . Unfortunately, the Catholic people of the United States are not citizens but *subjects* in their own religious commonwealth. The American Catholic people

themselves have no representatives of their own choosing either in their own local hierarchy or in the Roman high command.[20]

Having failed the congregational/democratic test that Blanshard offered as the self-evidently American way for all religious groups to organize themselves, the Catholic laity in the United States were then presented as an oppressed people, yearning to breathe free. Blanshard announced in tones reminiscent of Patrick Henry that it was for that very reason that he was addressing his book to Catholics "fully as much as to non-Catholics. American freedom is *their* freedom, and any curtailment of that freedom by clerical power is an even more serious matter for them than it is for non-Catholics."[21]

Blanshard's call to fellow Americans to resist and expose the "idolatrous source of oppressive power and overweening pride" that the Roman hierarchy represented fit into a perfectly coherent religious conceptual language. He argued that the three cardinal doctrines in this authoritarian belief system were papal infallibility (promulgated "while the political world was moving toward liberty and democracy"), the confessional (the "most important of the devices of priestly control"), and by far the most important, the Vatican's teaching on church-state relations ("the most important thing in the whole Catholic system because it determines the political and social policies"). It was in exposing this last Catholic "dogma" that Blanshard's Protestant dialectical imagination most clearly revealed itself.[22]

The Vatican's philosophy of church and state did rest on a theology that was churchly, as opposed to the sectarian congregational gathered model of religious organization shared by many North American Protestant denominations. Catholicism's sacramental worldview saw all of creation itself and all of human relations as under its purview. In this sense, Blanshard quite correctly saw that Catholicism's authority was not vested in a gathered community of individual believers who could democratically determine among themselves where the boundaries would be drawn between sacred and secular, between church and world. On the contrary, Catholicism's hierarchically and not democratically derived power flowed far outside of the safe channels of separation (one of Blanshard's favorite

words) that protected the individual from the "sinful oppression of social networks." A religious body with such a hierarchical, sacramental
self-understanding was insupportable in the United States:

> Much of the confusion in Catholic discussions of church and state is
> semantic. The Catholic bishop ... draws his definitions from a ready-
> made world, and the words "church and state" do not mean for
> him the same things that they mean to a non-Catholic, or even
> to many Catholics. The bishop begins by including in the concept
> "church" large areas of political, social, and educational life which
> the non-Catholic regards as part of the normal sphere of democratic
> government.[23]

For Blanshard, the word "church" represented an essentially private and
voluntary form of religious organization, centered on piety and worship,
in which the power and authority rose from the bottom up and in which
decisions were reached by a vote among all members who constituted it. It
was oxymoronic (as well as immoral) for one part of the church to impose
policy on its members on issues like education, sexuality, and divorce, as
there could be no higher authority within a gathered congregation than
the very people who constituted it. Further, the church was gathered for
personal and devotional purposes; public issues like education and divorce
were part of the secular ordering of society that transcended personal piety
and worship.

Blanshard pressed these fears of Catholic authoritarianism with weary-
ing consistency in a series of subsequent works: *The Irish and Catholic
Power* in 1953; *God and Man in Washington* in 1960; and even in his reflections on the Second Vatican Council, *Paul Blanshard on Vatican II*, in
1966. Even after its famous "Declaration on Religious Freedom" — perhaps the most important legacy of the North American church to world
Catholicism, a legacy in which Catholicism formally recognized the inviolability of individual conscience in religious matters — Blanshard still
wrote that

> in terms of twentieth century velocity, the Council brought Ca-
> tholicism from the thirteenth to the seventeenth century, no mean

achievement, but it still left this largest segment of world Christianity three hundred years behind the times. The non-Catholic world was happy about the result, and justly so. At last Catholicism was moving in the right direction, toward the reality of modern life. But Vatican II also revealed that the Church, with all its progress, was still pre-American both in the rigidity of its dogmas and the autocracy of its power structure.[24]

Blanshard's critique profoundly resonated with millions of other American Protestants who shared his "dialectical imagination."

The Catholic Position: A Reply

When *American Freedom and Catholic Power* was published, Murray was engaged in a discussion with Russell Bowie in the pages of the *American Mercury* on the topic of the growing tensions between Catholics and Protestants. Murray responded to Bowie's opening article in the exchange ("Protestant Concern over Catholicism") with "The Catholic Position: A Reply":

> [Bowie] asserts that it was the Protestant majority which founded this nation that "has given to it its particular genius of liberty." To this the only brief answer is to say: Historical nonsense. Again, he asserts that the Church of Christ is "that larger and unstereotyped fellowship of the spirit which includes Christians of different names." To this one can only reply: Theological nonsense. Again, he asserts that "the dignity of all human souls and liberty of mind and spirit are the only guarantee of truth." And to this one must simply answer: Epistemological and ethical nonsense. To go beyond this two-syllabled word would be to write a three-volume work.[25]

Murray pugnaciously chalked it all up to something "in the Protestant unconscious, in consequence perhaps of some natal trauma."[26]

Born in New York City in 1904 to a Scots-immigrant father and an Irish mother, John Courtney Murray entered the Society of Jesus at sixteen and quickly emerged as one of the order's future stars. After earning an M.A. from Boston College, he prepared for ordination at the order's seminary in Woodstock, Maryland, before being sent to the Gregorian University in Rome for a doctorate in theology. He then returned to Woodstock College as a professor of theology, where he taught North American Jesuits preparing for ordination, a position he held for thirty years until his death. One sign of his order's high regard for his intellectual acuity was his appointment as editor of *Theological Studies* in 1941, the quarterly journal published by the combined Jesuit theology faculties of the United States, which Murray transformed into the Cadillac of Catholic theology journals.[27]

The first period of Murray's scholarly career outside of teaching (1942–45) focused on the thorny issue of cooperation between Catholics and other Christians. For Catholics, such cooperation with other believers — even on the practical level of running food pantries and shelters for the homeless — raised the specter of what Catholics termed indifferentism, a theological heresy that asserted that all institutional forms of Christianity were secondary to a life of practical virtue, and thus of equal value. Conservative Catholic thinkers like Joseph Fenton (editor of the *American Catholic Review*) and Francis Connell (a professor of moral theology at the Catholic University of America) were already engaged in warning U.S. Catholics of indiscriminate affiliation with non-Catholics precisely because of the danger such mingling might have on the church's univocal claims. Murray offered an intellectually elegant end run around these concerns, arguing that not only could Catholics cooperate with Protestants and other believers in the corporal works of mercy, but that they were morally obliged to. He based his argument on the fact that cooperation took place on the plane of social interaction and need not affect the spiritual plane, the realm of doctrine. Murray recognized that the question depended on the need to balance two guiding principles: Catholic unity and the common good.[28]

Murray attempted to avoid "the temptation to be drawn to one pole of the tension" in responding to Blanshard in 1949. Monism — what Murray took to be the misguided philosophical and political attempt to absolutize one value system as the sole measure of individual and social meaning — appeared to him to define precisely both of the poles he sought to avoid. Murray saw social monism embodied both in the policies of the Soviet Union (just then closing Catholic churches and schools in Poland, Czechoslovakia, and Hungary), and in Blanshard's own monistic individualism (in which the individual becomes the one ultimate value). He sought to give expression to a Catholicism in which individuals achieved both meaning and identity precisely in communities of "rightly ordered liberty." In such communities, community and individual rights were balanced in divinely sanctioned ways. From Murray's point of view, the analogical loyalties of the Catholic were almost providentially relevant to a United States battling godless communism: the community of faith stood as a bulwark against both the disordered liberty of Blanshard and the disordered compulsion of Soviet ideology.

In his review of *American Freedom and Catholic Power*, Murray tied the welfare state pressed by Blanshard to the totalitarian ideal so feared by Americans during the Cold War, in the process elaborating on the anti-totalitarian position of the Catholic Church on these issues:

> In Blanshard's view, the "expanding conception of the democratic welfare state" has taken the fields [of science, medicine and social welfare, culture, the family, education, politics and law] under its exclusive sovereignty, and in them its action is ruled only by the norm of majority opinion of "the people," that is, the free people like Blanshard. He defends the absolute autonomy of the judicial process in Hungary; what is done by them is immune from question or judgment by a foreign power, such as the Church.[29]

Murray also noted that "behind the Nativist movement in both of its manifestations there lay the profound anti-Roman bias which has been endemic in the American republic." But he laid the blame for this bias at the feet of what he termed the "Continental liberalist tradition," which he believed provided Blanshard with his extremely problematic distinctions "first between priest and people, and second between Catholicism as a religion and as a 'power system'":

> The totality of man's community life is thus absorbed in the State and shaped and determined by that which gives form to the community — the State. From the State and from the all-governing democratic process man rescues only his "devotional" life. . . . Obviously the assertion of the political is only the implicit thesis of Blanshard's book. The explicit thesis is a denial that the Church

stands outside the political order and above it, and that she has a spiritual authority which, remaining spiritual, may reach into the temporal order, there to lay the protective grasp of its authoritative moral judgments on those elements of secular life which have a sacred aspect.[30]

The very idea that democratic principles might have religious foundations, and that Blanshard's idolatry of the democratic process itself rested on those religious foundations, eluded Murray's gaze. In retrospect, it is clear why Murray's identification of the Continental liberal tradition as the real source for Blanshard's secular critique of Catholicism convinced only the already-convinced — mostly other Catholics, who saw the world the same way.

From Murray's own standpoint, Blanshard had missed the social nature of the dignity of the individual, for in Catholic natural law discourse individual and social rights are both natural and healthy. The recognition of the rights and duties owed by individuals to the community in such an understanding of the world in no way undermined or diminished the dignity of individual persons; on the contrary, the individual achieves full identity and value only in community, which stands not against the individual, but rather offers the context for achieving full dignity and meaning. To pit individual rights against the demands and opportunities of community obligation was intellectually bankrupt.

It was inconceivable to Murray that anxiety regarding the intentions of the church in the public sphere could arise from legitimate religious impulses; such anxieties had to be based in the "aggressiveness of the secular faith." But many of the loudest supporters of Blanshard's book — Russell Bowie, Reinhold Niebuhr, Methodist Bishop Bromley Oxnam — whatever else their weaknesses were hardly in the grip of an aggressive secular faith.

While some of Blanshard's supporters in Protestants and Others United for Separation of Church and State (a group that Murray privately called "PU") undoubtedly shared his secular prejudices against organized religion, others justified their fears of Catholic authoritarianism on deeply felt and consciously expressed religious principles. These religious principles saw in the invisible fellowship of covenanted individuals freely bestowing authority on human representatives the true Christian definition of what the church was to be and saw the democratic process itself as one of the best defenses against institutional manifestations of idolatrous pride. As Reinhold Niebuhr observed, "man's capacity for justice makes democracy possible; but man's inclination to injustice makes democracy necessary." One of the more famous *obiter dicta* of the North American theological movement known as Christian Realism, this idea proceeded both from a profound political commitment to democracy in the midst of the Cold War and from the Reformed "dialectical imagination." The New Nativism that Murray derisively dismissed as resulting from an aggressively secular faith belittled the profound theological impulses that motivated churchmen like Oxnam and theologians like Niebuhr and led to even more anxiety about the Catholic problem among some Americans.[31]

Murray's own resolution for balancing the demands of Catholic theology with American constitutional principles would occur in the course of the next decade. His insight in his "Leonine articles" (written while studying the political thought of Pope Leo XIII) regarding the dangers of political establishment and his proposed resolution of those dangers for Catholics in the United States formed the basis of his now-famous essay in *We Hold These Truths*, "Civil Unity and Religious Integrity." This essay is the coda to the double fugue that Murray had been playing with Blanshard for over a decade by the of time the publication of *We Hold These Truths*. Its great insight was the recognition that historical context is crucial in making theological judgments about church-state arrangements.

There were two alternatives for the embattled Leo at the end of the nineteenth century: either to advocate governmental establishment of the Catholic faith, or to give in to the sectarianism of continental liberalism, which advocated the utter autonomy of the individual conscience and the radical privatization of religious faith. The result of the latter would be a political monism that gave political concerns precedence over the church; Leo, not surprisingly, chose the former option. Murray's insight was that Leo's choice was a matter of *historical prudence,* and not of unchanging *doctrine.*

Leo XIII did not compose his doctrine in the midst of academic quiet, in the leisure of a library, sealed off from the swirling struggles of the late nineteenth-century world. Rather, he hammered it out as the head of an embattled Church, which was under attack more radical and total than any that the Church had previously encountered in history.[32]

Murray recognized that the core issue in any question of Catholicism's relation to the state was the freedom of the church to proclaim its message and practice its communal life, not whether it had been accorded establishment status by the state. Legal establishment was only one among many other means of achieving this freedom, a means unnecessary in the United States, as the government was constitutionally prohibited from interfering in the church's life and duties. Indeed, Murray argued that the dangers inherent in the liberal option rejected by Leo were, finally, not altogether absent from the other pole — the state's establishment of Catholicism. He felt that the priority of the church over the state was better ensured by remaining free from all political entanglements, as it was in the United States.[33]

Murray argued that the old danger of cultural monism pressed by continental liberalism and so wisely rejected by Leo XIII had again reared its head in the mid-twentieth century in what he termed a "theology of the First Amendment" pressed by Americans like Blanshard and others. In this reading of the First Amendment, the American separation of church and state was read as an article of faith, offering ultimate truths very much along the lines of Blanshard's understanding of democracy as an ultimate category of value:

> There are those who read into [the religion clauses of the First Amendment] certain ultimate beliefs, certain specifically sectarian tenets with regard to the nature of religion, religious truth, the church, faith, conscience, etc. In this view these articles are invested with a genuine sanctity that derives from their supposed religious content. They are dogmas, norms of orthodoxy, to which one must conform on pain of some manner of excommunication. They are true articles of faith. Hence it is necessary to believe them, to give them a religious motivated assent.[34]

In such a false understanding of the First Amendment as possessing theological content — the belief that all religious groups should be democratically organized — Americans were somehow obliged, by the very fact of being citizens in a democracy, to affirm that democratic political processes possessed the authority and the competence to shape religious belief and practice. Democracy itself claims ultimate religious authority. This idea, of course, was repugnant to Catholics.

> These constitutional clauses have no religious content. They answer none of the eternal human questions with regard to the nature of truth and freedom, or the manner in which the spiritual order of man's life is to be organized or not organized. Therefore they are not invested with the sanctity that attaches to dogma, but only the rationality that attaches to law. It is not necessary to give them a religious assent, but only a rational civil obedience. In a word, they are not articles of faith but articles of peace; that is to say, you may not act against them, because they are law, good law.[35]

Catholics viewing the exchange between Blanshard and Murray from the safety of the post–Vatican II church might be amused by Blanshard's dark fears of Catholic subversion within the arsenal of democracy, given the alacrity with which North American Catholics joined in the affluent lifestyle and ideology of the middle class in the decades after World War II. Contemporary Protestants, on the other hand, might view Blanshard's fulsome praise of the naked public square with unease, given the uncomfortable degree to which his absolutist interpretation of Jefferson's wall of separation between church and state has made the living of a public life of faith difficult, even for Protestants.[36]

Chapter Six

The Power of Negative Thinking

The Peale Group and the Catholic Candidate

The front page of the *New York Times* on Thursday, September 8, 1960, announced a nasty theological turn in the already-heated presidential campaign well under way that fall. The *Times* offered an extended story, as well as a full-page "official statement" about the problematic religious affiliation of presidential candidate John F. Kennedy. The official statement had been released by a group calling itself the National Conference of Citizens for Religious Freedom, soon to be more familiarly known as The Peale Group after its convener, the Reverend Norman Vincent Peale of the Marble Collegiate Church in Manhattan.[1]

The group assembled on September 7 at Washington's Mayflower Hotel in what was characterized by Peale as "a very impressive gathering... more or less representative of evangelical, conservative Protestants." Among its 150 prominent members were Dr. Nelson Bell (editor of *Christianity Today* and father-in-law of evangelist Billy Graham); Dr. Charles C. Morrison (former editor of the *Christian Century*); Daniel Poling (editor of the *Christian Herald*); Dr. Glenn Archer (executive director of the libertarian group Protestants and Others United for Separation of Church and State); and Dr. Clyde Taylor (executive secretary of the National Association of Evangelicals). The group also included senior pastors from such nationally prominent Protestant congregations as the New York Avenue Presbyterian Church in Washington, D.C.[2]

The group's two-thousand-word manifesto announced that the religious issue posed by Kennedy's Catholicism was an issue in the campaign because a number of "actions and policies of the Catholic Church have given Protestants legitimate grounds for concern about having a Catholic in the White House." Harold Ockenga of Boston's Park Street Church

77

(himself a prominent evangelical on the national scene) appeared to be speaking for the whole group at the news conference at the close of the meeting when he was reported as saying:

> Senator Kennedy's statements upholding separation of church and state [are] analogous to statements made by Soviet Premier Khrushchev urging world peace during his last tour of the United States last fall. Mr. Khrushchev's meaning of the word "peace" equaled the world-wide victory of Marxism, and not what Americans thought it meant. Both men [are] caught in their respective philosophical "systems."[3]

In a series of articles on the Peale Group, *Time* magazine quoted Peale as warning the assembled evangelical notables that "our American culture is at stake. I don't say it won't survive, but it won't be what it was." Voicing similar concerns, Bell was reported as observing that "too many Protestants are 'soft' on Catholicism. Pseudo-tolerance is not tolerance at all but simply ignorance." Indeed, Bell observed that "Rome was little better than Moscow," and that "the antagonism of the Roman church to Communism is in part because of similar methods."[4]

The Peale Group's statement was quoted profusely in newspaper editorials and national magazine stories that September and beyond. It opened by observing that the ministers and laity representing the thirty-seven Protestant denominations present at the Mayflower Hotel conference felt that the religion issue had appropriately become one of the most contested points in the campaign between the Democrat Kennedy and (sometime Quaker) Republican candidate Richard M. Nixon. Indeed, "the candidacy of a Roman Catholic for President of the United States has aroused questions which must be faced frankly by the American people." Ringing the changes on the rather tired carillon tune already played by both Paul Blanshard and John Courtney Murray — that the Roman Catholic Church was both a church and a state — the Peale Group's statement noted that "the laws of most predominantly Catholic countries extend to Catholics privileges not permitted to those of other faiths," and then quoted at length canon 1374 of the Code of Canon Law regarding the church's prohibition against allowing Catholic children to attend mixed schools with non-Catholics. In response to these strictures on what canon law termed correctly formed Catholic consciences, the manifesto observed:

> These policies are clearly inconsistent with the American concept of separation of church and state, and to the extent that any candidate supports or endorses them, he is unfitted for the Presidency of the United States. To the extent that he repudiates these policies and demonstrates his independence of clerical control, he is entitled to our praise and encouragement.[5]

The Peale Group thus appeared to be offering Senator Kennedy the rather odious moral choice of either declaring himself a Roman Catholic devoted to "policies clearly inconsistent with the American concept of separation of church and state" and thus risking the presidential election in a predominantly non-Catholic culture, or "repudiating these policies and demonstrating his independence of clerical control," in the process casting himself as a less than faithful Catholic to fellow believers by the pre–Vatican II standards of the time.

Senator Kennedy was not alone in feeling outraged at being subjected to a religious test that only he was expected to pass. The outcry against Peale and his group was immediate and ecumenical. President Eisenhower (Nixon's most visible political supporter) denounced the idea of making religion a political campaign weapon the same day that the statement was issued. Both Reinhold Niebuhr and Paul Tillich — the best-known and most visible Protestant theologians in the United States, teaching at two of the Protestant Establishment's most revered bastions, Union Theological Seminary and the Harvard Divinity School, respectively — issued public denunciations of Peale and his group. Niebuhr's dean at Union Seminary, eminent theologian John C. Bennett, likewise denounced the Peale Group's manifesto in the journal *Christianity and Crisis* as the product "of a kind of Protestant underworld," while a number of Jewish rabbis made the Mayflower Hotel Conference the topic of their Sabbath sermons that weekend. Rabbi Maurice J. Bloom was reported in the *New York Times* the following Sunday as telling his Bronx congregation that

> the spirit of the statement issued by these 150 clergymen is the spirit of apartheid in South Africa, the spirit of the segregationists

in our Southland, the spirit of the cynics among us and in other lands who care nothing about the means as long as they serve their partisan ends.[6]

Peale later said that his part in convening the Peale Group that autumn was the worst blunder of his ministerial career, and one of the most unpleasant episodes of his adult life. By the morning of September 9, he was besieged by critics and members of the media seeking a response to the blistering criticism by Protestants, Catholics, and Jews. By that evening he and his wife, Ruth, were reported to have slipped out of town. Peale publicly severed his ties with the Citizens for Religious Freedom, spinning his attendance at the Washington conference not as convener but as an invited guest, and offering his resignation as pastor to the board of elders of the Marble Collegiate Church. The Montreux Conference of evangelical leaders that Peale had helped to organize the previous summer in Switzerland to galvanize Protestant preachers that coming fall to preach against a Kennedy presidency makes his claims appear, at best, disingenuous. The *Philadelphia Inquirer*, published by his friend Walter Annenberg and one of the earliest major national dailies to carry his "Confident Living" pieces, announced that it was dropping his syndicated column; about 10 percent of the 196 papers carrying it did the same. Peale finally emerged from his retreat on Sunday, September 18, to preach to his beleaguered congregation, which had refused to accept his resignation. The sermon he had originally planned to deliver that Sunday morning, "What a Protestant Should Do Today," addressing Kennedy's candidacy, was replaced by an oblique admission of his own mistaken judgment in a sermon entitled "What Christ Does for People" — namely, overlooking their follies by giving them grace and strength even when they make bad choices. Peale's packed and very supportive congregation gave him standing ovations at both services he preached that day.[7]

Although Peale's ministerial and publishing career, as well as the reputations of the other 150 evangelicals present at the Mayflower Hotel, took a serious downturn, Kennedy's campaign advisors nonetheless recognized the gathering's symbolic importance. The religion issue, which had dogged the young senator since his nomination and had followed him through tense election primaries in Wisconsin and West Virginia —

during which the press unweariedly reported the religious affiliation of voters leaving the polls with an acuity and interest that risked making the election a test of religious belief — refused to go away. "With considerable reluctance" but on the fervent advice of his closest advisors, Kennedy flew from California, where he had been barnstorming, to Houston, Texas, on September 12, for one of the more memorable evenings in the history of Catholicism in the United States.[8]

At 8:55 p.m., Kennedy sat down at the dais of the ballroom of the Rice Hotel to address a meeting of the Greater Houston Ministerial Association, a group of three hundred evangelical clergymen, moderated by a Presbyterian pastor. After Kennedy's acceptance of the Association's invitation, Ted Sorensen, one of Kennedy's closest advisors, told a friend that "we can win or lose the election right there in Houston on Monday night."[9]

The real issues that should constitute the legitimate focus of a presidential campaign, he announced at the outset of his speech, had been obscured by the noise raised by Protestants like Peale and his fellow cultural preceptors:

> The hungry children I saw in West Virginia, the old people who cannot pay their doctor's bills, the families forced to give up their farms — an America with too many slums, with too few schools, and too late to the moon and outer space. These are the real issues which should decide this campaign.... But because I am a Catholic, and no Catholic has ever been elected President, the real issues in this campaign have been obscured — perhaps deliberately in some quarters less responsible than this.[10]

Rather than judging him on a theological basis, Kennedy asked his audience to judge him on his fourteen years in Congress, "on my declared stands against an Ambassador to the Vatican, [and] against unconstitutional aid to parochial schools." When complex ethical issues like birth control, divorce, censorship, or gambling came before him as an elected representative of the American people, Kennedy said he would make his decision "in accordance with what my conscience tells me to be in the national interest, and without regard to outside religious pressure or dictates." He would not even concede "any conflict to be remotely possible" between his religious faith and the duties of public office, for "I believe in an America where the separation between church and state is absolute."[11]

This was the kind of America Kennedy announced he had fought for during World War II in the South Pacific, "and the kind of America my brother died for in Europe." Kennedy observed that no one at that anxious moment in American history "suggested that he might have 'divided' loyalty," that he did not "believe in liberty." His freedom to run for public office, in fact, was precisely the kind of freedom for which our forefathers died, "when they fled here to escape religious test oaths that denied office to members of less favored churches."[12]

It was on this understanding of church-state relations that Kennedy announced he was running for the presidency, not on the basis of pamphlets that "carefully select quotations out of context from the statements of Catholic Church leaders, usually in other countries, frequently in other centuries." To all such half-baked historical accusations and scurrilous insinuations, Kennedy announced: "I do not consider these quotations binding upon my public acts: why do you?"[13]

Kennedy's address to the assembled clergymen that evening was both an unexceptional instance of American political rhetoric ("I believe in an America that is officially neither Catholic, Protestant, nor Jewish"), and a rather extraordinary theological reflection on the place of religion in American public life ("I want a chief executive whose public acts are . . . not limited or conditioned by any religious oath, ritual, or obligation"). Kennedy's speech simply reiterated the hard-line separationist position on church and state that had marked his political career from its inception.[14] But he appeared to have offered a reasonably cogent answer to the question "How can a Catholic live in the White House?"

Kennedy's elucidation of an impassible wall between religious and political concerns was not just a hurried response to the Peale Group. In his April 1960 address before the American Association of Newspaper Editors in Washington, D.C., he had already asserted that

> there is only one legitimate question. . . . Would you, as President, be responsive in any way to ecclesiastical pressures or obligations of any kind that might in any fashion interfere with your conduct of that office in the national interest? My answer was — and is — no.

I am not the Catholic candidate for President. I am the Democratic party's candidate for President who happens to be Catholic. I do not speak for the Catholic Church on issues of public policy, and no one in that Church speaks for me.[15]

It is ironic that the issue of John Kennedy's religious loyalty should arise at all, since he had never been accused of being overly pious at any point in his life. Jacqueline had reportedly told journalist Arthur Krock that she was both mystified and bemused over the issue of her husband's Catholicism, as "Jack is such a poor Catholic." Likewise, Kennedy's advisors would later report that, while Kennedy resented his portrayal in the press as not deeply religious, "he cared not a whit for theology, [and] sprinkled quotations from the Protestant Bible throughout his speeches." Sorensen, himself a Unitarian, recalled that "during the eleven years I knew him I never heard him pray aloud... or, despite all our discussions of church/state affairs, ever disclose his personal views on man's relation to God."[16]

Whatever one's take on Kennedy's personal spirituality or depth of commitment to Catholicism, it is precisely because Kennedy was a Roman Catholic that he had to secularize the presidency in order to win it. The Houston Speech is a key moment in American Catholicism's "coming of age" and in the articulation of the terms of that rite of passage.

Kennedy's separation of religious duties from presidential political responsibilities was not aimed at the disappearance or denigration of religion or religious impulses; rather it took the form of a privatization of religion. The social and religious pluralism typical of complex modern societies like that of the United States almost inexorably leads to the removal of religious impulses from the public to the private spheres for the sake of social peace and political order. Read through that lens, Kennedy's speech represented a landmark in the secularization of American politics; it removed religion as an appropriate topic from the Oval Office. It is remarkable that presidential discourse between Kennedy and Jimmy Carter — that is, until the rise of what the secular press christened the new religious right — was marked by a singular absence of religious metaphors and Christian imagery.[17] The speech also represented the mainstreaming of American Catholicism.

Part of the irony inherent in the debate over religion is the fact that the Houston Speech, which marked an America well on its way to a secular White House no less than to a Catholic presidency, was the product of Protestants like Norman Vincent Peale, who had themselves made Kennedy's religion an issue. The issue they created helped insure the privatization of religion that they would later bemoan and attack as a betrayal of the close religious-political relations that had always shaped the presidential office.

Neither the Reverend Mr. Peale nor Senator Kennedy offered public performances that brought out the best in their respective religions. Peale's intellectually threadbare interpretation of Protestantism helped to make the revered tradition of evangelical cultural and political responsibility that had produced Abraham Lincoln, Woodrow Wilson, and Reinhold Niebuhr appear narrow, parsimonious, mean-spirited, and anti-Catholic. It was the piety of small-town Babbitts organizing behind closed doors to keep others from gaining power in city hall. Peale's post-election denial of being in any way anti-Catholic rings rather hollow; it was a disappointing performance for the pastor of "America's Hometown Church."[18]

Likewise, John Kennedy emerged from the 1960 campaign as less than compelling as the spokesman for the two-millennia-old Roman Catholic conversation about the duties of Catholics in politics. John Courtney Murray's "Catholic Reflections on the American Proposition" answered fears of a Catholic presidency far more brilliantly and far more faithfully to Thomistic natural law tradition than Kennedy's theologically thin answer.[19]

A number of Catholics (and non-Catholics, too) remarked on Kennedy's somewhat singular Catholic exposition of the religious duties of politicians at the time. Episcopal bishop James Pike labeled him the most thoroughgoing secularist ever to run for the nation's highest office. *The Nation* described him as "close to being a spiritually rootless man." Jesuit-edited *America* magazine had already observed that "we were somewhat taken aback by [Kennedy's] unvarnished statement that 'nothing takes precedence over one's oath.' Mr. Kennedy doesn't really believe that. No religious man, be he Catholic, Protestant, or Jew, holds such an opinion." But it is not clear, in fact, that Kennedy did not believe precisely that.[20]

Both the Protestant Peale and the Catholic Kennedy offered problematic interpretations of their faiths in 1960, and the political culture of the United States has been the poorer for it since. Peale's baldly tribal presentation of the contours of Protestantism failed to call up the quite healthy distrust of oppressive organizations to the big and powerful tribe that Peale was ostensibly defending. The result has been that evangelical Protestants (today often lumped together as the "Religious Right" by the media and academics, regardless of actual theological positions) have since had to bear the political burden of being perceived as oppressive and judgmental cultural bullies. And in an ironic sense, Kennedy's very success in winning the presidential office on secular terms has helped to categorize Catholic politicians as either hypocritical opportunists — professing a very public faith while denying the obvious social implications of that faith for public/ political policy — or as unthinking slaves of the hierarchy on sexual and reproductive social issues. Both religions deserved better.

A Guide to Confident Living

What religious historian Sydney Ahlstrom christened "The Phenomenon of Pealeism" emerged from the very heart of evangelical Protestantism, despite the later distrust of Peale's theology among evangelical Protestants and secular liberals. Many religious conservatives came to dismiss Pealeism as pop psychology masquerading as religion or as the most successful artifact of the mentalistic self-help tradition, while liberals and the psychoanalytic establishment saw his gospel as a religion attractive to pathological yahoos.[21]

It is certainly the case that Peale came to rely increasingly on therapeutic and psychological tools in defining his ministerial responsibilities as the most famous pastor in the Reformed Church of America, especially by the time he helped to found the American Foundation of Religion and Psychiatry adjacent to Marble Collegiate Church. His therapeutic turn, however, was based on resolutely evangelical impulses: as a pastor Peale came to feel that the pastoral skills he had been taught in seminary had been too academic and theoretical to actually help cure his parishioners' troubled souls. Peale sought out Dr. Smiley Blanton, a psychoanalyst trained by

Sigmund Freud in Vienna; together they established a religio-psychiatric clinic.

Peale himself emerged from what his most perceptive biographer has termed "a thoroughly Methodist beginning."[22] He was raised in a succession of small-town parsonages in the Ohio Conference of the Methodist Church. His pastor father was eulogized at his death in 1955 as a lifelong Republican, a passionate evangelical who had been an active participant in the Anti-Saloon League's crusade for prohibition, and the father of three successful sons — two in the ministry and one in medicine. Norman took the Wesleyan heart religion with him to Ohio Wesleyan University in 1916, a denominational school where he received substantial scholarship aid as a preacher's kid. The university adhered to the standard Methodist ban on the customary trilogy of smoking, drinking, and dancing, required attendance at weekday chapel and Sunday church services, and supplemented the curriculum with on-campus revivals, prayer meetings, and hymn-sings.[23]

Peale studied William James and Ralph Waldo Emerson, both of whom became objects of a lifetime fascination. From Emerson, Peale learned that it was possible to be a practical idealist, addressing the opposing impulses of service and satisfaction, self-denial and reward that the undergraduate Peale saw within himself. James's influence was both psychological and pragmatic. His optimistic healthy-mindedness mixed well with the benevolent worldview Peale had imbibed in his parsonage home.

After graduating in 1920, Peale had a fifteen-month satisfying tenure as a reporter for the *Detroit Journal,* and then returned to the college to attend the annual Methodist Church Conference with his parents in September of 1921. Back in familiar surroundings, with the sermons, hymn-singing, and witnessing that had bracketed so much of his familial and college years, he was prompted to enter the ministry, an urge that had always been at the back of his consciousness. Returning with his parents to his boyhood town at the close of the conference, he walked until late into the night past boyhood haunts until finally, as he would later recount, "the conviction came, illuminated by the Presence of Jesus."[24]

That fall Peale moved east and began taking courses at the Methodist-affiliated Boston University School of Theology, which was committed to the dual heritages of Walter Rauschenbusch's social theology and the metaphysical celebration of individual worth (called "personalism") taught by Borden Parker Bowne. Peale remained at the time and subsequently largely impervious to the impulses of the social gospel. Bowne's almost mystical emphasis on the psychic and spiritual possibilities of the human person, on the other hand, nurtured the benevolent understanding of personal potential to which he had already been introduced. More fulfilling than the academic theology to which he applied himself with dogged if flat-footed devotion, however, was Peale's position as a student pastor at a Methodist church in Berkeley, Rhode Island, where he learned firsthand both the joys and discipline of parochial ministry. On leaving Boston, Peale was appointed pastor of a fledgling congregation in the Flatlands section of Brooklyn, New York, in 1924, whose unsteady membership Peale was expected to build up.[25]

His pastorate in the King's Highway Methodist Church in Brooklyn established a ministerial pattern that would define the rest of Peale's career: a laser-like focus on the recruitment and retention of new church members; a clever utilization of advertising techniques (a "Buy a Brick" campaign for a new church building) in publicizing and expanding facilities; and a prescient use of radio and newspaper media to publicize programs. In Peale's three-year term as pastor, the King's Highway congregation grew from just over a hundred members to nearly nine hundred and came to sponsor the fourth largest Sunday School in Brooklyn. Also foreshadowing liturgical things to come on Fifth Avenue, Peale abandoned the last vestiges of evangelical Methodist informality in worship for a more formal, even grand, style, juxtaposed against his own populist brand of preaching — theologically amorphous, anecdotal, and focused on developing a personal, transformative relationship with Jesus.[26]

So successful had Peale become in Brooklyn that he came to the attention of the bishop of Central New York, Adna Leonard, who invited the rising young pastor to preach a trial sermon from the pulpit of the University Avenue Methodist Church in Syracuse, New York, a church adjacent to the Methodist-founded Syracuse University with a large congregation that included students and professors as well as a fair sampling of the city's professional elite. Peale preached in April of 1927 and within a month was invited to become the pastor.[27]

Peale more than lived up to his reputation, partly from the replication of the techniques he inaugurated in Brooklyn, and partly from his preaching, which he redesigned in Syracuse. Under the tutelage of Hugh Tilroe, the dean of the university's School of Speech and a member of Peale's congregation, Peale learned to deliver animated, humorous, and informal sermons. He picked up on local political concerns among the elite in Syracuse and among the most pressing were

> the implications of the 1928 campaign, which resurrected nativist themes around [Catholic] Al Smith's run for the presidency.... Peale was convinced that the church had an important role to play in the culture, not least as the preserver of Protestant cultural hegemony. He told his Syracuse congregation that "only the Christian Church can keep alive free institutions, the rights of man, and the sacredness of personality." He suggested euphemistically that the "better people" needed to take their religious responsibilities more seriously.[28]

He eventually caught the attention of those outside the Methodist fold and in 1932 was invited to preach at New York City's affluent Marble Collegiate Church. A remnant of the establishment of the Dutch Reformed Church in seventeenth-century New Amsterdam, it was the third largest property owner in New York City, with a tiny (if tony) congregation of a few hundred members and very little visibility either in New York or nationally. All that was to change dramatically. The church's search committee for a new pastor was deeply impressed by Peale's performance and offered him a package that included a very generous salary, long summer vacations, and limited ministerial responsibilities focusing on preaching, with home visitation and other pastoral duties falling on ministerial associates who would leave Peale free to craft his Sunday "messages."[29]

The fly in the ointment was that Marble Collegiate's offer meant leaving his Methodist fold for a Calvinist one at the other end of the Protestant theological spectrum. But the psychological and emotional ease with which Peale accepted the offer evinces Peale's own dismissive attitude toward formal theology and his increasing emphasis on what he called "practical Christianity." As Peale's biographer Carol George has noted, in a real sense Peale never really left Methodism at all; rather he created a new style of ministry, its synthetic message shaped by his Methodist heritage to be sure, but now open to the language of Calvinist orthodoxy and the harmonial optimism of metaphysical spirituality. His symbolic break with Methodism... released him to create a ministry that cut across denominational lines. It eventually became a movement of which he was the sole designer.[30]

A central component of Peale's new style of ministry at Marble Collegiate, which would come to cut across denominational lines to address a broad national audience, was his quite effective joining of the traditional Protestant sense of responsibility for the democratic culture of the United States and an increasingly therapeutic and psychological evangelical message.

This is best evinced by the extraordinary popular success of his book *The Power of Positive Thinking,* published in October 1952 — a month before Dwight Eisenhower's landslide presidential victory over Adlai Stevenson. Peale's book has been labeled by one of the mind cure movement's most respected students as "the Bible of American auto-hypnotism," although its author then and thereafter claimed a biblical source for its inspiration: Jesus' assurance, "Be of good cheer. I have overcome the world."[31]

The book, which sold over two million copies between 1952 and 1960 alone, wove the themes of power, status, and material success into a vague evangelical sense that "faith is stronger than will." Peppered with numerous anecdotes about top-level executives and military heroes who overcame a "negative attitude" with "positive thinking" (in the process achieving career success, peer respect, and inner assurance), the book appeared to be saying that God will give you what you want if you believe in yourself while asking it. This automatic functioning on the basis of inner power functioned as the very heart of what Peale termed his "applied Christianity":

> The greatest secret for eliminating the inferiority complex... is to fill your mind to overflowing with faith. Develop a tremendous faith in God and in yourself and that will give you a humble yet soundly realistic faith in God and in yourself. ... Simply affirm, "God is with me; God is helping me; God is guiding me." Spend several minutes

each day visualizing His presence. Then practice believing that affirmation. Go about your business on the assumption that what you have affirmed and visualized is true. Affirm it, visualize it, believe it, and it will actualize you. The release of power which this procedure stimulates will astonish you.[32]

Peale himself did not address the social and political implications of this kind of faith, although critics at the time, like Reinhold Niebuhr (and since, like Donald Meyer) have termed Peale's message "a gospel of nonpolitics."[33] But this therapeutic answer of turning inward to address the deficiencies of social location, existential uncertainty, and business reverses was not completely so, for Peale's ministerial career was marked by a succession of quite concrete alliances with political forces well to the right of center to effect the concerns of the Protestant establishment in the United States. Peale had always believed that politics and religion were necessarily interdependent. In a 1956 exchange with a parishioner who had taken exception to Peale's pulpit attack on Adlai Stevenson, the Democratic candidate in that year's presidential race, Peale announced that "I totally disagree with your idea that [politics] has no place in the pulpit.... I completely insist on not only the right but the duty of the preacher to deal with any subject which, in his judgment, should be discussed."[34]

Peale's increasing national visibility as chaplain to conservative political forces can be charted chronologically: in 1936 Peale was sought out by newspaper publisher Frank Gannett to become a founding member of the National Committee to Uphold Constitutional Government, a conservative group organized by Gannett to block Franklin Roosevelt's court packing plan to increase the number of progressive Supreme Court justices. Peale's participation was followed by his membership in a number of other groups that fostered capitalism, Protestant cultural hegemony, and the Republican Party: Peale was asked to join Spiritual Mobilization in 1944, the Christian Freedom Foundation in 1948, and H. L. Hunt's Fact Forum in 1951.[35]

Peale's decision to join other evangelical conservatives on behalf of Richard Nixon's presidential campaign in 1960 hardly constituted lightning in a cloudless sky. But equally important in understanding Peale's participation in the campaign was his long-standing friendship with Richard Nixon, which stretched back to the 1940s. Although describing himself as Quaker-born and Quaker-raised (he attended Friends-sponsored Whittier College as an undergraduate), Richard Nixon had been a devoted congregant at Marble Collegiate while stationed in New York during the Second World War, after which Peale and Nixon stayed in regular contact. During his eight years as vice president, Nixon and his wife, Pat, attended Peale's church whenever they happened to be in New York. Thus, when the election year opened in 1960, it surprised no one that Peale sent Nixon a letter assuring him of "how deeply interested I am in your present campaign," and promising the Republican candidate his "earnest prayers...that victory will crown your efforts."[36]

Early August 1960 found Peale and his wife traveling in Europe. He sent Nixon a letter with his thoughts on the campaign, offering to do whatever he could to help the effort and noting that "recently I spent an hour with Billy Graham...we must do all in our power to help you." As things turned out, doing "all in our power" came to include considerably more than their prayers. Peale and Graham, along with prominent members of the National Association of Evangelicals like Harold Ockenga and L. Nelson Bell, had already agreed that the upcoming election was a vital matter and required their efforts. Peale had already decided to preach the sermon "What a Protestant Should Do Today" on his first Sunday back at Marble Collegiate in September. Some 350,000 copies of its text would immediately be distributed to the press and to other Protestant leaders nationally — a long-distance publication project already underway that summer. Peale's planned sermon was noteworthy in a number of respects, most obviously for being carefully argued and deliberately worded — unlike his usual pulpit performances. Likewise, for one usually so cavalier about theological distinctions, the sermon offered a detailed set of contrasts between Protestantism (a "thoroughly democratic faith" that had broken the shackles of an "authoritarian hierarchy" centered on a "supposedly infallible man") and a corrupt European tradition that had sent thousands of martyrs devoted to "unchaining the Word of God" to the stake. The sermon would end by asking its listeners to remember that "American freedom grew directly out of the Protestant emphasis upon every man as a child of God."[37]

But by mid-August Peale's distress about the outcome of the election had increased considerably. In a letter dated August 19, 1960, Ruth Peale said that

> Norman had a conference yesterday at Montreux, Switzerland, with Billy Graham and about 25 church leaders from the United States. They were unanimous in feeling that the Protestants in America must be aroused in some way, or the solid block Catholic voting, plus money, will take this election.[38]

Subsequent accounts have offered various narrations of what exactly transpired at the Montreux Conference, as the group met in secret and none of its participants ever spoke of it publicly. (Some later claimed that Peale felt abandoned by Billy Graham, whom he considered the conference's convener). From the arrangements made afterwards it appeared that two decisions had been reached during its meeting: the group delegated Peale to arrange a meeting between Nixon and a select group of ministers, including Peale, to discuss what the Protestant clergy might do to help the Nixon campaign in this surprisingly close race. Far more importantly, the participants decided to sponsor a public meeting, in conjunction with a group organized by the National Association of Evangelicals (the NAE), that would publicize Protestant concern over Kennedy's candidacy. The NAE had already delegated Donald Gill to organize a campaign interest group for the presidential race under the designation Citizens for Religious Freedom, and the young Baptist minister was reportedly delighted to learn that Peale himself would preside at the proposed public meeting. In the event, the planned meeting between Nixon and the clergy members, which had been scheduled for September 8, never took place. The second meeting was held in the Mayflower Hotel barely three weeks later.[39] What neither Peale nor any of the other organizers apparently knew was that two reporters, John Lindsay of the *Washington Post* and Bonnie Angelo of Long Island's *Newsday,* were also present.[40]

The five-point statement that had been prepared in advance of the meeting was unanimously accepted by the attendees. The points were a series of scatter-shot concerns regarding John Kennedy's Catholicism. One point observed that "it is inconceivable that a Roman Catholic President would not be under extreme pressure by the hierarchy of his church to accede to its policies with respect to foreign relations." Another asked: "Is it reasonable to assume that a Roman Catholic would be able to withstand altogether the determined efforts of the hierarchy of his church to gain further funds and favors for its schools and institutions, and otherwise breach the wall of separation of church and state?" In its most fire-breathing point, the document argued that

> in various areas where they predominate, Catholics have seized control of the public schools, staffed them with nun teachers wearing their church garb, and introduced the catechism, and practices of their faith. In Ohio today — a state with a Roman Catholic governor — according to an attorney general's ruling, Roman Catholic nuns and sisters may be placed on the public payroll as schoolteachers.[41]

In fact, the Ohio governor who in 1958 had allowed nuns in habits to teach in the public schools, William O'Neill, was both a Republican and a Protestant and had simply reaffirmed a state tradition that had been on the books for thirty-nine years, that had originally been approved by another Protestant governor, and that had never involved anyone teaching the catechism on public property.

But in summing up its deep concerns about the election that fall, the statement observed in what passed for its conclusion: "that there is a 'religious issue' in the present campaign is not the fault of any candidate. It is created by the nature of the Roman Catholic Church, which is, in a very real sense, both a church and a temporal state."[42]

The unanimous vote was followed by a soloist's singing of an old favorite on the revivalist circuit, "I Want to Be a Christian in My Heart." Peale then jokingly asked the group to "pray for us while we are talking to those reporters" and "strode off to the lions' den of waiting newsmen."

Peale opened his meeting with reporters immediately following the closed conference with the observation that it had been a very successful philosophical discussion about the "nature and character of the Roman Catholic Church." But Peale was quickly forced to confess in response to some pointed questions that no Catholic had been invited to the meeting, even as a resource on the nature and character of that church. Further, in response to a question about why no one had raised any questions about

Nixon's Quaker background in light of the Friends' consistent denunciation of the Cold War then raging, Peale said of Nixon's inferred pacifist
principles, "I didn't know that he ever let it bother him." But most problematic was Peale's response to the question of why other Protestants —
fellow believers somewhat to the left of those assembled at the Mayflower
Hotel — had not been invited, particularly as the group had portrayed
their meeting as a pan-Protestant concern. The name offered to Peale as
a logical candidate was Union Seminary's Reinhold Niebuhr, a theologian
with solid liberal and even socialist credentials who had taken an active
part in political issues for several decades. Peale's somewhat bare-faced
response was, "If he were here, we'd never get anything done."[43]

On one level, Peale and his fellow self-proclaimed guardians of the
individual conscience were voicing revered concerns of both the Protestant and the U.S. constitutional tradition regarding the salutary clauses
of the First Amendment. But the monolithic way in which Peale defined
those concerns for American culture as a whole and the hostile manner in which he projected his fears onto individuals who happened to be
Catholic but who consistently professed sincere allegiance to the principles of the First Amendment seems (in retrospect, anyway) a betrayal of
the deepest impulses of Protestantism. The fact that the Montreux and
Mayflower conferences welcomed only individuals from certain religious
groups within Protestantism and excluded all individuals from other groups
raises a number of profound questions about the degree to which the Protestants convening the conferences actually understood the implications of
their own faith.

Peale's demand that others conform intellectually to his own group's
presuppositions as a condition to their taking part in the public forum
came very close to the kind of ideological coercion he expected from
Catholicism. But this appears to have eluded Peale, at least until the
morning of September 8. It could be argued that Peale's cavalier attitude
to doctrinal niceties helped to inure him to the ways in which he was
betraying some of the deepest convictions of the faith in whose service he
was ostensibly organizing his crusade.

Quite ironically, what Peale never understood was that Kennedy advocated a more solid wall of separation between church and state than
did either Peale or any of his ministerial protégés. They would never have

condoned anything like Kennedy's idea of absolute separation. Thus, despite their rhetoric of concern over church-state separation, it can be compellingly argued that the Peale Group was less concerned with the individual conscience contending against oppressive social networks than with enforcing the standards of their own politically conservative group — a group behaving in ways that might fairly be termed socially oppressive.

Protestants who took theology more seriously served their faith far better that September. As Union Seminary's John Bennett remarked, the concerns and actions of the Peale Group represented less the voicing of Reformation principles than an attempt to return to a time when "we" told "them" what to do. Protestant theologians like Bennett, Reinhold Niebuhr, and Paul Tillich recognized more clearly than the Peale Group that the profound themes of divine judgment, individual responsibility, and salvation from tribal loyalties advanced so compellingly by the dialectical imagination were not well served by the events on September 7.

Niebuhr and Bennett issued a statement that was published on the front page of September 16's *New York Times*, denouncing both the bigotry of the Peale Group's statements and its presumption in claiming to speak for all American Protestants. The Niebuhr-Bennett statement observed that "most of the people in the forefront of the attacks on Roman Catholicism as an influence on the Presidency are social conservatives who generally oppose liberal policies and candidates." They claimed that using Protestantism to mask political motives was both bad theology and bad politics:

> Even if the Protestant statements are based upon innocent misunderstanding of the inner dynamics of Roman Catholicism today, they still violate the principles of fairness and of individual and group responsibility that are the hallmarks of Christian ethics. Protestants, in particular, by virtue of their belief in individual freedom of conscience and of judgment, are compelled to be fair in dealing with the beliefs and practices of others. There is also a failure in these attacks on the Roman church to realize the freedom of the Catholic layman in civil affairs. It is imperative that all voters realize that the persons who are raising the religious issue in this Presidential campaign certainly do not represent American Protestantism as a whole.[44]

When Peale reappeared in his pulpit for the first time since the events in Washington, he announced to four thousand sympathetic congregants that he still sincerely believed that he had done nothing wrong. Jack Marsh, leader of the church's Young Adult Group, in an interview with a *New York Times* reporter on the steps of the church after one of the services, said: "I insist on the right of a Protestant to say that there is something in our Protestant background and ethic that makes a Protestant better equipped to be President of the United States. We must have the right to say this without the danger of being called a bigot."[45]

Profiles in Secularization

At least since the presidential election of 1928, when the anti-Prohibition Catholic Democratic governor of New York, Al Smith, lost the election by a landslide, many in the Democratic Party leadership believed that a Catholic candidate would lose them more votes than he could gain. This common wisdom was one of the most discussed and debated issues in the Democratic Party — especially given Roman Catholicism's status as the largest religious body in the nation and its majority status in key presidential election states like New York, Pennsylvania, New Jersey, and Illinois. The party discussion had reached a critical point by 1956, when two Roman Catholics, along with two Dixiecrats, were being considered by the party leadership for the number two spot on the ticket: New York City mayor Robert Wagner and John F. Kennedy.[46]

Kennedy (and a number of politicians who supported his bid that year) believed that his Catholicism would defend the Democrats' ticket against Republican charges that they were soft on communism, as well as counter the fact that Adlai Stevenson was divorced, then a big issue. John Bailey, state chairman of the Connecticut Democratic Party and fervent Kennedy supporter, sent a memorandum to party officials in 1956. It contended that millions of Catholic Democrats who had voted for Eisenhower in 1952 would return home to the Democratic Party if a Catholic were chosen as Stevenson's running mate. The report also challenged the so-called "Al Smith Myth" by presenting statistical and historical arguments to show that the 1928 candidate lost not because of anti-Catholic bigotry, but for a host of factors unrelated to Smith's religion. The report asserted that

Kennedy would bring into the party fourteen pivotal Catholic states, which carried between them 261 electoral votes.[47]

As it turned out, Bailey's memorandum failed to galvanize party support for Kennedy. Several political scientists on the party's payroll claimed to have discredited its statistical data, while others observed that it had made no ethnic distinctions among Catholic Democrats, thus raising questions about the veracity of its conclusions. Further, liberal Protestant journals who were sympathetic to the Democrats' political agenda, voiced their own set of questions about a Kennedy candidacy. The *Christian Century* editorialized just a few days before the party's convention that their questions had more to do with the style of Wagner and Kennedy's religion than its brand. They noted that neither potential candidate offered much independent thought, religious or otherwise, during their political careers, so that Protestant worries in the case of these specific Catholic candidates were hardly put to rest. In the event, of course, neither Wagner nor Kennedy was nominated for the Democrats' number two spot.[48]

Kennedy supporters turned their eyes to the 1960 race. In preparation for that campaign, Kennedy began to reiterate his strict constructionist reading of the separation of church and state in a number of interviews and speeches, perhaps most famously in his interview with Fletcher Knebel in *Look* magazine in March 1959. Answering a question about possible conflicts between his Catholic conscience and the presidential oath to uphold the Constitution — a tendentious and insulting question — Kennedy answered that "whatever one's religion in private life may be, for the officeholder, *nothing* takes precedence over his oath to uphold the Constitution in all its parts — including the First Amendment and the strict separation of church and state."[49]

The Catholic press took immediate exception both to the questions asked and the answers. Why, they asked, should Kennedy have submitted to a loyalty test for Catholics only? The Diocese of Baltimore's *Catholic Review* said that Kennedy "appears to have gone overboard in an effort to placate the bigots"; John Cogley, in a column in the left of center Catholic weekly *Commonweal*, intimated that Kennedy had leaned a little too far in the direction of accommodation, as any Catholic in political office "would have to acknowledge that the teachings of the Church are of prime importance to him."[50]

There were also rumors of widespread opposition to the Kennedy ticket in the hierarchy of the American Catholic Church, but it rarely manifested itself in a public way — for instance, when New York's Francis Cardinal Spellman publicly and warmly welcomed Richard Nixon to his city. Whether American Catholic bishops considered Kennedy's political and religious views too liberal, whether they feared a backlash of anti-Catholicism that a Catholic president could engender, or whether they felt that a Protestant candidate would be more likely to woo their support than one of their own flock, the hostile silence of many U.S. Catholic bishops to the Kennedy ticket belied Protestant fears of an organized clerical plot behind the Kennedy campaign.[51]

On Saturday, January 2, 1960, the forty-two-year-old Kennedy announced his candidacy, challenged by Hubert Humphrey. The Wisconsin and West Virginia primaries would be decided on the religion issue. In Wisconsin Catholic and Protestant voters were about evenly divided, in West Virginia 95 percent of the voters were heavily evangelical Protestants.[52]

Although Kennedy tried to sidestep the issue in Wisconsin, the local and national press would not let it go: pictures of Kennedy greeting groups of nuns were printed across the country; other shots were left on the newsroom floor. Questions from student audiences regarding his religion were extensively reported; questions about labor and agriculture were ignored. One newspaper's political analysis of Kennedy's campaign mentioned the word "Catholic" twenty times in fifteen paragraphs.[53]

The Wisconsin primary results confirmed Kennedy's hopes and fears: he won the race with more votes than any other candidate in the history of the state's primary. But pollsters, hard-pressed to explain how his 56 percent of the Wisconsin vote had exceeded the 53 percent predictions, attributed the difference to Catholic Republicans voting on religion alone. Wisconsin threatened to make religion the only issue in the campaign: a Harris poll showed an increased awareness of the religion issue among voters in West Virginia, the state hosting the next crucial primary.[54]

Before that primary even got underway, the Episcopal bishop of Wheeling announced his opposition to a Catholic candidate for the presidency on religious grounds alone, forcing Kennedy to launch a new tactic: if religion was to be the deciding issue in the contest, he would pick the terms. If being a Catholic disqualified an American citizen from public office, he told a West Virginia audience, "I shouldn't now be serving in the Senate, and I shouldn't have been accepted into the U.S. Navy," for the oath was the same in all cases: an oath sworn on the Bible to defend the Constitution.[55]

Kennedy carried the state with 61 percent of the vote and carried districts dominated by the United Mine Workers and districts in farm and urban areas; most significantly, he had carried the white Protestant vote. That evening, Kennedy accepted Hubert Humphrey's withdrawal from the race. The religious issue, Kennedy announced, had been "buried in West Virginia." On July 9, two days before the Democratic National Convention in Los Angeles, Kennedy said on *Meet the Press* that he was certain the *bête noir* in the campaign had been silenced, and that he would win the nomination.[56]

While much has been made of Protestant-Catholic tensions during the 1960 presidential race by scholars, most students of that political campaign have overlooked the singular fact that neither religious group followed the logic of its respective theological imagination. Few noticed that in the most famous incidents in the campaign Protestants behaved in remarkably "communal" ways toward another group, and the Catholic who caused the commotion in the first place outlined the most private model of piety's place in public life ever advanced by a presidential candidate until Michael Dukakis. What has elicited considerable comment is the fact that Kennedy's razor-thin victory ushered in the end of ideology — religious ideology included.[57]

Chapter Seven

The Death Cookie and
Other Catholic Cartoons

Comic Book Theology

The morning Jack Chick borrowed $800 from a local credit union to publish his cartoon "Why No Revival?" the landscape of North American anti-Catholicism changed forever. Chick, who was working at the AstroScience Corporation in southern California at the time, was sitting in his car reading Charles Finney's classic nineteenth-century work on revivalism, *Power from on High,* when inspiration struck. Chick said that Finney's book "pushed his button." Shortly thereafter, Chick attended some churches in his neighborhood "and saw all the deadness and hypocrisy, and I thought, 'That's why there's no revival.' So I started making these little sketches. My burden was so heavy to wake Christians up to pray for revival." These themes defined his Christian cartoon empire for the next three decades.[1]

The format of the first little sketch determined the shape of the four hundred million cartoons in seventy languages that followed: two-by-four-inch, twenty-four-page booklets soon to be christened Chicklets by his fervent devotees. The simplistic theology of "Why No Revival?" spawned an entire genre of evangelical cartoons. The first frame announced that

> many pastors are unable or unwilling to say the things that appear in this book. Many things will make you angry and upset (I hope so), but I pray it will lead to repentance and to revival. I direct this book to myself, but I also believe it applies to all of us. Yours for the lost, J.T.C.
>
> Please note: This book is for Christians only — not for the unsaved![2]

100

The following frames depict images like "the family altar," a *TV Guide* resting on top of the Bible on a living room endtable, both next to a smoldering cigarette; another, called "Sunday Morning," shows Charlie teeing off at a golf course while saying to himself, "Lord, I couldn't stand another one of the pastor's dry sermons today. *He* must be out of fellowship with You. *Now remember, Lord*, I'm just as close to you out here as I am in church!"[3]

But it is frame 24 of the first Chicklet that is richly prophetic of the anti-Catholic things to come: a soberly attired televangelist couple are welcoming a mitre-clad figure and say, "We are so blessed to have our brother with us on Christian television." To which the prelate responds, "Thank you, heretic... Oops, I mean my brother." The bishop then prays in the "bubble" at the bottom of the frame, "May Mary Immaculate, the patroness of the United States, bless you and intercede with her Son for you." Below is Chick's disapproving response, quoted from the third chapter of the Epistle of Jude: "Is this contending for the faith once delivered to the saints?"[4] Chick presented his own gospel in response to this tepid ecumenical Protestantism and to Roman Catholicism, which Chick would shortly thereafter denounce as the "Whore of Babylon" prophesied in the Book of Revelation.

Mr. Chick's fervent hope that many things in his message would make people angry and upset was fulfilled a hundredfold shortly after the opening of his evangelical cartoon ministry. Along with the appearance of an almost-immediate following of Bible Believers carefully collecting each Chicklet (which appeared every ninety days, reportedly to beat the Jehovah's Witnesses, who published their tracts every six months), there appeared an equally fervent host of opponents. Chick's anti-disciples — avowed Christians, as well as militant agnostics and convinced atheists — accused the cartoon evangelist of bigotry, paranoia, and worse. The fiercely negative style that Chick's detractors say marks his literalist reading of the King James Bible is reflected in the equally spirited web-based denunciations of his universe of hermetic paranoia. Richard von Busack, in "Comic Book Theology," reports that

> everyone has seen Chick's comics, those grisly little rectangles of pulp epitomizing the violently paranoid, apocalyptic side of fundamentalist Christianity. Chick has carpeted the globe with his tiny

comic-book pamphlets, each about the size of a dollar bill....In Chick's scheme, the Catholics are currently busy creating the One World Government. This reign of terror will bring with it disease, decadence, famine, and $5 glasses of water — a horror seen only in some supper clubs, at present.[5]

As von Busack drolly observes, while the demonic forces contending against true Bible Christianity are farmed out in an equal opportunity kind of way in Chick's cartoons as really being behind the Masons, rock music, Jews, homosexuals, and big city culture in general, it is the Catholic Church that represents the very epicenter of the synagogue of Satan. Scott Adams laments online at *teleport-city.com* that in Chick's world

Satanists, vampires, rock and rollers, Shriners, and evolution-teaching eggheads lurk around every corner. The only thing more frightening than this army of darkness, however, is the fact that they are all controlled by one of two entities, the Catholic Church or Satan. Actually, in Chick's mind there is not much difference between these two, as the Devil is using the Catholic Church to lead people astray....But to tell the truth, if the Catholic Church orchestrated the two World Wars, why couldn't they stop that Kevin Smith movie (*Dogma*) that came out last year?[6]

Chick's dire warnings about the satanically led Vatican conspiracy grew progressively more shrill and hyperbolic during the 1970s, when compared to earlier cartoons that merely glossed Catholic infidelity. A classic example of Chick's comparatively mild early Catholic bashing is seen in a 1971 Chicklet entitled "The Thing," in which the holy water sprinkled by a Catholic priest on the demon-possessed "Maria" is thrown back in his face. By the end of the decade Chick had launched his "Alberto" series — overtly anti-Catholic comic books of dozens of color-filled pages — as well as his "Smokescreens" series, which featured a white-clad papal figure (looking very much like Pope John Paul II) extending his arms in a threatening way over the entire world. "Most of you know from studying your Bibles that Satan will build a false superchurch — the whore of Revelation, chapters 6, 13, 17, and 18," Chick wrote in the Introduction to the latter work. "I believe that an assault is coming by the whore of Revelation. I believe they are setting up smokescreens." Indeed, "that whore of Revelation is the Roman Catholic Institution." Likewise, the third installment of the "Alberto" series, entitled "The Godfathers," is advertised on the Chick Publications website as promising to uncover "how the Roman Catholic Institution, as the 'Mother of Abominations' (Rev. 17) caused many wars. This is the book the Catholic press is afraid to mention."[7]

The reader of these works learns that Karl Marx, Stalin and his *gulag* henchmen, and Adolf Hitler and the entire Nazi S.S. corps were actually secret members of the Jesuit order plotting the overthrow of Western democratic culture to set up a One World Government under the despotic control of what Chick persistently called the "Pope of Rome." Exactly why, in light of such a goal, communists and Nazis should engage in the mid-century slaughter of each other of the 1940s, or why the Vatican would spend the century after the publication of *Das Kapital* consistently and vociferously denouncing communism, is left to the reader's own fertile imagination, although there are many dark hints offered that this is simply one more brimstone-smelling component of that mystery of iniquity foretold in scripture.[8]

But if Chick's book-length cartoon works like "Alberto" and "Smokescreens" offered a sustained glimpse of the seamy underside of the Jesuit-led Vatican conspiracy against what Chick termed "Bible Christianity," it was the Chicklets — published in the millions — that served as the most effective popular engines of his message. These evangelical works, which were passed out on buses and subways, left in laundromats and gas station restrooms, offer a pellucid picture of the individual alone in a hostile cosmos, surrounded by demon-inspired temptations (like the International Order of Odd Fellows and rock music at church services) that inevitably led to being cast into thousand-degree lakes of fire, rendered in disturbing detail in tract after tract.[9]

This is an individual Christianity without community, sacraments, intellectual nuance, or forgiveness, in which Satan — invariably portrayed as a goatee-wearing man chortling over the lost with capital-letter "HAW, HAW, HAW" guffaws — and God fight over individual sinners, one soul at a time. Church — that is, any institution claiming divine warranty — is regularly portrayed as one of the most damnable snares that leads unsuspecting souls astray, especially when these institutions are led by demonically inspired (read progressive) pastors trained in seminaries. It is no surprise that the Church that comedian Lenny Bruce once described as always beginning with a capital "C" should be targeted as the very gateway to the Bottomless Pit.[10]

Against the ever-changing background of ceaseless demonic plots, two elements remain reassuringly constant: the revelation that most elements of modern civilization (especially egg-headed university professors teaching Darwin, every translation of the English Bible save the 1611 King James Version, and rock music) are simply fronts for a satanically led conspiracy against human souls; and the warning that the embodied form of that conspiracy is the Roman Catholic Institution. Indeed, Chick's insistence on labeling Catholicism an institution gives the distinct impression that even calling it a church risks reader complicity in the nefarious plot.[11]

Since this plot remains unknown to most North American Catholics, it might be useful to give a short course in Chicklet theology, if only to illustrate its amazing consistency over time (in which it is later than you think).

Three elements of the Catholic tradition are identified by Chick as proof positive of its satanic origins. The first regards the primacy and infallibility of the Pope of Rome, who most visibly embodies the apocalyptic predictions in the Book of Revelation regarding The Beast who fights God's saints just before the Second Coming of Christ and the end of history. Frame 10 of Chick's cartoon "The Beast" quotes the thirteenth chapter of Revelation — a far more important biblical book to Chick than any of the gospels themselves — which warns that Satan will "raise up a leader that the world will love." Below this scriptural warning is the cartoon depiction of a vast crowd in St. Peter's Square, gazing lovingly at a papal figure. "Can I show you a very scary thing?" frame 16 of this cartoon asks the reader, and then quotes Pope Leo XIII, who is presented as having taught that "he held the place of God Almighty on this earth." Chick reminds his readers about biblical warnings against false prophets "who would come in His name."[12]

A second element in the Catholic tradition that Chick regularly denounces is devotion to the Virgin Mary, which he claims originated in Babylonian worship of the goddess Semiramis. Chick's historical recovery of this fact is offered in "Why Is Mary Crying?" which includes a commendably short four-frame cultural anthropology lesson and an answer to the title's question — because, of course, "people are bowing down to statues of her." According to Chick's richly detailed if historically fact-free account of the real origin of Catholic devotion to the Virgin Mary, Satan found a beautiful witch, Semiramis, who single-handedly

> came up with the idea of confessionals, and celibacy for the priesthood. . . . Satan's phony virgin gave birth to another child and claimed that Nimrod had been reincarnated. She became a goddess with many names such as Baali (The Madonna), Queen of Heaven, the Mediatrix, and the Mother of Mankind.[13]

Satan utilized this Babylonian temptress "to create a satanic cult so powerful that it spread around the world." When Roman Catholicism came into existence (around 300 A.D. according to Chick's reckoning) its leaders immediately recognized that "if they could adopt the worship of the goddess mother, then countless pagans" could be tricked into converting to their perverted form of Christianity. This, of course, is precisely what transpired in the powerful Mary cult in the Catholic Institution. Catholics themselves are not to blame, but rather are to be pitied and forced to face the awful truth, as "Catholic families have been betrayed for centuries" by this demonic sleight-of-hand. "The 'Mother of God' that Catholics worship is not the Mary of the Bible," but rather the "counterfeit goddess that Satan has deceived them into worshiping."[14]

Catholic teaching about the sacraments, and especially about the eucharist, forms the third element of Chick's denunciation of Catholic idolatry and blasphemy. In the Chicklet "Last Rites" we see Henry and Hazel hit poor John Sullivan with their car on a rainy night; Hazel immediately calls for a priest to hear his confession and get him "right with God." The unfortunate Mr. Sullivan expires immediately thereafter. But when the angel comes for John's soul, poor John discovers to his horror that he's not "going up." "OOPS, I think I'm in trouble," John thinks to himself after being tipped off by the angel sent to escort him to God's Judgment Seat. "I spent my whole life doing good works," John pleads with an oversized and faceless Jesus figure sitting on the Throne of Judgment. But the faceless divine Judge responds (quoting St. Paul in the King James

Version), "for by grace are ye saved through faith and not by yourselves. It is the gift of God, NOT OF WORKS, lest any man should boast." A panicked John then tries another tack: "But I prayed to the blessed virgin, just like the pope does." But the implacable Judge responds, in language somewhat more colloquial than the previous "King James" quote, "That's idolatry, John, and no idolater shall enter heaven." Things go from bad to worse until the punch line is delivered near the end of this sorry tale. John finally asks the Judge, "Don't you *love* the Roman Catholic Church?" "How could I, John? Her false teachings are why you are going into the *lake of fire.*"[15]

But it is the Catholic doctrine of the eucharist that draws Chick's special enmity, embodied in classic form in the offensively named "Death Cookie" Chicklet. The "cookie" referred to, of course, is the small round wafer used for communion in Catholic churches. The reader learns that these cookies did not originate with Jesus at the Last Supper (which Catholics mistakenly believe) but rather Satan himself. The first dozen frames of this cartoon render a goatee-sporting Satan conferring with one of his chief henchmen about how he might "gain control of people without an army." The answer, of course, is that he needs a "God people can see and touch and pray to," at which point Satan pulls out the answer from his brimstone-laden pocket to announce, "And here it is — a cookie!" To his incredulous henchman's response of "Are you insane? Nobody would believe that!" Satan responds with an extended if somewhat singular history lesson about the pagan origins of Catholic sacramental practice:

> They did it in ancient Egypt and it WORKED! Our hardest job will be to convince people that this is their God, and we'll do it with magic. . . . Egyptian priests would pray over the little wafers to make them holy. They told the people that a miracle had happened. They claimed that the wafers had turned into the flesh of the sun god, Osiris. The priests of Egypt called this miracle "transubstantiation," and then the people ate their God.[16]

All of this would work, Satan announces, if only the presiders at these rites would act "very mysterious and different. Speak things that no one understands, and burn a lot of candles." The trajectory of the history lesson is thereby established, and the reader quickly notices that the vaguely

Egyptian outfitted priests in the cartoon are immediately replaced with mitre- and chasuble-wearing figures resembling medieval popes. One such figure is presented standing behind a darkly clad and hooded figure (who is reciting "Hocus Pocus Domi Nocus" over a wafer) while the mitre-wearing prelate announces to the rapt multitude watching this drama, "Watch children, this Holy man is calling God out of heaven into the cookie. We call this transubstantiation." The people thereafter learn that the only way to heaven is through "Mama Church," which controls this magical rite. But the Reformation arises just three cartoon frames later in a dizzying historical fast-forward. "One day a big problem arose," the reader is informed in bold print. A crowd of poor, unhappy burghers — soon to become true Christians — realize they've been duped by both Mama Church and Holy Papa and exclaim "we've been tricked!"

> And so the blood bath began. From 1200 to 1808 unspeakable tortures and deaths stalked the Catholic world, with 68 million victims. Satan was in complete control of the Roman Catholic Church.... To hold their people in bondage the Catholic system passed some diabolical laws at the Council of Trent.... Cutting through the gobbledygook, it says when the priest says mass and magically turns the cookie into Jesus, if "Joe" says the cookie is only a symbol of Jesus and really isn't the actual body, blood and soul of Jesus Christ, then "Joe" must be killed.[17]

The creation of this wafer god represented the "greatest religious con job in world history. One billion people live in terror that it will cost them their salvation if the priest denies them their wafer god." But not to worry, "The Vatican is marked for judgment and destruction by the Lord for her blasphemy." The reader is warned in the very last frame of the cartoon that "there is no salvation in the Roman Catholic system (Acts 4:12). You must come out."[18]

These three demonic elements of the Catholic system are brought together for the reader in a systematic way in a Chicklet entitled "Are Roman Catholics Christians?" In the very first frame of this "summation of Catholic theology" Chicklet, the reader is asked, "Is there a slight chance that the Roman Catholic Church is really NOT Christian?" If there is such a chance, think of the horrifying consequences! If it is not, then billions of people have been deceived. If it is not...then the Ecumenical Movement is not of God. If it is not — then the Roman Catholic Charismatic Movement is not of God. If it is not...then Roman Catholics are headed for a spiritual disaster. Let's study Helen's life as a devout Catholic.[19]

The eternal fate of poor "Helen" emerges as brimstone-laden because of her mistaken trust in that hellish Institution. The reader is walked through her sacramental history with an ever-growing sense of foreboding: We see her as a child being baptized (which makes her "a citizen of two countries" with "two loyalties"). We witness her first confession ("part of an occult religious system...used to find out what was going on, and to control and blackmail"), and first communion ("Helen takes the wafer god"). We see a bishop slapping Helen's cheek as part of the rite of confirmation ("Is Rome a militant 'church'? Very much so."), and a much older Helen receiving the last rites ("if [only] she had believed in the Bible!"). After the curtain has fallen on poor Helen's sad life as a carnal Christian, the moral of Helen's pilgrimage is laid out with unmistakable clarity — just in case the reader missed anything along the way:

> How can Helen possibly be filled with the Holy Spirit? She can't be. She is not even saved (Ephesians 2:8–9). Helen is very religious in a worldly sense. She can now tell the Protestants that she is a Christian [and] has been "born again." [But] poor Helen is completely brainwashed. What a dismal failure. The sacraments didn't help her. **She was betrayed.**[20]

Readers wishing to avoid a similar betrayal are not only informed about what the Bible says about getting to heaven, but are told what to pray after reading about Helen's betrayal: "Dear God, thank you for showing me what You think about Catholicism. **I also reject it!**"[21]

Are Roman Catholics Christians?

Jack Chick's fundamentalist cartoon gospel offers what might be termed the dark underside of Protestantism — particularly as it is manifested in an extreme individualistic and biblically literalist North American form. Jack Chick's stripped down version of the dialectical imagination simply represents a more extreme (or, at least, more offensive) version of a diffuse distrust of Catholics shared by a number of contemporary evangelical Christians in North America across the denominational spectrum.

It is tempting to dismiss Chick's message as a paranoid pulp gospel, or as an especially offensive example of U.S. popular culture gone laughably astray on a bizarre religious tangent, as a number of Chick's online critics argue. But his tracts can be examined as full-scale theological works, if for no other reason than because just one of these comic books reaches more believers than many preachers and theologians might hope to reach over the course of an entire career. These little evangelistic comics, however intellectually distasteful and theologically simplistic they may be, are in fact informed and structured by a well-developed intellectual understanding of how the universe operates, and how the Holy One operates in it.

What David Tracy recognized as the Protestant imagination's emphasis on the broad gulf separating the Holy from all human purposes is graphically portrayed in Chick's renderings of a larger-than-life, faceless "Jesus as Judge," righteously (if not positively gleefully) sending misguided souls to hell for reading the New American Bible or saying the rosary. The rupture between God's ways and those of humanity is taken to a logical extreme. Not only is the knowledge of such revelation central to the message, but a specific scriptural translation is key to avoiding the vast caverns full of screaming victims portrayed with almost sadistic detail. It is the magically empowered 1611 Authorized Version of the Bible or nothing for hearing the Good News. This totally ahistorical understanding of the mechanics of biblical translation — one that betrays almost total ignorance of the challenges of translating Greek into English, and one to which none of the translators of the Greek Testament into what we know as the 1611 Authorized Version would have subscribed — informs Chick's quite specific and singular meaning of "The Word."

Likewise, the grace and salvation that come only after divine judgment and rejection becomes in Chick's hands a pathological emphasis on eternal wrath directed against even good-willed believers betrayed by their institutions. All reasonable efforts at living the Christian life — save Chick's own revelation about trusting in the all-saving King James Version — are doomed from the get-go, not because of any sophisticated understanding of conflicted human consciousness, or because of profound psychological insights into the necessary but always-selfish nature of human political and social activity (insights appreciated by the great representatives of this tradition like Augustine, Calvin, and Reinhold Niebuhr) but rather in Chick's world because of a vast global conspiracy overseen by Jesuits lurking everywhere from the United Nations to the United Way.

God's "no" to our pride-filled efforts to save ourselves — a "no" that brilliant Protestant expositors like Karl Barth argued becomes the dazzling and joyous "yes" of redemption when sinners accept that judgment as valid — metastasizes into a vast global cloud over all of human culture. In Chick's hands, almost all of human culture, especially those aspects overseen by institutions, becomes, literally, the devil's playground. The individualistic tendencies vaguely inherent in the Protestant religious worldview are brought to a logical conclusion: the dramatic locus of revelation and redemption, the place where sinners see the truth and are converted, is never communal or liturgical. Rather, the individual stands alone in a fallen universe, on his own save for the King James Bible, the one life-line revealing God's evacuation plan from planet earth. Chick's cartoons, at their most communal, show saving knowledge of this plan being passed on from individual to individual — almost in secret, and almost never in church. Indeed, churches — including obviously Protestant churches using contemporary music, high church trappings like candles and altars, or therapeutic preaching — are as often as not portrayed as being under the firm control of the Prince of Darkness himself.

A profound Protestant "Augustinian" distrust of the Catholic confidence about the similarity between humanity and the Holy One becomes, in Chick's scheme of salvation, an across-the-board denunciation of all sacramental activity as a demonic strategy that displaces the internal scrutiny and doubt that should accompany the pilgrim's progress. Thus, the Catholic Institution's tradition of baptizing babies is revealed to readers as a pagan rite that trusts in human ritual rather than in that shattering conversion that palpably makes us different from unredeemed humanity.

Communion as the real presence of Christ is thus shown as eating the Death Cookie, as no human being — as Moses was reminded — could encounter such a Presence and live. Likewise going to confession is a mockery of Christ's commandment to repent by making repentance simply one more mundane human activity — something one does on Saturday afternoon between the yard sale and dinner.

According to Chick, Christianity in its purest form is reduced to individuals reading the King James Bible by themselves, then carefully selecting those few-and-far-between Bible fellowships that have nothing to do with institutional religious networks — the National Council of Churches and the General Assembly of the Presbyterian Church no less than the Pope of Rome.

The question posed in the title of Chick's most theologically synthetic work — "Are Roman Catholics Christians?" — is so obvious as to need only a cartoon answer. Poor Helen obviously isn't a good Christian, or even Christian at all, because she isn't even saved! And she isn't saved (obviously) because she has quite mistakenly entrusted her eternal welfare to that oppressive social network. This ability to grasp the nature of the True Gospel, as opposed to the false teaching of the Roman Institution, is — quite literally in Chick's theological universe — the key to Christianity and salvation. Since poor Helen has missed or been blinded to that truth, her eternal fate is sealed, despite her best intentions.

A Private Man with a Private Message

At least part of the force of Chick's preaching is that the man behind the message is almost invisible. The cartoon evangelist himself is so secretive that some of his most vocal critics have speculated that "Jack Chick" is actually a fictional character, invented by a team of conservative Christians for the express purpose of furthering their own right-wing agenda through the cartoons. However fictive the man behind the message may be, the official "Biography of Jack Chick" available at *chick.com* offers a brief but comprehensive life story. Readers are informed that Chick's ability to draw was manifested early in his childhood, a precocious talent so marked that he failed first grade "because he was so busy drawing airplanes in battle." Jack was a wild lad in an unnamed school, and "none of the Christians would have anything to do with him because of his bad language." They were convinced that Chick "was the last guy on earth who would ever accept Jesus Christ."[22]

After graduating from an unnamed high school, Jack won an acting scholarship to the Pasadena Playhouse, but his thespian career was interrupted for three years by military service in an unnamed conflict. He served in the Army in New Guinea, Australia, the Philippines, and Japan. After his discharge from the military, Jack returned to the Playhouse, where he met and married his wife, Lynn, "who was an instrument in his salvation." While visiting Lynn's parents in Canada during their honeymoon, his mother-in-law insisted that he sit and listen to Charles Fuller's *Old-Fashioned Gospel Hour* on the radio. According to Chick's own recollection, "God was already working on my heart, but when Fuller said the words, 'Though your sins be as scarlet, they shall be as white as snow,' I fell on my knees and my life was changed forever."[23]

Somewhat later, Chick had his famous experience in his car while reading Finney's *Power from on High.* After he self-published *Why No Revival?* Chick

> was driving down the road, when his eyes were drawn to a group of teens on the sidewalk. Jack remembers, "at the time, I didn't like teenagers or their rebellion. But, all of a sudden, the power of God hit me and my heart broke and I was overcome with the realization that these teens were probably on their way to hell. With tears pouring down my face, I pulled my car off the road and wrote as fast as I could, as God poured the story into my soul." Within 15 minutes, *A Demon's Nightmare* was written. After going home and drawing the art, Jack Chick's very first soul-winning gospel tract was completed.[24]

The packaging of Jack's tracts in the form now recognizable to millions was actually suggested by Bob Hammond, a missionary broadcaster at an evangelical radio station called "The Voice of China and Asia." Hammond told Chick that millions of Chinese peasants had been won over to Chairman Mao's brand of communism through the mass distribution of cartoon booklets. "Jack felt that God was leading him to use the same technique to win multitudes to the Lord Jesus Christ." Chick had been invited to present the gospel to a group of inmates at a prison near his home, and decided to draw several cartoon illustrations as well as a chart to illustrate his talk. At the conclusion of what turned out to be an extraordinarily successful preaching/cartoon presentation, "nine of the eleven inmates present trusted Christ as their savior, [and] Jack became convinced that God had given him a method of reaching people with the gospel that worked."[25]

Using his kitchen table as both an office and an art studio, Chick began producing new tracts "as God gave them to him." Chick persevered through what are termed in the website biography the rough early years — made rough in part by the fact that "many bookstores were reluctant to accept this revolutionary concept. They thought it was sacrilegious." But demand for the Chicklets grew without a bookstore network, and Chick Publications was formed as a self-supporting ministry under Jack's inspired leadership. Indeed, "the Lord assembled a dedicated staff and the work grew." Thus,

> for nearly forty years, the work has flourished. Jack Chick has written and published hundreds of illustrated gospel tracts in close to one hundred different languages. Copies of Chick tracts are even displayed in the Smithsonian Institute as an integral part of American culture. Hundreds of millions of copies have been read world-wide.[26]

The official biography takes some pains to testify to the success of Chick's idiosyncratic cartoon ministry by noting that "testimonies continue to pour in from around the world." Many of these testimonies, we are informed, recount how Chick's tracts were "instrumental in their salvation thirty years ago, then in their children's salvation, and now in the salvation of their grandchildren." The international nature of these testimonies is especially cherished by Chick, who wanted to be a missionary himself after his oversees military duty, but whose "new wife wanted no part of missionary life." God (we are informed) had other plans for this artistic evangelist, bringing Jack home to produce "effective gospel literature that missionaries could use to win the lost."[27]

The official biography ends with a testimonial by a pastor who used the Chicklets in his own ministry:

> The thing I most appreciate about Jack Chick is that thirty years ago when I read my first Chick tract, it was a pure soul winning tract, presenting the gospel in a simple format that anyone could understand. Today, thirty years later, he hasn't changed a bit. While

many other Christian leaders have left soul winning far behind, Jack Chick is still faithfully producing easy-to-understand soul winning gospel tracts with a salvation message that anyone can understand. He has never swerved or strayed from his calling to share the gospel with the lost multitudes around the world.[28]

The good pastor's testimony is the gospel truth: Jack presented the gospel "in a simple format that anyone could understand" that "hasn't changed a bit" over the course of three decades. Thus an entirely new genre of evangelization was born. The entire range of complex Christian theological concerns could now be addressed in twenty-four page cartoon booklets in a style that could be easily read, understood, and passed on by the simple expedient of leaving your own already-read Chicklet on a park bench or in a phone booth!

The features so beloved by Chick's followers — the simple content and format; the unvarnished soul winning message; the one-to-one nature of the evangelism — are the focus of attack by Chick's vociferous detractors. Adam Bugler, in an online critique entitled "Christ Comics," notes that while Chick's tracts are available by mail order from Chick's Ontario, California, offices, they are just as likely to be found in the men's rooms of highway rest stops, passed out by "men with shifty eyes on street corners," and in strip malls. Their distributors, indeed, more likely than not are "irony starved hipsters who get a rise out of goofy religious iconography." Further, Bugler observes that Chicklets' artwork

> is reminiscent of *Mad* Magazine, particularly the "Lighter Side of" series. Excluding dialogue, a Pepsi challenge comparison of a frame from "This Was Your Life" would result in confusion. Both are drawn in depthless line style and both seem stuck in a perpetual 1979 feathered hair and hip hugger bellbottoms time loop. . . . But where the drawings are absurd and pathetic and offer seeming visual evidence of humor or fun (like Satan's natty van dyke facial hair in the anti-Catholic treatise "The Death Cookie"), the comics are emphatically not very funny at all.[29]

Bugler goes on to note that Chick's anti-denominational faith is aimed at readers who are undoubtedly already good Christians and not the lost multitudes spoken of in the official website's rhetoric. After repeated attempts to speak to Chick at his office, Bugler was finally led "to suspect something which, when it hit me seemed so obvious that I was actually ashamed for not having thought of it earlier": that Jack Chick was either dead or never existed at all. Chick's almost-paranoid avoidance of any and all public interviews, the "eerie sameness of the plot construction of the comics," and the regular aesthetic changes in drawing style, led Bugler to suspect that "a majority or perhaps all of his works are products of different writers and artists, united only by a collective pseudonym":

> There is nothing celebratory, nothing transcendent about Chick's comics. The comics are uniformly stern moral reprimands. There is no joy of knowing Jesus in the world of Chick. This is not about love. This is about hate. Chick casts aspersions on other religions, but neither has nor endorses one of his own. In exposing the world as an interlocking construct of Satan, he leaves little room for solace. This is not the kind of Christianity that will make you a better person; there is no compassion. There are barely any other people; just you and the warmth you feel from knowing you're probably not going to hell. It's Christianity as an amalgam of solipsism and fear.[30]

Dwayne Walker, in "Jack Chick, a Private Man with a Public Message," offers a caustic evaluation of the Chick empire:

> The followers of Ian Paisley, the anti-Catholic friend of terrorists and all-purpose windbag from Belfast, Ireland, are fond of Chick tracts and pass them out from time to time.... [These] tracts are cruel, entertaining, evil, wonderful, lustful, deceitful, hypocritical, and the best example of the mindset of the average fundamentalist: paranoid, fearful, and filled with longing for the world that is rejecting you.[31]

The Catholic League for Religious and Civil Rights has likewise attacked Chick's anti-Catholic tracts. *The Catalyst,* the League's newsletter, offers its own "Survey of Chick Publications," which opens with the observation that while the "most invidious form of anti-Catholicism is that which emanates from elite circles," there is also a quite healthy form of the animosity that "comes from less urbane quarters" and targets the "undereducated."[32]

The *Catalyst* article takes special aim at Chick's "Alberto" series of comic books, especially vile because they are

> aimed primarily at teenagers. [They are] based on the work of Alberto Rivera, a man who claims to be an ex-Jesuit from the Diocese of Madrid. Past research by the Catholic League, however, shows no record of Rivera ever being a priest. Vintage Chick in content, the comic books are strewn with vile anti-Catholicism.[33]

The *Catalyst's* doubts regarding the veracity of Alberto's story were in fact confirmed by reports in resolutely Protestant organs like *Christianity Today* and the *Christian Century*. In a 1982 article in the latter journal, Aubrey Holmes explained that Alberto Rivera is supposedly a Spanish priest who served the church in the 1950s and 1960s, but who became disillusioned with the duplicity of both the Vatican and his own Society of Jesus, and decided to leave both in 1967 to "expose the ecumenical plot [of] Catholics' attempt to infiltrate and destroy Protestant churches." As a direct result of these decisions, Rivera claimed to have been incarcerated by Catholic officials in a Barcelona sanitarium, where he was starved and given shock treatments. On release, Alberto "resolved to bring the truth to people about the villainous work of the Catholic hierarchy."[34]

Likewise, in a 1981 article in *Christianity Today*, Gary Metz brought Protestant readers up to speed about this villainous work, with tongue in cheek. If *Christianity Today's* readers were unaware of this nefarious plot, Metz said it was because Protestant churches had been infiltrated by Jesuits. Metz then explained that both the "Alberto" Chicklet (1979) and its sequel "Double Cross" (1981) conveyed the story of how the protagonist rescued his sister, an English nun, from the convent — where she was bleeding to death from flagellation. Metz offered other secrets uncovered by Alberto — like the fact that radio evangelist Kathryn Kuhlman was a secret agent of Rome, and that the ill-fated cult leader Jim Jones was secretly a Jesuit. Perhaps the most astonishing piece of information of all was that the "name of every Protestant is kept in a computer file in the Vatican, and that the Catholic church is preparing for a twentieth century Inquisition."[35]

What Metz uncovered was that Alberto Rivera was in fact from the Canary Islands and not Spain, had traveled widely, and had been associated with numerous Christian organizations, including several in California. The Archdiocese of Madrid-Alcalá had no record of Rivera ever being ordained as a Catholic priest, nor had any other diocese in Spain. Further, Metz noted that, at the time of his writing, Alberto was being sued in Los Angeles by a man who claimed that Rivera had borrowed $2,025 from him to purchase land for a Hispanic Baptist church; when the donor asked for his money back after the land purchase never materialized, he received a bank receipt acknowledging his contribution. Further, while Rivera claimed to have numerous academic degrees — including three doctorates — a hometown friend told Metz that Rivera had never finished high school and had been in a special program for non–high school graduates at the evangelical Protestant Seminario Bíblico Latinoamericano in Costa Rica. A letter from that institution said that Rivera had been expelled for "continual lying and defiance of seminary authority."[36]

In the teeth of these devastating accusations, Rivera issued a sworn statement declaring that his story regarding his past and present activities was a "true and factual account and I will face a court of law to prove the events actually took place." *Christianity Today*'s Metz dryly observed that

> he may get his chance. This reporter's investigation shows that not only was Rivera not a Jesuit priest, but also that he had two children during the time he claimed to be living a celibate life as a Jesuit. Neither, it seems, does he have a sister in England who was a nun. Rivera has been sought by police for writing bad checks in Hoboken, New Jersey, and for stealing a credit card in Florida. Those revelations taint the credibility of the fantastic stories Rivera tells in the comic books.[37]

At the same time that these respected Protestant journals were producing their exposés, *Our Sunday Visitor* — the largest Catholic weekly newspaper in the United States, published in Huntington, Indiana — offered a $10,000 reward for proof of any of the allegations about the Catholic Church made by Alberto, or even for verification of the assertions made by Rivera regarding his life as a Catholic priest. Two decades after that generous offer, no one — not even Chick himself — has attempted to claim the money. But as Richard McMunn, editor of the *Visitor*, observed at the time, Rivera's lies were "so huge and monstrous that they are very difficult to refute."[38] These devastating exposés notwithstanding, Jack Chick has resolutely refused to discontinue publication of the "Christian Crusader" series in which Rivera stars.

Chick can afford to cavalierly ignore the accusations brought by the Catholic League and other organs of institutional religion, since the Alberto series is said to have sold in the hundreds of thousands (a figure offered by a Chick employee who declined to be identified). But Jack's personal nonchalance notwithstanding, by 1981 even that bedrock of transinstitutional evangelicalism, the Christian Booksellers Association, had had enough. The CBA — a congeries of large evangelical Protestant publishing firms, smaller Fundamentalist printing houses, and independent Christian publishers like Jack Chick himself — was brought into the debate by Michael Schwartz of the Catholic League, who had formally complained to the booksellers' organization that as a CBA member Chick was able to display and sell his literature at their conventions. Schwartz noted in his complaint that

> because he maintains membership in good standing with the CBA, Chick has been able to gain a measure of credibility for his lies.... Accusations like [his] are not matters of doctrinal disagreement, on which conscientious Christians may differ in good faith. They are not arguments for the truth of Protestant Christianity. They are vile, outrageous lies. They are the seeds of fear, hatred, and sectarian violence.[39]

Schwartz also argued that many Christian booksellers considered Chick respectable precisely because he was a CBA member, although some had voiced reservations about the kind of material found in his tracts, especially the "Alberto" series. Some members of the CBA had already suffered financial loss; after purchasing the comics, they had read the *Christianity Today* article and subsequently refused to sell them. John Bass, executive vice president of the association, commented in the CBA's *Bookstore Journal* that the controversy over Chick was "not only injuring and retarding the growth of the Christian literature movement, but is creating divisions that are not Christian in nature." Bass excerpted several letters he had received from Christian bookstore owners complaining about Chick, like one who reported how disappointed he had felt on finding a Chick publications booth at a CBA convention, "spilling out such hatred and untruth."[40]

The CBA sent a letter to Chick "asking him to reflect on the division [his] books were causing in the Christian community" and a delegation to discuss with him the many complaints it had received from members about his tactics. Chick subsequently resigned from the CBA, after denouncing it as having been infiltrated and weakened by Catholics.

Deceived!

The paranoid secrecy, simplistic biblical literalism, and hard-edged sectarian narrowness informing Chick's theology have been parodied and dismissed by mainstream Protestants and Catholics as an insignificant and marginal aberration in an ecumenical age. Likewise, libertarian commentators (like many of Chick's critics online) have been lulled into a sense of having slain the dragon of ignorance by portraying Chick's career as just another adolescent object of humor, to be taken no more seriously than *Mad* magazine. Many view Chick's ministry as beneath mainstream intellectual contempt. But such a dismissal misses the intellectual mark by a considerable margin.

Chick's work reaches more readers than mainstream religious publications. Although he may inflate the numbers for his own purposes, millions of Americans can nonetheless recall coming across at least one of these booklets. Such ubiquity should not be taken lightly.

Furthermore, he has successfully tapped into the rather large reservoir of anger and cultural suspicion underlying the rise of Protestant Fundamentalism in the United States. This resolutely militant form of Protestant evangelicalism, characterized more by its militancy than by any specific theological position, was crafted in twentieth-century North America and emerged onto the cultural stage in the 1920s, most famously in the Monkey Trial in Dayton, Tennessee, in 1924. But the old time religion championed by this movement was in fact a resolutely modern phenomenon that drew discontented believers into its ranks by the millions, largely because of the perceived apostasy and betrayal of mainstream churches in their embrace of theological modernism, ecumenism, and a critical approach to the Bible after World War I. One of the classic embodiments of this militantly modern faith was Charles Fuller's *Old Fashioned Gospel Hour,* the radio program that Chick himself claims was instrumental in his own conversion.[41]

Chick has managed to craft his anger over the diffuse sense that something has gone fundamentally wrong in U.S. culture into an easy-to-understand product that millions of simple but anguished believers can understand. The rage, suspicion, and sense of cultural betrayal characterizing Chick's tracts reflect and minister to the widespread sense of alienation of his readers.

Most importantly, to dismiss Chick's cartoon preaching as simply kooky or amusing is to miss the well-developed theological base on which it rests. The Chicklets and the "Crusader Comics" series offer an extraordinarily successful embodiment of Protestantism, albeit a truncated and simplistic one, absent of that profound Christian tradition's nuance, scholarship, and intellectual sophistication.

The individual stands alone before an especially vengeful and angry God, undoubtedly reflecting the deep anger and betrayal of Chick's readers; the forlorn individual must always battle the sinful oppression of social networks on a vast array of fronts: rock music, the Masons, the National Council of Churches, and, most sinister of all of course, the Jesuits — who mysteriously number in their ranks everyone from Adolf Hitler to Jim Jones. Sin is all-pervasive and entices the vast majority of humankind through the broad gate that leads to vast caverns full of screaming victims burning in furnaces; grace is attained through arcane knowledge of the cosmic plot that enables one to pass through the narrow gate to bliss, where one can gaze on an immense, faceless Redeemer — an Other too different from humanity to see even in the afterlife.

Chapter Eight

Catholicism and Science

The Non-Catholic Origins of American Scientists

While Jack Chick was launching his evangelical cartoon ministry in California, the academic business of explaining U.S. culture to itself was proceeding apace. The August 9, 1974, issue of *Science* magazine — one of the most prestigious academic journals published in the United States — carried an article by Professor Kenneth R. Hardy of Brigham Young University entitled "Social Origins of American Scientists and Scholars." The article's potential for controversy was more truly gauged by the synopsis printed just below its title, which said that "scholarly doctorates come disproportionately from religious groups having certain beliefs and values."[1]

Hardy, a member of Brigham Young's psychology department, began his article in standard social-scientific fashion by reviewing statistical studies that had offered fairly consistent data over several decades. Scientists in the United States, in disproportionately significant numbers, tended to come from Protestant family backgrounds, and had attended "small (often Protestant-related) liberal arts colleges." The statistical data also showed a geographical bias. U.S. scientists grew up, again, in disproportionately significant numbers, in the Midwestern and Rocky Mountain states.[2] His account of the consistent patterns rested on well-known studies dating back decades. Hardy reported that the groundbreaking 1931 study by Harvey Lehman and Paul Witty that examined 1,189 scientists described as "eminent" in the 1927 edition of *American Men of Science* found that subjects claiming affiliation with "liberal Protestant faiths" (a category that included Unitarians, Congregationalists, Friends, Episcopalians, and Presbyterians) were over-represented in both percentages and sheer numbers among American scientists. The study also reported that scientific professionals reared in "fundamentalistic" Protestant faiths (a category that included Methodists, Disciples of Christ, Baptists, and Lutherans) were described as markedly under-represented. Scientists reared in, affiliated with, or educated in the Roman Catholic faith were grossly under-represented. Hardy also reported the findings of Ann Roe's 1952 study of highly distinguished scientists: fifty-eight of the sixty-four professionals had a Protestant upbringing or attended schools founded by Protestant denominations. Five were Jewish; the parents of one scholar were described as free thinkers. None came from a Catholic background or had attended a Catholic institution.[3]

But it was Robert Knapp and Hubert Goodrich's 1952 study, *Origins of American Scientists*, that Hardy found most useful for his own work. The trustees of Connecticut's Wesleyan University appropriated funds in 1946 for a long-range study

> to assess statistically the relative scientific-production efficiency of some 490 universities and colleges by determining what proportions of their graduates had entered careers in science, and, by means of statistical analysis and case studies, to attempt to discover what factors had contributed to effective production.[4]

Knapp and Goodrich studied the academic origins of scientists listed in the 1944 edition of *American Men of Science* and then ranked the fifty most productive educational institutions. These fifty institutions included science- and technology-oriented schools like the California Institute of Technology and M.I.T.; Ivy League powerhouses like Cornell; large state universities like Wisconsin and Montana; and small junior ivy elite institutions like Haverford, Swarthmore, and Wesleyan. But the surprising fact about the top fifty list was that the largest single group of schools producing scientists — well over half — were small, mid- or far-western Protestant-sponsored liberal arts colleges — Kalamazoo, Hope, and De Pauw; St. Olaf, Wooster, and Wabash; Muskingum, Westminster, and Brigham Young; the Wesleyan universities of Iowa, Nebraska, and West Virginia. A simple observation in the next-to-last-paragraph of the chapter describing the types of institutions found in the top fifty notes:

> this list does not include any institutions controlled by the Roman Catholic church, though a variety of private institutions of Protestant

affiliation, as well as a number of state-supported institutions appears. A closer examination of the Catholic institutions reveals that, without exception, they lie among the least productive 10% of all institutions, and constitute a singularly unproductive sample.[5]

After a careful review of a number of possible factors, Knapp and Goodrich offered two possible explanations for their surprising findings: they speculated that Catholicism had "maintained a sharper ideological discipline over its adherents" than Protestantism, so that Protestant-related institutions were perhaps freer to explore unanswered questions in more creative and thus more secular ways. The authors argued that Protestants perhaps had "more readily abandoned their fundamentalist religious outlook," making them freer to accept scientific explanations of the universe. But a second possible interpretation of their data referred their readers to the considerable sociological literature — most famously exemplified by Max Weber — that argued that Protestantism (and especially Calvinism) possessed inherent value systems including a commitment to rational empiricism. This inherent value system "might be described as a theory of the *intrinsic association* of science and Protestantism."[6]

Hardy, over two decades later, was clearly convinced by Knapp and Goodrich's data, as well as by the explanations they offered for it. Now he wanted to explore whether the data still held in the 1970s, which was witnessing the explosion of science faculties and facilities on university campuses across the United States. His own study (based on exhaustive data gathered over a forty-year period) sought to extend, confirm, and clarify the patterns embedded in previous studies.[7]

What Hardy found in the hard data he collected confirmed the findings of his predecessors. Table 5 in his 1974 article offered the productivity indices, comparing the findings of his predecessors and his own data. The results were reassuringly similar. Quakers, Presbyterians, and Congregationalists (liberal Protestants) remained at the top of both lists. Jews had moved from second-to-last to second. The group that ran Hardy's own institution, the Mormons, remained among the top ten, but had dropped from third to seventh place. The most consistent piece of data was that Roman Catholics still remained at the very bottom, going from last to next-to-last.[8]

In summarizing the data, Hardy hypothesized that "certain broad *cultural* influences are sharpened in particular religious sects, social classes, and individual families, and that these influences account, at least in part, for the marked geographical, institutional and religious patterns" in the forty years of data. By casting his analysis in terms of cultural factors, Hardy moved his discussion from theology onto the safer ground of habits inculcated in the socialization process. Hardy speculated that

> from the reservoir of talent found in any sizable population, cultural influences operate to stimulate or dampen the capabilities of its members. I suggest that there is a set of cultural values that promote scientific and scholarly activity, and that these are found most clearly in those groups highest in the production of scientists and scholars. These values appear to be less pronounced in groups of moderate productivity, and the antithesis of these values is found most clearly among those groups who are least productive of scientific and scholarly workers.[9]

The cultural values ostensibly sharpened or dampened by particular religious groups were set out in Table 7 of the article. The values of "High Productivity" — purportedly making adherents of particular denominations more likely to enter careers in science — were set out in the left-hand column of the table, and "Low Productivity" values — making devotees of certain sects less likely to become scientists — were listed on the right-hand side. Hardy then matched up specific religious groups with these values.[10]

> Highly productive groups share a certain set of values; unproductive groups hold the antithesis of these.... Tentatively, the common beliefs and value systems of high producers seem to include naturalism, intrinsic valuation of learning and the individual quest for truth; emphasis on human dignity, goodness and competence; a life path of serious dedication of service to humanity; humanistic equalitarianism; a pragmatic search for better ways of doing things unfettered by traditional restraints. Historically, the scientists (or their immediate ancestors) have broken away from the traditional orthodoxy, broadened certain values, and retained others. It appears that eminent

scientists often emerge from devout Protestant homes emphasizing learning and responsibility, but that such scientists frequently depart from the parental religious faith.[11]

Hardy offered a relatively simple and accessible social scientific model for understanding the relation of religious belief, scientific progress, and academic prestige in terms of cultural values. His article eschewed the issues of theology, personal ability based on race or ethnicity, and the touchy question of the academic rigor of specific educational institutions. The apparently ideologically neutral category of cultural values was the level playing field on which he would measure his teams. The productivity of the teams that both he and earlier social scientists had tracked over a number of decades could thus be measured by the reasonably neutral yardstick of productive and nonproductive cultural values.

The usual groups were placed in pretty much the same categories in Hardy's match up table as in earlier studies, with a few new wrinkles — for instance, Jews now joined Unitarians and Quakers in the highly productive group. Also like earlier studies, Hardy listed Roman Catholics at the very bottom of his table, by themselves, under the category "very low productivity."[12]

The unspoken inference from a Catholic point of view was that Roman Catholics in the United States were formed in a religious tradition that did not foster, or positively hindered, the cultural values of human dignity, egalitarianism, service to humanity, and the valuation of learning for its own sake; they were products of a tradition-bound, authoritarian, and world-wary institution that sought answers to life's pragmatic challenges in authority. Hardy's article confirmed what some academics and intellectuals had held for a number of decades: that Catholics were intellectual and cultural outsiders. Catholics appeared fated to be in, but not of, the democratic, pragmatic, and humanitarian cultural experiment.

What Hardy failed to mention in his article was that a number of American Catholic intellectuals, including John Tracy Ellis, Gustav Weigel, and Thomas O'Dea, had themselves attacked throughout the 1950s and 1960s precisely the anti-intellectual character of many Catholic colleges and universities, as well as their failure to produce scholars in the physical sciences. In the opinion of these Catholic critics, the Catholic higher educational enclaves of immigrant children and grandchildren tended to produce far too many lawyers, businessmen, and salesmen, and not enough artists, musicians, and academics.

John Tracy Ellis, the dean of American Catholic church historians, had published the most famous insider critique of Catholic intellectual life in a 1955 issue of Fordham University's *Thought* magazine. The prefatory statement announced that the "failure to develop a strong intellectual life may become the great scandal of the [Catholic] Church in the United States."[13] He went on to accuse Catholic higher education of being far more devoted to vocationalism and athleticism than to serious intellectual inquiry and research.

Jesuit scholar Gustav Weigel likewise observed in 1957 that the recruiting of some younger Catholics to academic careers seemed to be for what he termed missionary purposes — that is, to attract Catholics who would remain loyal to Holy Mother Church in what was perceived to be a hostile culture. Weigel argued that such reasons for entering the intellectual or academic life — however historically understandable, given American Catholicism's immigrant character until the twentieth century — were sociologically disordered. Missionary purposes clearly met certain immigrant needs to define the boundaries between "ours" and "theirs," but they witnessed to a failure to understand the true end of the intellectual life, which was — as the Catholic theological tradition had always asserted — for knowledge of the truth for its own sake.[14]

Thomas O'Dea noted a troubling form of authoritarianism in Catholic educational circles in his 1958 inquiry into Catholic intellectual life, a disturbing tendency "to rely on the sanction of custom and convention to support majority opinions or the views of institutionalized authority."[15]

In O'Dea's estimation, at least some of what had passed for education in Catholic institutions tended to reduce the necessary creative tension between scholars searching open-endedly for truth and the community seeking clear answers to its identity. This reduced the relation of real Catholic scholars to their religious community to something like the "relationship between a mischief-maker and a policeman." The search for truth in such an approach to education restricts "by its very rigidity the activity of the exploring mind, by conducting it only to safe and shallow channels."[16]

By 1974, then, a number of Catholic intellectuals had noted the failure of American Catholicism to produce intellectuals and academics in numbers appropriate to the size and resources of their community. But all of these loyal if tough internal critics interpreted the disappointing Catholic educational record in producing scientists and academics as having more to do with the social position of their co-religionists than with their essential religious beliefs. Their explanations were along the understandable sociological lines of immigrants wanting their children to enter the verdant pastures of middle-class affluence rather than the underpaid fields of academe; of pastors more concerned with forming loyal churchgoers than critical intellectuals in their parish schools. These factors clearly had, in the eyes of these Catholic critics, shaped a U.S. religious tradition in which intellectual and academic excellence played second fiddle to impulses focused on vocational preparation, on safe obedience to church authority, and on brick and mortar concerns that measured success more in terms of buildings put up on campus than on research projects undertaken in its laboratories.

The first scholar to really bring Catholic critics of Catholic academic lassitude into some kind of conversation with external studies of the problematic Catholic educational record in the United States was Andrew Greeley. But Greeley took as axiomatic one of the oldest insights of academic social science: that correlation does not equal causation. Greeley reminded his readers that they should avoid reducing correlated data — Catholics being dramatically under-represented among physical scientists, to causative explanations — because Catholic cultural values were inimical to science. He noted that Hardy's article contained some problematic flaws: Hardy's most recent data was already fifteen years old at the time of his article's publication, and Hardy had not felt the need to include in usual social scientific fashion contrary evidence from a substantial body of sociological literature produced during the two decades after his latest data. Several important studies had raised questions about Hardy's findings. Greeley says that the two most sophisticated articles, by Bockel (1969) and Bogue (1959), provided little support for Hardy's thesis of lower Catholic achievement, and that little attention had been paid to either article among social scientists generally.[17] These studies suggested that after the mid-1950s younger Catholics were more likely than white

Protestants to move into academic careers, and likewise more likely to have tenure in major (although not elite, private) universities.[18]

Greeley's extended rejoinder to Hardy's study was published in 1976, two years after the *Science* article, as *Ethnicity, Denomination, and Inequality*. Greeley utilized data collected since 1961 by the National Opinion Research Center at the University of Chicago, on the basis of which he argued that Catholics in fact ranked below Jews, Episcopalians, and Presbyterians, but above Lutherans and Baptists in terms of average years of per capita education. If one judged by another factor, that of educational mobility — that is, if one compared by denomination the average number of years of education of parents to their children's years of schooling — then Jews, Catholics, and Presbyterians were the most mobile educational groups in the United States in 1976, while Lutherans, Episcopalians, and Baptists were the least mobile. Since the children of the latter three groups were far more like likely to have been raised in households with college-educated parents, and Jews and Catholics were far less likely to have college-educated parents, the significant increase of college education among second generation Catholics and Jews was, statistically speaking, quite impressive — indeed, far more impressive than those Protestant groups that Hardy had argued inculcated cultural values that led to the valuation of education. In other words, Greeley's data found that Catholic parents were more likely than Protestant parents to send their children to college — appearing to value education in a way that raised questions about the cultural values Hardy had attached to educationally unproductive Catholic beliefs.[19]

Greeley also observed that Irish Catholics were the best educated Gentile group in the United States, ranking just below Jews in per capita years of education, but above the next religious grouping, British Protestants, by almost a full year of education. Greeley's data threw down an academic gauntlet to fellow social scientists and raised the question of discrimination not on the part of hooded men burning crosses in the night or of evangelical ministers warning their flocks about papists, but rather on the part of academic elites in the United States.

Greeley asked why dispassionate, data-seeking social scientists like Hardy were so hesitant to utilize, or even refer to, statistical studies that pointed to Catholic educational and occupational parity with other religious groups after World War II, even when those studies were more recent than studies quoted to argue opposite conclusions. He also raised the old specter of anti-Catholic prejudice among a surprising group of supposedly impartial cultural observers: Greeley's monograph raised the possibility of a late-twentieth-century form of North American culture's most ancient prejudice among the academic cultural elite. This newer manifestation of the bias was much harder to discern, since it was embedded not in discussions of doctrine, theology, or church structure, but in apparently quantitatively based academic discussions of cultural values inculcated during the socialization process.

Scientific Data and the Religious Imagination

It is extremely unlikely (or, in any event, unprovable) that social scientists of the academic stature and personal integrity of Robert Knapp and Kenneth Hardy would consciously shape their methods or data to conform to preconceived or distorted conclusions. It is equally unlikely (or again unprovable) that a premier academic journal like *Science* — which sends out articles submitted for publication to blind referees who remain unknown to the authors of the pieces submitted — would even consider publishing data that was perceived to be flawed. It is at least as unlikely that tenured academics, in a research pattern that stretched over four decades, would willingly propagate tainted data that could damage carefully constructed professional careers predicated on good scholarship.

How to account, then, for the decades-long pattern of interpreting Catholic scholarly and scientific underachievement in terms of flawed cultural values? This question is more troubling because such a pattern had to be read into otherwise opaque statistics that might have been explained in a number of other sociological ways — like the predictable (and documentable) desire of immigrant parents to have their children get ahead rather than to become intellectuals.

Equally puzzling in light of the review of the literature offered by Andrew Greeley, why were pertinent sociological studies offering dramatically different data than Hardy's on the academic career paths of

U.S. Catholics not even mentioned in scientific articles about Catholic underachievement?

We might also raise another set of troubling questions based on the findings of Catholic critics. Why did second- and third-generation progeny of Catholic immigrants seem willing to settle for moral formation over creative inquiry, vocationalism over artistic production, and loyalty to the tradition over cultural engagement? How to explain the concerns of Catholic intellectuals like Ellis that much of what passed as Catholic education in the United States — at least until the late 1960s — was marked more by rote learning than by the pursuit of truth and creative experimentation, precisely at a time when the great majority of American Catholics were no longer immigrants, or even the children of immigrants? How to explain why Catholics (unlike, say, eastern European Jews, who arrived in the United States in the very same immigrant wave as Catholic Italians and Poles, shortly before or after 1900) were so much less likely to become university professors, journal editors, or research scientists in the same proportions as their Jewish fellow-immigrants? This set of uncomfortable questions was asked not by secular intellectuals or by hostile critics of the church, but by respected clerics in Catholic-run journals.

The Religious Factor

There already existed a considerable body of literature on the issue of Catholic academic underachievement well before the publication of Hardy's article in 1974. Among the most famous voices from the Protestant side was that of noted social scientist Gerhard Lenski, who in 1961 published a monograph entitled *The Religious Factor: A Sociological Study of Religion's Impact on Politics, Economics, and Family Life.* This much-awaited study sought to uncover religion's impact on the culture of Detroit, Michigan — based on data gathered in a 1958 "Area Study." Lenski suggested that his project might be understood as a dialogue with a long-deceased conversation partner, Max Weber, one of the founding fathers of the discipline that would become modern sociology.

Weber's 1904 classic work, *The Protestant Ethic and the Spirit of Capitalism,* argued that Protestants and Catholics in post-Reformation Europe had developed distinctive economic ethics, specifically that Protestant (and especially Calvinist) belief — which happened to be the religious affiliation of Weber's family — carried within it a distinctive work ethic that ingrained and rewarded the values of hard work, sobriety, honesty, and the stewardship of material resources as signs of divine favor and election. Weber suggested it might not have been an historical accident that nations where Calvinism had achieved its strongest hold — England and Scotland, Germany and Switzerland, and especially the United States — were also the cultures in which capitalism, which depended on the same values, had achieved its most successful forms. Weber posited a correlation between the cultural dominance of Calvinism and the economic growth of capitalism without arguing that the one caused the other, and even rejected the hypothesis that Protestantism was a necessary condition for the emergence and survival of capitalism. Rather, he argued that Protestantism offered certain cultural conditions that made the emergence and flourishing of capitalism more likely. Lenski sought to explore "the relevance of [Weber's] theory for the contemporary scene"[20] and opened his conversation by noting that

> no one who has read Weber's analysis of the historical significance of religion for economics can help wondering what relevance his theory has for the contemporary scene. Are the major religious groups in America today the carriers of distinctive economic ethics? Do the economic values and actions of Protestants and Catholics in mid-twentieth-century America differ as much as Weber suggests they did in post-Reformation Europe? Are Protestants more inclined to view their work as a sacred calling? Do they practice the pattern of worldly asceticism Weber identified with the Puritans and Pietists of an earlier era?[21]

Lenski noted that "more recently, several scholars have challenged the assumption that Protestants are more successful than Catholics, at least when opportunities for advancement are equal." He was referring to a 1959 monograph by noted sociologists Seymour Lipset and Reinhard Bendix, who had used a national sample of Americans interviewed in connection with the 1952 presidential election to test for social mobility among religious groups participating in that election. They found that there were no appreciable differences in the economic mobility rates of Catholics and Protestants in the years immediately after World War II. Lenski did not agree. He argued that "their analysis of these data is somewhat cursory, and therefore their conclusions cannot be accepted at face value." According to Lenski the authors had focused on urban areas, where more than half of U.S. Catholics lived, but in which only a quarter of white Protestants were to be found. "Thus the Protestants in their sample competed under a severe handicap," since the majority of Protestants lived in the under-studied rural and small-town areas overlooked by the authors.

What makes Lenski's questioning of Lipset and Bendix's analysis arresting is his own admission that it was not their data that was problematic, but their interpretation of it, which he dubbed cursory because it put Protestants (like himself) "under a severe handicap." What Lenski failed to note in his own corrected analysis of their data was that the United States was, according to census data gathered for five decades, becoming progressively more urban and less rural.[22]

Lenski then referred his readers to an article published in the *American Sociological Review* in 1956 by three eminent social scientists, Mack, Murphy, and Yellin, which had argued that there were in fact no statistically significant differences between Catholics and Protestants in either occupational advancement or aspirations for such advancement. The study was based on questionnaire responses from salesmen, engineers, and bank officials of both Protestant and Catholic faiths. Lenski again noted that "a careful analysis of their data indicates that their conclusion is not warranted." He claimed that statistically significant differences did exist in the data that Mack, Murphy, and Yellin themselves had misread. Thus Lenski observed that

> our evidence from the 1958 Detroit Area Study is consistent with the actual findings of the Mack, Murphy, Yellin study and indicates that white Protestant men rise further in the class system than Catholics. When white Protestants were compared to Catholics who began life at the same point in the class system, the former rose to (or stayed in) the ranks of the upper-middle class more often than the latter. At the opposite extreme, Catholics wound up in the lower half of the working class more often than Protestants three out of four times.[23]

When the same data utilized by Mack, Murphy, and Yellin were viewed with a different set of references, Lenski drew very different conclusions. Lenski argued that there were four major socioeconomic groups in postwar U.S. culture whose socioeconomic mobility could be statistically corre-lated by religion. American Jews, in Lenski's "correct" reading of the data misread by Mack, Murphy, and Yellin, appeared to be the most mobile religious group in the United States; white Protestants ranked second; Catholics ranked third; and Negro Protestants were the least mobile.[24]

Lenski allowed that this ranking might be read to imply that economic and occupational mobility were associated with the social acceptability of the groups under consideration. That is, it might appear that those groups who were more socially acceptable found it easier to navigate to higher social positions than groups laboring under the onus of some social bias. But he deflated this perception, pointing out that "the marked success of the Jewish group clearly indicates that the problem is more complex." For if social acceptability was the determinative factor, then the Catholics in the sampling — as fellow Christians — should have ranked above the Jews.[25]

Lenski built on and expanded the Knapp and Goodrich study, which he commended. Scientific activity, Lenski noted, demands intellectual auton-omy, and the college student who constantly looked to others for detailed direction and guidance would probably not choose a career in science in the first place. Important in understanding the disinclination of Catholics to enter scientific careers

> is the basic intellectual orientation which Catholicism develops: an orientation which values obedience over intellectual autonomy. Also influential is the Catholic tendency to value family and the kin group above other relationships. In brief, at both the conscious and sub-conscious levels of thought and action, membership in the Catholic group is more likely to inhibit the development of scientific careers than is membership in either the Protestant or Jewish groups. The implications of this for the future of American society are not difficult to discover.[26]

The "implications of this for the future of American society" were patently clear for Lenski: in those measurable areas of career achievement and mo-bility demanding initiative, independence of thought, and self-direction,

Catholics consistently "operate at some disadvantage in modern society." And this marked Catholic disadvantage, in Lenski's opinion, had less to do with immigration history, urban location, or ethnic background than with something he labeled the intellectual orientation that Catholic believers absorbed through their religious tradition.[27]

According to Lenski's reading of the hard data in the Detroit Area Study, then, Catholic and black Protestant Detroiters were statistically far more likely than either Jews or white Protestants to be "responsive to appeals to limit individual freedom and increase authority." Jews and white Protestants, on the other hand, could be counted on to favor efforts in the precise opposite direction — that is, they would be far more likely to limit hierarchical authority and to increase individual freedom. Indeed, Lenski argued, the "classical, liberal democratic theory" that underlay American democracy was tied to the intellectual orientation found among the white Protestants and Jews in his study, which

> is what is required *from all citizens* if we are to maintain a stable and effective democratic society. More recently some political theorists have come to speculate that democratic systems function best where there is a diversity of political tendencies. However . . . the differences in intellectual orientation found among the socio-religious groups [in this study] are certain to have consequences for the operation of our political system.[28]

What is surprising, of course, about the academic literature of the 1950s and 1960s studying Catholic scientific and academic underachievement is that a number of Catholic intellectuals reached conclusions not far removed from that of Lenski. Thomas O'Dea, then a professor of sociology at the Jesuit-run Fordham, offered what is arguably the most thoroughgoing internal critique of Catholic underachievement in his 1958 monograph, tellingly entitled *American Catholic Dilemma*. Indeed, in parts of his monograph, O'Dea came very close to sounding like he agreed with Lenski and Hardy as to the reasons for the dilemma in the first place. He argued that the Catholic worldview, while recognizing the importance of the intellect in religion, nevertheless had a tendency to subordinate rationality to what he termed a "more holistic orientation" of human beings toward God. And while it "was not in any sense anti-intellectual, under certain circumstances it was nonetheless subject to misinterpretation in a more or less anti-intellectual direction."[29]

O'Dea believed such misinterpretation about the role of the intellect in religion on the part of his fellow-believers was in large part to blame for the sorry intellectual pass of U.S. Catholicism. Quoting Notre Dame's president, John Cavanaugh, who lamented that "the 35,000,000 Catholics in this country and our Catholic educational system are not producing anywhere near their proportion of leaders," O'Dea noted the "almost complete failure" of American Catholics to distinguish themselves in terms of scholarship. This failure was "revealed each time the National Science Foundation Fellowship Awards are distributed." O'Dea noted the derivative nature of even the best Catholic scholarship in the postwar United States. At academic institutions like his own, he observed that fellow faculty members seemed obsessed with writing footnotes to a largely European-based neo-Thomistic revival that was itself somewhat derivative. Indeed,

> There is a simple test that every reader may make for himself. Let him simply examine the shelves of any Catholic bookshop in this country. A simple count will reveal that an overwhelming proportion of the serious books on every subject are of European origin. The fact is that, although American Catholics have the largest and most expensive educational system of any national Catholic group in the world, a genuine Catholic intellectual life is still dependent upon translations of European works and books of British origin.[30]

O'Dea admitted that it was fairly easy to understand why U.S. Catholics, "with their long history of minority status," had failed to develop a vibrant intellectual tradition and reprised the familiar story of the immigrant, working-class status of a large proportion of the U.S. Catholic community until well into the twentieth century. He also noted the overwhelming and immediate pastoral duties of clergy scrambling to care for needy flocks, with little or no time for scholarship. He recognized that the defensive ghetto mentality of the Catholic community in the United States had emerged in response to a Protestant cultural mainstream that was perceived to be, and to some extent was, hostile to and prejudiced against Catholics. All of these factors, in O'Dea's estimation, played their part in militating against the development of distinctive Catholic intellectual life in the United States, as well as explaining why North American Catholics "react defensively to criticisms which point up their shortcomings." Given the history of the community, "it is even easy to sympathize with such a reaction." However, he said, "when that reaction descends to anti-intellectualism, then one must ask not for intellectual standards but merely for the simple, common, sound standards of honest discussion."[31] The Catholic community in the United States had finally arrived at something like its cultural adulthood, and it was now time to analyze its own shortcomings honestly and without varnish.[32]

O'Dea targeted five impulses in American Catholic culture that he believed inhibited the development of mature intellectual activity in Catholic educational institutions, seminaries, and journalism. First, he noted the formalism of much American Catholic educational theory and practice, in which the memorization of the correct formulaic answers replaced genuine debate and the active and messy interchange of ideas as the core of learning. Philosophy and theology as taught in such a manner became safe but restrictive disciplines. Such formalized learning "often fatigues the mind and leads to boredom" on the part of students, and to second-rate and derivative research on the part of scholars.[33]

Second, O'Dea noted an authoritarianism that derived in part from an essential misunderstanding of the correct role of ecclesiastical authority. This impulse tended to impose altogether too easy and quick solutions to complex problems by the simple expedient of pronouncements by those in power — especially those in power in the church. This second impulse was likewise incarnated in a troubling tendency among U.S. Catholics to accept the received answers of their past to support the views of institutionalized authority. This tendency

> combines with formalism to produce a worldview in terms of which the statement of a problem bears the solution in it, thus closing the door to lively debate. Each thing can be put in its proper category; there is no question which cannot be answered (not to mention the question which cannot be framed). The result is the *illusion* of a neat universe in which nothing eludes the conceptions of a searching mind. Such a tendency too often subtly penetrates into teaching,

preaching, and other activities, where it creates unintellectual habits of thought.[34]

Third, O'Dea identified what he termed a troubling impulse toward clericalism in the U.S. Catholic community. Such an impulse over-relied on ecclesiastical officials to define the mission of the Christian life in the world and worked toward collapsing all Catholic questions into institutionally clerical issues to be solved by the clergy. In O'Dea's view, this impulse tended to deny the secular world of creation its proper place, as "the secular seems, in such a view, to have been created in order to be avoided." It likewise tended toward reducing the role of laypeople — that 99 percent of the church without whom, as Cardinal Newman once observed, the church would look silly — to "pay, pray, and obey." By thus creating "intellectual dependency on the part of the laity," such a clericalism "further inhibits intellectual activity."[35]

O'Dea likewise identified a pervasive moralism in the North American Catholic worldview, which emphasized obedience to the rules — especially the rules that kept one pure of contamination by the world — as the essence of Christian living. Instead of presenting the vocation of lay people as the exciting and demanding challenge to build God's Kingdom in the world through their work and family life, much in the American Catholic intellectual tradition seemed to present the life of the Catholic laity "as a series of moral dangers which are to be shunned." Such moralism fed into an ecclesiastical legalism, in which every new challenge could be answered by turning to the already elucidated rules offered by the church. "Does it count?," for instance, became an important question in determining how late one could appear at mass and still have it fulfill the requirement for attendance. "From such a lower-middle-class mentality," O'Dea observed, "little can be hoped for in terms of intellectual activity."[36]

Finally, O'Dea identified a troubling defensiveness in the U.S. Catholic community that derived from its long history as the object of prejudice and even persecution, in which "all the foregoing tendencies are reinforced by the strongly felt need to repulse attack, whether real or imagined." However understandable from a historical standpoint, O'Dea felt that it kept the U.S. Catholic community from examining its own strengths and weaknesses frankly and honestly.[37]

The American Catholic Intellectual Dilemma

Hardy's interpretation of Catholic educational underachievement in the production of scientists had been addressed a dozen years before by Thomas O'Dea; Andrew Greeley presented quantitative data at least as convincing as Hardy's to dispute not only the latter's conclusions, but his data as well. Greeley also observed that "while [this] debate has gone on for a long time, the data never seem to provide a definitive conclusion." The definitive conclusions sought by social scientists cannot, of course, be decided by data alone, as they involve questions of value and judgment that transcend statistics. That is, the meaning of facts carefully compiled and scrupulously numbered is not self-evident in the data itself; that meaning must be lifted out of the facts by scientists who always bring their own worldviews and preconceptual languages to bear. This is not to say that all interpretations of data are purely subjective, nor that all of the meanings are equally true, depending on one's point of view. It does mean that the point of view of the scholar doing the interpreting is itself a factor in assessing the validity of the resulting interpretation.[38]

For example, O'Dea's critique of the clerically ridden, overly defensive, and moralistic character of U.S. Catholic intellectual life posited historical and sociological factors as the culprits in the problematic Catholic life of the mind in the New World, rather than negative cultural values in their religious tradition.

The historical and sociological factors set out by O'Dea had, in fact, found material perhaps too pliable in a Catholicism so concerned with safeguarding the purity and integrity of the inside that it could not listen to well-founded criticisms offered from outside the community. When one brings the insights of Tracy and Greeley to bear on O'Dea's critique of the American Catholic dilemma, we might allow the possibility that such a worldview contributed to an authoritarianism and clericalism that preferred the safe results of derivative scholarship to the messiness of genuine debate and experiment.

Further, the sacramental and historically shaped nature of the community's worship and polity can be seen as contributing to a formalism of thought, in which, as O'Dea noted, "demonstration replaces research, abstractions replace experience, formulae replace content, and rationalistic elaboration replaces genuine ontological insight." The desire to form students in the tradition of the community undoubtedly played its own part in helping to shape an educational network in which making students docile and respectful toward authority was more important than teaching them to think critically and independently about complex issues.[39]

At the same time, however, the dialectical presuppositions of scholars like Gerhard Lenski and Kenneth Hardy, in which large and hierarchically ordered institutions like the Catholic Church were understood to inevitably stifle individual initiative and freedom of thought, led them to over-read their data and to ignore data that pointed to a less monolithic, more nuanced relationship between American Catholicism and the production of scientists.

Andrew Greeley's data, based on wide demographic samplings constructed according to sophisticated models of sociological research, limned a changing pattern of Catholic involvement in the mainstream academic and scientific discussion in the United States. Indeed, by the time of the appearance of Hardy's article in 1974, Greeley had found that Catholics were more statistically likely than Protestants to pursue academic careers in science as well as in the humanities, more likely than Protestants to hold progressive political positions, like opposition to the Vietnam War, and considerably more likely than Protestants to espouse the liberal social policies of the Democratic Party, American Catholicism's traditional political party preference.

Greeley's observations about the continued perception in both the popular press and the academy of Catholicism's working-class, anti-scientific, and politically reactionary habits — a perception that he identified as a late-twentieth-century form of America's anti-Catholicism — tell us more about the way non-Catholic academicians see the real world than about Catholics.

Chapter Nine

"Why Does He Say Those Awful Things about Catholics?"

"Just because Jimmy Swaggart believes in God doesn't mean that God does not exist." — Catholic novelist Walker Percy, "Science, Language, Literature"

"A Letter to My Catholic Friends"

June 1983 was hotter than usual in Baton Rouge, Louisiana, a city an hour and a half north of New Orleans, where the humidity index in June often rested lazily in the high double digits. The widely respected Roman Catholic bishop, Stanley Ott, had arranged a behind-closed-doors meeting for the end of the month with the pentecostal preacher the Reverend Jimmy Lee Swaggart. In a conciliatory gesture to that revivalist whose preaching style bore a striking resemblance to the performing style of first cousins Jerry Lee Lewis and Mickey Gilley, Bishop Ott had agreed that the meeting would take place on the 257-acre campus of Jimmy Swaggart Ministries in Baton Rouge. Swaggart's campus on World Ministry Avenue served as an architectural testimony to what the evangelist termed his God anointed success: it included the Jimmy Swaggart Bible College, the ten-million-dollar Zoe Vance Teleproduction Center (where his telecasts originated), and the seven-thousand-seat Family Worship Center.[1]

At forty-eight, Swaggart had surpassed Oral Roberts, Robert Schuller, and even Jim and Tammy Fay Bakker of PTL fame to become the king of the TV evangelists. The *Jimmy Swaggart Telecast* was watched by 2.6 million people weekly; his monthly magazine, *The Evangelist*, was read by eight hundred thousand readers. The preacher's appeal was not limited to the southern small-town world of "crackers" too readily dismissed by some

140

secular journalists: Swaggart's two largest TV markets were reportedly New York and Los Angeles, and a 1982 Bible crusade in Manhattan's Madison Square Garden was forced to turn away five thousand at the door. The Arbitron Ratings Company, tracking television viewing for the period from November 3 to 30 in 1982, had found that Swaggart's telecast had an audience of 2,653,000, ranking second among the top ten televangelists to Robert Schuller's *Hour of Power,* with 2,667,000 viewers, but running ahead of *Oral Roberts and You* by 150,000 viewers. Ranking after those were Rex Humbard and Jerry Falwell's *Old Time Gospel Hour.*[2]

What was on Ott's mind was a piece entitled "A Letter to My Roman Catholic Friends" that Swaggart had published in the January 1983 issue of *The Evangelist.* Swaggart had advised his faithful Catholic readers and viewers — in language borrowed from St. John the Divine in the Book of Revelation — to "Come out from her and be separate!" and quickly generated a storm of protest from Catholics in both Louisiana and across the country. Swaggart claimed that he had issued this call to Catholics because the Roman church was not a Christian organization. Not only were all of its claims false; it was "a false religion. Whosoever follows its errant doctrines will be deceived and end up eternally lost."[3]

One can only wonder what Swaggart's Catholic readers, who had made up a small but loyal group of followers, made of their favorite televangelist describing them as pitiful for thinking that "they have enriched themselves spiritually by kissing the Pope's ring." Swaggart allowed that his Catholic friends and followers might very well "be furious and vow to never again turn sets to our telecast," and it was with a "very real sorrow that I accept this fact." But, he added, "how much more tragic if I didn't write this — and one Catholic soul that could have been saved was lost."[4]

In a city that was more than a third Catholic, Swaggart's "Letter" was too much, and an immediate rejoinder was printed on the front page of the Baton Rouge diocesan newspaper, the *Catholic Commentator.* The uproar was picked up by other Catholic diocesan and national publications. But from Swaggart's point of view, his portrayal as anti-Catholic bad boy was not a bad thing. The majority of his followers — obviously Protestant pentecostals like himself — liked his diatribes against the cult of Catholicism, along with his other attacks on secular humanism, the National Council of Churches, the press, and rock and roll.[5]

Anne Seaman, Swaggart's unauthorized biographer, noted that by the 1980s Swaggart had assumed the role of policeman for the rest of the charismatic world, rampaging against other popular Assemblies of God ministers — "in particular those who pastored churches with large congregations and who had sizable television and radio ministries" — as well as against ministers and leaders of other denominations. In his self-anointed role as protector of Bible Christianity, Swaggart had filed charges within the Assemblies of God against fellow minister Karl Strader (pastor of a seventy-four-hundred-member congregation in Lakeland, Florida) for taking up the healing teachings of Oral Roberts and had brought a complaint against Assemblies pastor Glen Cole (head of an eight-thousand-member church in Sacramento) for inviting Robert Schuller to present his "health and wealth" gospel in his California superchurch. Much better known than these two instances, however, was Swaggart's public denunciation of fellow Assemblies of God televangelist Jim Bakker as "sissified" and "worldly," and his leaking to denominational overseers his suspicion that Bakker was either bisexual or homosexual. Swaggart also broadcast a nationwide denunciation of the United Methodist Church for apostasy for considering ordaining homosexuals. Crossing the line into what many (even in his own denomination) perceived to be dangerous territory, Swaggart showed gruesome photographs of Jewish victims of the Auschwitz death camp on his TV telecast in October 1983, drawing a chilling theological moral from the Holocaust in the process: "When a person does not accept Jesus Christ, he takes himself away from God's protection . . . and places himself under Satan's domain." This led two Boston TV stations (among others) to cancel his show. Vicky Gregorian, WLVI's programming manager in Boston, in response to possible charges of press censorship, said that Swaggart "has a right to say whatever he wants, but not on *our* air."[6]

Allowing for Swaggart's equal opportunity approach to lambasting theological opponents, Roman Catholics had long constituted a special target of his rhetorical wrath. During one mission telecast, Swaggart observed that "most Catholics are Catholics two times a year: once at Mardi Gras and once at . . . I can't think of the other." On another he announced that in countries where Catholicism dominated, "the people have been led into ignorance, superstition, and sin," while their moral behavior was marked by the "vilest immorality and intellectual apathy." It came as no surprise that during an interview shortly after the publication of his letter, Swaggart responded to the question, "Who are your greatest enemies?" with this answer:

> Catholics are my greatest enemies. It's not malicious, bless their hearts. I had to take a strong stand, I felt. I've had most of my Protestant brethren to say that I'm making a mistake. I would hope that's not true. I love the Catholic people, and we have probably the largest Catholic audience for television. . . . They may not like me for what I say, or they may still love me, but I've got to say it.[7]

But it was not only Swaggart's remarks against fellow North American Catholic citizens that roused the ire of Catholic leaders like Ott. Swaggart had also targeted Central and South American Catholic countries like El Salvador, Costa Rica, Chile, and Guatemala as the special objects of his missionary ("Holy Spirit Anointed") crusades for some time before the offending letter. Swaggart's success in those countries led Lucas Neves, the archbishop of São Salvador da Bahia in Brazil, to note that "the springtime of the sects could also be the winter of the Catholic Church."[8]

Journalist Penny Lernoux, in an article on the "Fundamentalist Surge in Latin America," noted that the challenge posed by Swaggart in the region was a serious one:

> The Catholic Church's own surveys show how serious is the challenge: every hour 400 Latin Americans convert to the Pentecostals or other fundamentalist or evangelical churches. One-eighth of the region's 481 million people belong to fundamentalist or evangelical churches, and in some countries, such as Guatemala, it is estimated that half the population will have switched into those churches by the end of the century. Not since the mass baptisms of Latin American Indians by the conquering Spanish in the 16th century has Latin America witnessed a religious conversion of such magnitude.[9]

Unlike Latin American Catholic parishes — where there was often only one priest to serve as many as ten thousand faithful in a parish — Swaggart's missions in Latin America planted hundreds of small congregations in their wake, usually led by fervent but largely unschooled pastors ordained for their preaching skills rather than their seminary erudition. Such pastors were nothing if not vocal in their denunciations of what Swaggart called a religion centered on the "liturgical religious monstrosity" of the Catholic mass.[10] Swaggart gloated publicly about his success in saving Latin American Catholics from a false religion.

Swaggart's ministry-long attack on Catholicism is best laid out in his book *Catholicism and Christianity,* published in 1983. It offers his usual accusations but in expanded and biblically footnoted form and shows a carefully thought out theological position on the subject as well as a surprisingly extensive knowledge of Catholic theology — although now and then the Catholic reader is rewarded with genuine laughter in his interpretations of Catholic belief and practice. It is also an example of the rhetorical power and canny turn of phrase that brought Swaggart acclaim and a following, despite having only an eighth grade education and a complete lack of seminary training.[11]

Swaggart opens *Catholicism and Christianity* by admitting that he has been branded anti-Catholic by many, although he does not "consider this to be a valid assessment of my feelings." He professes to love the Catholic people with a deep and abiding love, because the "ultimate test of love is to work for the eventual good (and happiness) of those we love." The term "anti-Catholic," in his estimation, appropriately describes someone who "does not approve of or like someone simply because he is Catholic," and he has "never met a Catholic I disliked." His own statements on Catholicism, which represented the most widely televised form of anti-Catholic rhetoric in North America, did not proceed from personal feelings. His critiques proceeded from his belief that Catholicism offered "a fraudulent path to salvation, and I can think of nothing more *tragic* (however well-intentioned) than a *promise* of salvation that delivers *eternal torment* instead of *eternal life.*" He asserted that "I do *not* feel that pointing out errors in basic doctrine — caustic as it may seem at the moment — is anti-Catholic." Thus his hostility to Catholicism was not personal but rather based on his belief that its errors in doctrine have

> been responsible for the deaths of multiplied [sic] millions of martyrs over the centuries, but is *even now responsible for damning the deceived souls of multitudinous millions!* In America alone there are over 50

million Roman Catholics, and in the world, over 600 million Roman Catholics — FOR WHOM CHRIST DIED.[12]

"Am I not," he continues, "demonstrating love to my Catholic brethren when I warn them of impending doom if they persist in following the erroneous teachings of the Catholic Church? Was Jesus cruel when He warned His disciples against the leaven of the Pharisees?"[13]

One example of false teaching is infant baptism, which he claims is not only unscriptural but "responsible for sending more people to hell than any other doctrine or religious error," because Catholics quite mistakenly believe that they have been somehow made right with God because of this exterior ritual performed on them as infants.

His tirades against the teachings of the Roman church were analogous to nineteenth-century evangelist Charles Grandison Finney's justification for preaching fire-and-brimstone sermons to terrified listeners in upstate New York during the Second Great Awakening. Finney believed that human beings were asleep in a burning house, and his job was to shout Get out! in the loudest possible voice. The fact that such shouting annoyed some by waking them up was not only not a bad thing, but rather represented a dutiful fulfillment of a direct command from the Lord Jesus himself to do precisely that. Thus, for Finney and Swaggart both, such offensive shouting was based not in differing theological interpretations of doctrinal details, nor in any personal animus against Catholic believers.[14]

Swaggart based his fervent revivalist style (and his equally fervent denunciations of false Christians like Catholics) on what he took to be the core message of the Gospel itself: "unless you are born again, you will not enter the Kingdom of God." It was this shattering individual experience of being born again that made people Christian, not being sprinkled with water either as a child or an adult. The gathering of these born-again believers into fellowships constitute true churches, not an institutional structure focused on sacraments.

After the meeting on July 1, 1983, between the bishop and the televangelist, Bishop Ott observed to reporters that he came away from the meeting with some hope because "real progress was made on both sides toward reducing the misunderstandings between the Catholic Church and the Swaggart Ministries." He nonetheless observed that "there is still a very serious problem. I believe that Rev. Jimmy Swaggart continues to harbor views and judgments and make statements about the Catholic Church and our faithful which do not represent our condition with truth and fairness." This, Ott observed with commendable understatement, "makes mutual relations more difficult." They planned to meet again, however, and Ott asked that "all parties join me in asking for everyone to pray that we may succeed in accomplishing God's will in these further efforts at understanding and reconciliation."[15]

From Swaggart's point of view, however, God's will had been fully and finally represented by him at that first meeting. He announced in the July 1983 issue of *The Evangelist* that he did not regret a single word of either the January letter that had caused all the ruckus in the first place or anything he had said at the July meeting. He had spoken "only what God [was] compelling me to say," and "every word contained within this message is God's truth." How could anyone, he was quoted in the *New Orleans Times-Picayune*, "remain in this tradition as they become familiar with the Bible and realize that the Catholic tradition is in complete contradiction to the Word of God?"[16]

The Gospel According to the "King of Honky Tonk Heaven"

Jimmy Swaggart's letter and his ministries empire as a whole offer a classic instance of Protestant conceptual language — with a distinctive southern, evangelical, and pentecostal twang. But the outlines of that dialectical language are readily discernible in his rhetoric nonetheless.

As Swaggart himself has so tirelessly preached, his gospel is almost exclusively concerned with individual salvation — an individual salvation achieved by encountering the Lord Jesus personally in scripture and in preaching, and then accepting him as one's personal Lord and Savior. This clear-cut understanding of how salvation is to be achieved — one that Swaggart, like most of his televangelist brethren, finds in a literal reading of the New Testament — judges the entire Catholic tradition and finds it wanting. By the standards of this scriptural yardstick, the "average [Catholic] priest has never met the Lord Jesus Christ as his own personal savior." Because of this, when Catholic priests even attempt to share the gospel message with the laity, what is really communicated is a "shared ignorance — which can be catastrophic." This weakness in the Roman church has led to the demonic situation in which "the Bible is a captive of the institutional church hierarchy." In this captivity — the same captivity outlined by Martin Luther in the sixteenth century — "there is no room whatsoever for the marvelous operation of the Holy Spirit" on individual believers. In Swaggart's estimation, Catholics

> are actively discouraged from delving into God's Word themselves — and thus developing a personal relationship with Jesus Christ. Instead they are advised to leave this "potentially dangerous" or "positively disturbing" practice to "experts." When they do, they then are delivered a product that is certified by the same people who prepared it.[17]

Far more demonic is the theology of church that results. The Catholic understanding of church as incarnated in an authoritative, hierarchical structure makes "union with this organization, in some manner, necessary for salvation." This directly contradicts what Swaggart takes to be the clear voice of scripture on this question, which defines the church as a "universal and *invisible* community of born-again Christians" whose chief mission is the "witness to Jesus Christ crucified" and "proclamation of the authoritative, written Word of God." Bible Believers see

> the church in a secondary degree, with its visible congregations as a vehicle instituted by Christ to preach the Word, to celebrate the ordinances of Water Baptism and the Lord's Supper, and to *gather saved Christians in fellowship for mutual edification.* . . . [The church] supports no intricate, external, contrived, hierarchical structure, but conforms to the pattern of the simple pastoral framework revealed within the New Testament.[18]

It is not the community as such that constitutes the locus of saving grace but rather the one-to-one relationship between believer and the Word. The misplaced Catholic focus on community, sacrament, and hierarchy has resulted in a form of religion that "has changed the substance of the greater part of the teachings and doctrines of the Lord Jesus Christ." The apostles and evangelists, he says, "would be horrified to see the changes that the Roman Catholic church has instituted in the Word of God." As Swaggart reads it, the Catholic sacramental understanding of the created world, and its understanding of the Holy as mediated in community, have no basis in scripture. "Consequently, all hopes that the Roman Catholic may place in these avenues to salvation lack substance. Those trusting in rituals will be shattered on the day they must stand before the Supreme Judge."[19]

Swaggart's denominational affiliation (until 1988) with the Assemblies of God — one of the fastest-growing Protestant groups in the United States during the last quarter of the twentieth century — provided firm institutional support for his theology. A spin-off of the Wesleyan holiness tradition organized in Hot Springs, Arkansas, in 1914, the Assemblies are the best organized and most unified group in the sometimes confusing network of Protestant groups devoted to practicing divine healing and the charismatic evidence of the Holy in daily life. This is most dramatically witnessed during worship services when individuals are baptized in the Holy Spirit and prophesy in tongues. The eleven thousand congregations affiliated with the denomination are overseen by a General Council in Springfield, Missouri (which also credentials the thirty thousand ministers it recognizes), but specific matters of church organization and congregational worship remain in the hands of the local congregations. They must remain, though, within the general perimeters of certain fundamental doctrines: a belief in the Bible as the inspired and literal Word of God; a gathered church membership based on believers baptism; a celebration of speaking in tongues and divine healing during worship; and a biblically literalist doctrinal emphasis on Christ's imminent return to earth and on the thousand-year rule of the saints under him (termed premillennialism by church historians).[20]

Almost everything about the Assemblies' structure, worship, and theology — especially its emphasis on charismatic evidence of the Spirit in individual believers — was heaven-sent for Swaggart's mission and message and helped to nurture his deep misgivings about Catholicism. The decentralized structure of the Assemblies allowed Swaggart to develop his own effective preaching style and message, but offered him the support of a fast-growing network of preachers who sought out the dynamic young preacher for guest visits to their own pulpits. The decentralization that

made the young denomination so flexible also claimed biblical warrant —
appearing much closer to the early Christian communities described in
the Acts of the Apostles than the over-routinized structures of Catholicism. The informal and sometimes folksy nature of Assemblies worship
allowed Swaggart to utilize and develop his considerable musical abilities within the context of his ministry, a happy marriage of native talent
and ministerial ambition that represented a not-insignificant part of his
success with audiences from Quebec to Quito. This style had the sole
aim of delivering the precious word of salvation to sinners who could
then be reborn and saved, as opposed to the Catholic emphasis on dead
ritual and sacramental magic. Evidence of the rebirth preached and received was immediate, concrete, and personal: speaking in tongues and
witnessing healings. Given the individualist presuppositions of Swaggart's
theology and cultural context, an intellectual appeal to apostolic succession or transubstantiation (found nowhere in scripture anyway) could not
measure up to the democratic invitation to undergo a literally ecstatic
experience.[21]

Swaggart's ministry perfectly matched the *medium* — television — and
the *message* — individual believers gathering in fellowship to experience
rebirth. Janice Peck, in a very perceptive study of Swaggart's televangelistic
career, has noted that his message to an invisible TV audience necessarily
deemphasized the communal, sacramental, and hierarchical elements of
Christianity. Opposing these emphases is a focus on an individualized,
verbal, and democratic approach to getting the Holy Ghost through the
ministrations of the preacher on whom the camera alone focuses.[22]

Swaggart's packaging of the Christian message, Peck believes, is perfect
for the television culture of North America, in which complex and thickly
contextualized realities are simplified and neatly packaged in thirty- or
sixty-minute segments. The sense of being alone with Jimmy Swaggart
in one's living room — achieved by the TV camera's laser-like focus on
Swaggart at the pulpit — dovetails perfectly with Swaggart's theology of
personal conversion: it is you personally that the televangelist wants to
win for Jesus.[23]

Precisely because of the formatted nature of televised media, a single
message must appear to speak to every individual's personal situation. But
as Peck shrewdly observes, Swaggart knows his TV medium extraordinarily

well, offering clearly drawn and demarcated moral choices for his viewers, who know how to respond appropriately to Swaggart's narrative of what ails them: the good/bad dichotomy that defines so much television drama (and even news reporting) is brilliantly crafted into insider/outsider categories that fit in perfectly with the televangelist's theology:

> One is a "Christian" or a godless humanist, good or evil, saved or damned. Solutions to social problems are dichotomized. In this worldview, the complexities of cultural difference, the international economic structure, class antagonisms, and structural inequality simply disappear. In this respect, religious programming is not too different from secular television. Drama and comedy series are structured on a principle of closure that reduces all problems to personal difficulties and solves them within the space of a program. Television news simplifies social reality by reducing it to isolated "events," turning deep social conflicts into disputes between prominent personalities, and dramatizing rather than analyzing issues. If televangelism offers an alternative story to counteract the narrative of secular society, the packaging of both tales is strikingly similar.[24]

The dialectical presuppositions of Swaggart's theology are just as clearly visible to the thousands gathered in person at the Family Worship Center. The worship program is also structured toward individual conversion: from the gospel music that opens the program (modeled on nineteenth-century camp meetings and intended to excite the congregation's emotions and bring them to their feet to welcome Jimmy into the pulpit) through Swaggart's informal but emotionally intense sermon addressed to individual sinners to the call to the altar at the end of the service of those seeking to receive the Lord Jesus into their lives. This ritual is quite consciously scripted to create an interaction between the preacher and the individual listener that militates against any sacramental or communal understanding of church. For the worshipers on World Ministry Avenue, only the preacher and the individual auditor constitute a true church. Any sense that the community *as such* might be the locus of grace, or that communal ordinances like the Lord's Supper might actually mediate the Holy, is rejected out of hand, or more likely never appears at all. The one thing necessary in that seven-thousand-seat worship center is that every single individual present become a spirit-filled, Bible believing, tongues talking Christian.[25]

From Swaggart's point of view, those Bible-believing Christians are themselves the solution to society's ills. One reason why Swaggart was so warmly welcomed on his missions into Latin America by dictators like Chile's Augusto Pinochet is his regularly voiced belief that the solution to society's problems is neither political nor social, but rather spiritual and individual. Such a gospel message ineluctably contains within it an implicit social passivity. Neither Washington, nor the educational system, the legal system, nor unemployment insurance — nor any other belief system than Swaggart's own — can solve problems like crime, abortion, drugs, divorce, and teenage pregnancy. They can be changed only by a change of heart.[26]

Swaggart's answer to the problem of Christianity's relation to the world and history, then, stands at the opposite pole from Catholicism's communal answer. The Catholic model of church that sees organized Christianity as ministering to the problems of history (even to those who are not and will never be Catholics); Swaggart sees the gathered church of redeemed individuals in constant, direct tension with the world around them. For Swaggart's followers, as Janice Peck noted,

> the pleasures and the problems of the world "have nothing to do with you." Christians experience tension in their choice of separation . . . because they are "going against the prevailing currents of the world." In this sense, Swaggart preaches a dualist version of Christianity that is anti-modern and anti-materialist.[27]

The emphasis on divine action in and through creation that pervades the Catholic understandings of sacrament (God actually in the bread and wine), institution (the Holy Spirit operating through specific communal offices), and theology (analogical human language actually transmitting a reliable knowledge of the Holy, even apart from scripture) is seen by Swaggart as a betrayal of the Gospel itself. Further, Swaggart's call represents a stance directly opposed to Catholicism's churchly tradition of taking responsibility for the human cultures in which it finds itself. As the great scholar of world religions Mircea Eliade put it in his own definition of Catholic Christianity, the opposite of Catholicism is not Protestantism, but rather sectarianism. By this Eliade means that intrinsic to Catholicism's social stance is a very this-worldly focus on the material aspects of belief, on institutional structures, and on communal sources of identity. According to Eliade's definition of Catholicism, then, conversion becomes a lifelong process of encountering the Holy in material forms (i.e., sacraments) and in the community itself. The past of the institution is analogous to the written scripture itself as mediating God's purposes; and the "mysteries" celebrated by the community are efficacious even without worthy ministers (what the tradition defines as *ex opere operato*).[28] These aspects of Christianity shape a religious sensibility that stands at the opposite extreme to Swaggart's come-outism. Far from asserting that the "pleasures and problems of the world have nothing to do with you," Catholic Christianity — at least since the emperor Constantine in the fourth century — has consistently worked toward building God's kingdom in this world. Thus the vast cathedrals with wide portals inviting all to come in; the university faculties of theology and philosophy attempting to mediate the faith in the best and most sophisticated categories available to human reason; the worldwide network of hospitals, orphanages, and schools serving any and all who appear at the door.[29]

To someone with Swaggart's dialectical approach to the Gospel, not only is such an incarnated version of Christianity incomprehensible; it represents a profound betrayal of the faith. The Catholic message — which has consistently condemned any and all forms of come-outism — is paganism pure and simple. Thus does Swaggart, like Jonathan Edwards and Charles Finney before him, feel driven by God's Spirit to stand up in the burning house of this world and shout "Get out!" in the loudest possible voice.

"Everything Changed"

According to his spiritual autobiography, *To Cross a River* (named after a gospel hymn), Jimmy Lee Swaggart felt called since God first spoke to him as a young boy. His parents had been converted under an Assemblies of God tent erected by Mother Sumrall and her daughter, who had come to Jimmy's home town of Ferriday, Louisiana, in 1936, when Swaggart was two years old, to preach gospel holiness in that ostensible sinkhole of iniquity. Swaggart's father — who had never been in any church before — heard the spirited singing one night and decided to join in and play his fiddle. Soon his mother, an accomplished rhythm guitar player and singer, came to the tent also. "Night after night as they sat through the services, the Spirit of the Lord dealt with them." After a great deal of soul-searching, one night "with tears on his face, daddy walked down the aisle and surrendered his life to Christ. Following him, only a few steps behind was mamma. Behind her were daddy's parents. Everything changed."[30]

The young Swaggart regularly accompanied his parents to both the services and Sunday School, but continued in his chief worldly vice: he "loved going to the movies at the Arcade Theater on Fourth Avenue," where on Saturday afternoons he watched Johnny Mack Brown, Gene Autry, or Hopalong Cassidy. Swaggart's mother was a frequent moviegoer too, "but once she became a Christian she decided to quit going. But it had been a real battle." On a particularly auspicious Saturday afternoon, when he was waiting to meet his cousins Jerry Lee Lewis and Mickey Gilley outside the Arcade, everything changed for him too. As he stood in line to buy his ticket, an entreating voice spoke to him. The voice said to him, "Do not go in this place. Give your heart to me. I have chosen you a vessel to be used in my service." The voice was so strong that he looked around him to see if anybody was actually speaking to him. But "something inside seemed to say it was God speaking to me." And like the young prophet Samuel in the Old Testament similarly called of God — only now at a distinctly American kind of temple — Swaggart responded immediately and wholeheartedly: "I will, I'll do what you said. . . . I'll accept you." He stepped out of the ticket line and skipped home, singing, "I've got a home in glory land that outshines the sun." His mother was surprised to see him back so early. Her reborn son told her, "I gave my heart to the Lord and I'm not going anymore."[31]

A second blessing occurred when Jimmy was eight years old, when "Brother" Cecil Janway came to the Ferriday church. Janway preached a fervent message, spoke in tongues, and was a skillful pianist who played hymns with such passion that "life flowed throughout the church building." Watching these musical ministrations, Swaggart recalls: " 'Lord, I want you to give me the gift of playing the piano' I prayed the entire time Brother Janway was playing." Whether the Holy Spirit created the gift *ex nihilo* or built on that gene that Swaggart seems to have shared with his musical cousins, his youthful prayer was answered a hundredfold: Swaggart himself was given the gift of writing and singing soul-melting gospel tunes as well as the ability to speak in tongues. He recorded his first gospel album in 1959, and by 1988 he had recorded fifty-four albums, earning (according to his own report) $200 million. He was reported to be the best-selling gospel artist in record history by the recording industry. By the 1980s, Swaggart observed to an interviewer, it was fruitless to even try to quantify how much his success owed to his music and how much to his rhetorical style:

> You're talking about the right arm and the left arm. One without the other is almost unthinkable. During the great Moody revivals, Moody had Sankey. Billy Sunday had Homer Rodeheaver, and it just goes hand in hand. Somebody said Christianity is the only religion, even though we don't really look at Christianity as a religion, but the only one that has a songbook in it, because Buddhism, Shintoism, Confucianism, have nothing to sing about. And so music of necessity plays a tremendously important part.[32]

Swaggart began his "spirit anointed" ministry by witnessing on a street corner in Mangham, Louisiana (a town of five hundred), on market day. His dire biblically inspired message that afternoon — that America's coming judgment day was considerably closer than those sleeping souls appreciated — met with surprising success, and the young revivalist eventually began preaching in his home town of Ferriday on a flatbed truck fitted with a microphone and loudspeakers. On January 1, 1958, when he was twenty-two years old, Swaggart entered full-time evangelistic work and undertook to bring his gospel to a string of small towns in Arkansas, Tennessee, Mississippi, and Louisiana. He freely confesses that he often boosted attendance at these itinerant revival meetings by "letting it be known that he was the 'preacher cousin' of Jerry Lee Lewis." And as a result "scores of people came to hear about Jerry Lee and wound up accepting Christ as Saviour." That same year he married Frances Anderson, a devoted spouse who has been described as Swaggart's most ardent supporter and most listened-to advisor.[33]

But as Blan Stout has observed, Swaggart's early rhythmic musical style — sort of rockabilly applied to gospel music — and his relation to Jerry Lee Lewis caused him to be perceived as too folksy even for the leadership of the Assemblies of God. His first application to the Assemblies of God leadership for ordination was denied, despite the fact that he had already met their standards — a successful record of preaching and soul winning. But Swaggart refused to be daunted by the stinging rejection and continued his itinerancy throughout the Southeast. His popularity as a pentecostal preacher continued to grow. A year later he was accepted for ordination.[34]

On January 1, 1969, Swaggart began preaching on the radio, and in August he was selected to address the biennial meeting of Assemblies' preachers. This marked Swaggart's transition "from primarily a musician who preached to a preacher who sang." After this event, Swaggart was vouchsafed yet another divine epiphany. It was undoubtedly deeply consoling that the good Lord had the same Louisiana drawl and style of speech as Swaggart himself: "Son, I'm pleased with what you're doing," Swaggart recalls the Lord saying to him. "But you're going too slow with the radio effort. I will return before you get the job done. You must hurry. I want you to go on every radio station possible that will air a gospel program daily."[35]

In order to implement God's plan, by 1972 Swaggart stopped holding his meetings in individual churches and instead sponsored weekend crusades in auditoriums and civic centers to reach more people. In 1973 he also undertook a weekly thirty minute television program. Recorded in a studio in Nashville, the country music capital of the world, Swaggart's broadcast foregrounded Jimmy's considerable musical talents. As Swaggart remembers, "The first fifteen minutes of the show was music, another ten minutes was used for a Bible message, and the remainder of time for announcements of meetings and album offers."[36]

Swaggart continued to look for ways to implement God's command to hurry. In 1973 he bought a radio station in Baton Rouge for full-time ministry outreach — with others soon following in Dallas–Fort Worth, Oklahoma City, Pensacola, Florida, and Bowling Green, Ohio. By 1981 Swaggart's voice could be heard on 550 stations nationally. Even so, he took a major step that year. In May he abandoned his radio ministry to appear exclusively on television. He claimed that he felt "led of the Lord to do it."[37]

By 1983, Swaggart's televised broadcast was carried by over 225 local stations and was watched by 2.6 million people every week. His Baton Rouge headquarters (now with its own zip code) received more mail than any other organization in the state of Louisiana, and its mailing list had one million names, a telemarketer's dream. The average donation was fifty dollars; the Jimmy Swaggart Ministry's income for 1982 was $57,448,000, and of this, $15,726,000 was spent on television time and production.[38]

But the millions of dollars that Swaggart spent on his new television ministry ranked behind his personal appearances at weekly crusades in terms of importance. This ranking of ministerial exertions was based on an unofficial seven point plan that had evolved by the early 1980s, according to which his weekly revivals ranked as most important in carrying out the good Lord's command to hurry. Behind this came his televised ministry, in which his son Donny came to occupy an increasingly important place as the point man in asking for donations on camera. Ranking behind those two were the building of foreign churches and Bible schools (chiefly in Latin America); literature distribution in both the United States and abroad; and support for missionaries. Taking up last place was the Jimmy Swaggart Children's Fund — the most recent of his ministries. Swaggart's television ministry generated the capital to build his World Ministry Center in Baton Rouge. When the Jimmy Swaggart Bible College opened for business the year after Swaggart's letter to Catholics, eighteen thousand students applied for the four hundred seats available. Staffing the college, the worship center, and the radio and TV programs provided twelve hundred jobs for residents in the area.[39]

In the fourteen years after he began full-time ministry work, Swaggart had moved from preaching on the street corners of small southern towns on market day to being one of the most watched and admired religious leaders in the United States. By almost any standard, the pace and breadth of his success might have reasonably been termed miraculous. Swaggart, of course, consistently claimed that all the glory belonged to God alone, who had made good on his word.[40]

Swaggart's "Letter" in 1983, then, represented a challenge to both Catholic self-respect and to ecumenical relations in a uniquely Catholic enclave in a Baptist South. However outrageous or even nonsensical by Catholic theological standards, his call to Catholics to come out of that hell-bound institution had to be taken seriously, and seriously answered. For the challenge was tendered not by a southern preacher on the fringes of mainstream culture (as was sometimes portrayed in the northern press). Rather, in 1983 Jimmy Lee Swaggart was one of the two or three best known and most watched religious personalities in the United States. Only Mother Angelica would come to have the kind of televangelistic visibility that Swaggart had then; but her rise to religious media superstar status was to occur later in that decade.

In the event, it would be neither the ecumenical efforts of Bishop Ott to pour oil on waters made turbulent by Swaggart, nor editorials in Protestant mainstream journals like the *Christian Century* that would silence his anti-Catholic rhetoric. A series of tawdry newspaper stories about Swaggart's meeting with a prostitute at the Travel Inn on Airport Highway in New Orleans in October of 1987 — stories that provided camera footage of the encounters — forced Swaggart to turn his attention to his own survival as a preacher. Swaggart's vociferous denunciations of Catholic perfidy and anti-biblical foundations fell silent after the autumn of 1987. The Tempter apparently was operating at much closer quarters than Vatican Hill in Rome.[41]

Catholicism and Christianity

Bishop Ott's efforts to reach accord with Jimmy Lee Swaggart during the summer of 1983 came to naught. Within a year of his "Letter," Swaggart denounced a four-day North American Congress on the Holy Spirit and World Evangelism held in the New Orleans Superdome — an event expected to draw upwards of fifty-five thousand — because of its anti-biblical compromise in allowing fifteen thousand Catholic charismatics to attend. Swaggart cancelled his much-awaited appearance at that congress. "There is absolutely no way that ministers of the Gospel can stand on a platform with Catholic priests in some type of professed unity without compromising the Word of God." In a letter published on the op-ed page of the *New Orleans Times-Picayune* on August 13, 1987, that is, just two months before the devastating exposés of his sexual sins and on the eve of a visit by John Paul II to New Orleans, Catholicism was described by Swaggart as being "in a seriously declining position worldwide." Catholics, he announced, probably had a "greater spiritual hunger for God than their Protestant brethren" because of the starvation rations they had been fed. He also cited "an unparalleled exodus from the Catholic Church." He continued:

> Millions of sincere Catholics who have faithfully kept the sacraments of the church have found that hunger remains. Many more, while versed in Catholic doctrine and honest in their beliefs, are discovering that dogma alone will not fill the spiritual void. Others have begun reading their Bibles, and what they have found is that the traditions they were raised with are often not scriptural, and certainly not prerequisites for salvation.[42]

He added that he welcomed the pope to his own missionary territory and was confident that he had nothing to fear from the visit of the pontiff; indeed, the pope himself couldn't do anything to stem the flow of converts leaving the Roman church for real Christianity. This was a miracle that "the pope is simply not going to be able to stop." Swaggart could only hope that both the pope and his church "will accept the blowing winds of revival."[43] Two months later, the blowing winds threatened the collapse of his own house of prayer The ironies informing the threatened collapse of that house of prayer, in fact, were rather broad and deep. Perhaps the most graphic of them was the fact that the sign behind the manager's desk at the Travel Inn that Swaggart frequented for his assignations with Debra Arlene Murphree ("NO REFUNDS AFTER THE FIRST 15 MINUTES") faced a large billboard on the other side of the highway that read: "JESUS SAID UNLESS A MAN IS BORN AGAIN HE CANNOT SEE THE KINGDOM OF GOD: JOHN 3:3. YOUR ETERNITY IS AT STAKE."[44]

From the standpoint of pentecostal demonology, however, perhaps it was not coincidental that Swaggart chose this way to give himself up to his enemies. Here, as Lawrence Wright has noted, "in this highly charged battleground between God and Satan, he found a twenty-six-year-old mother of three with a crucifix tattooed on her right arm" to perform sexual favors for him. Ms. Murphree was later exposed fully in *Penthouse* magazine. And it did seem that Satan won the battle that particular day in his never-ending war with the armies of the Lamb.[45]

Swaggart admitted to only a single instance of what he termed his moral failure, but Murphree set the number closer to twenty-five over a long period of time. The General Council of the Assemblies of God showed little interest in the exact number. It likewise remained deaf to Swaggart's famously teary "I Have Sinned" confession on February 21, 1988. In that extraordinary performance in front of eight thousand worshipers and millions of TV viewers, Swaggart "cannily admitted to an unspecified sin and begged his congregation's, his wife's, his family's, and, of course, almost as an afterthought, God's forgiveness." His disturbingly rent clothes and mussed hair can be viewed as either effectively scripted, pathologically distraught, or a telling combination of both. Striding feverishly from one side of the stage to the other, Swaggart proclaimed: "My sin was done in secret, but God said to me, 'I will do what I do before the whole world.'" Without ever divulging to his stunned audience what exactly it was that was being made manifest to the whole world, he said, "I don't plan to whitewash my sin. I don't call it a mistake. I call it a sin. I have no one to blame but myself."[46]

It was a dramatic performance, even for Swaggart. At the time, only a handful of close associates and denominational leaders knew what Swaggart was confessing to. What his vast audience didn't know was that Swaggart had had four months to plan it. Assemblies' leadership was not amused. While the Louisiana District Council of the denomination had decreed that Swaggart should step down from his pulpit for three months to atone for his sin — during which time Swaggart's wife, Frances, would serve as his emissary to his far-flung missionary empire — the Assemblies' national leadership refused to accept such a light penance. The General Council decreed that Swaggart should be suspended from preaching and personal appearances both on and off the air for one year. Swaggart had agreed to the District Council's decision (which would allow him to return to the pulpit and the airwaves on May 22, 1988), but the harsher strictures of the General Council — the same as those applied to Jim Bakker, whom Swaggart had helped to convict of sexual and financial irregularities the previous year — seemed far too heavy. When Swaggart announced his refusal to abide by this ruling, the National Council dismissed him from the church.[47] His *Sunday Crusade,* viewed in 1.96 million homes in 1987, was down to 851,000 households a year later; by 1989 his annual revenues were 50 percent of what they were in 1987; and by 1991 the *Jimmy Swaggart Telecast* had dropped from second to seventh place among religious broadcasts.[48]

But the eventual disappearance of anti-Catholic rhetoric in Swaggart's personal and televised appearances should not be construed to mean that the televangelist somehow saw the light and changed his mind, about the likelihood of Catholics getting into heaven or on the relation of Catholicism and Christianity. His book of that title may still be purchased from his Baton Rouge headquarters, and he has never recanted a single pithy phrase hurled at the Church of Rome.

The anti-Catholicism of Swaggart's ministry lies at the very core of his theology — a theology that Janet Peck asserts "prevents the formation of genuine community" precisely because the only community allowed is one between himself and the individual listener or viewer. Swaggart's premillenialist, biblically literalist, pentecostal gospel is, Peck avers, perhaps the most individualistic religious message on TV:

> Swaggart's communion occurs in relationship with Christ and the Holy Spirit; as he often says, "Christianity is not a religion. It's a relationship with Jesus Christ." Swaggart proposes a challenge of sorts to contemporary society. His ideology is a negation of modernism. Progress, enlightenment, and material accumulation have failed to fill humanity's deepest desire — the desire for cosmic connection and for an "ultimate relevance of being." Swaggart condemns modern society because it has robbed human life of meaning, and he offers a story of the world that restores premodern significance and transcendence.[49]

Peck's read of Swaggart's ideology can be extended in an overtly theological direction, so that his theology can be read as a challenge of sorts not only to contemporary society, but to Catholic Christianity as well. At its very core, Swaggart's message contains undigestible individualist, unmediated, and anti-sacramental impulses — whatever the timbre and frequency with which they are proclaimed — that see in the Catholic tradition of Christianity a profound betrayal of everything the Gospel proclaims.

The resolutely individualistic presuppositions of Swaggart's theology — Christianity being simply an individual's relationship with Jesus Christ —

fly in the face of Catholicism's deeply communal and institutional traditions. There is no such thing as saved believers in Catholic Christianity — at least in the sense of individuals coming to salvation on their own: the community is the locus for both the celebration of the mysteries and of the encounter with the Holy. Likewise, Swaggart's unmediated understanding of salvation and sanctification — that individuals can encounter the Word of God directly in scripture and in the word preached (especially by him), acceptance of which makes individuals born again — represents the polar opposite of Catholicism's mediated approach to holiness. In the latter approach, individuals almost never encounter the Holy directly, but rather through God's good creation — the world of nature and ideas, other people, bread and wine, and the word proclaimed in community. It is precisely the context of that last activity that makes it effective, for Catholic Christianity has always asserted that the Community came before the Book: indeed, the Community, under the prompting of the Spirit, created the Book. The idea that individuals can use the Book apart from the Community — or even to justify dispersing the Community, as happens in come-outer forms of sectarianism like Swaggart's — is heretical, or even nonsensical, to the Catholic mind. Finally and by no means least importantly, Swaggart's reference to baptism and eucharist as ordinances rather than sacraments is not just semantic preference: his understanding of what happens in those events that Catholics call sacraments represents the opposite pole of the sacramental imagination.

In Swaggart's dialectical imagination, God — by definition — cannot be present in fallen creation or in that creation's material creatures like bread and wine, because "the flesh availeth nothing; the spirit is all." Rather, God stands apart from and in judgment on created reality. History and nature are headed for a fiery end, from which Bible Believers will be spared by the Rapture. It is not the water of baptism, the bread and wine of the Lord's Supper, nor the intention of the community that celebrates them that makes such ordinances effective. It is rather the faith vouchsafed by the Spirit to those born again that makes them ordinances in the first place. Thus, in a real sense, these ordinances aren't even celebrated by a community at all, but rather by a collection of individual Christians, gathered together from a fallen world for mutual edification, who have undergone the world-changing experience of rebirth. Such a gathered understanding of worship and celebration militates against a sacramental worldview from the get-go, seeing in the Catholic understanding of sacrament only magic and pagan superstition.

The Reverend Jimmy Lee Swaggart continues his ministry in Baton Rouge, calling sinners to accept Jesus and become born-again, speaking in tongues, witnessing disciples of the Lord. And an important part of that call to "Get out" of the burning building of the fallen world is addressed to Catholics both in the United States and abroad, How could it be otherwise, given that Catholics are his "greatest enemies — bless their hearts."

Part Two

CRISIS IN
AMERICAN
CATHOLICISM

"That some should criticize my earlier decisions I can easily understand. Judgments were made regarding the assignment of John Geoghan which, in retrospect, were tragically incorrect."   — Bernard Cardinal Law

"The bishops gathered wood for this current conflagration every time they turned away from the human condition to emphasize wayward genitalia. They must be amazed at how harshly they are now judged after all those years of deference, when they were allowed to make their own laws. Perhaps they sense that they are being judged with the ferocity of those accustomed to being judged harshly themselves."
                                                — Anna Quindlen in *Newsweek*

"It is pointed out that the [Boston] *Globe*, like its owner the *New York Times*, is no friend of the Church... [that] the messenger is not a neutral party. All that is true; but it is of limited pertinence. It is also true that Catholics should not be apologetic about wanting to defend the Church. It is their duty. Doing that duty, however, is not incompatible with, but in fact requires, a recognition that, in this case as in so many others through history, leaders of the Church are guilty of giving ammunition to those who would attack her.... What has happened in Boston is inexcusable. Those responsible can be forgiven, but they cannot be excused."   — Richard John Neuhaus in *First Things*

"From the start, the archdiocese [of Boston] has been incredibly stupid in the way they have handled this crisis. And as hard as it was to do, they have managed to make things worse."   — Carmen Dorso, Boston attorney
                                                representing alleged victims of priests

"I dig this Catholic stuff. I dig the orthodoxy. I view myself as a very orthodox, very conservative Catholic. Call me a young fogey at 44. I can't imagine things ever being the same as before. I want to believe these are good guys, and I can't anymore."   — Brenda Becker, Catholic laywoman, in the *New York Times*

"I can speak only for myself, not the half a dozen other Catholics in the room. But the American bishops have lately succeeded in inflicting something on me I have not previously experienced. They made me ashamed of being a Catholic."
                                    — Arthur Jones in the *National Catholic Reporter*

"The cardinal said canon law had to be considered. We just looked at one another. Whatever we had just told him didn't seem to be registering. Canon law was irrelevant to us. Children were being abused. Sexual predators were being protected. Canon law should have nothing to do with it. But they were determined to keep this problem, and their response to it, within their culture."
                                        — Carolyn Newberger, child psychologist and
                                                special advisor to Bernard Cardinal Law

Chapter Ten

Betrayal in Boston

"The bishops appointed [under Pope John Paul II] have been the kind of men who are, with some happy exceptions, not nimble enough to deal with the sexual abuse crisis or even to be aware of it. They are, in the parlance of the Curia, *safe men*. Who could be safer than Bernard Cardinal Law of Boston, who just this weekend refused yet again to apologize for his gross mishandling of abusive priests. Only it turns out that in times of ongoing crisis, safe men are not safe at all." — Andrew Greeley, "'Safe' Men Put Church in Its Crisis"[1]

"Inexcusable"

"Inexcusable" is a strong word, one of the strongest that can be used by individuals against disappointing institutional behavior in a democratic society. But the spectrum of Catholic voices using that word to describe what has come to be designated as the "clergy child molestation scandal" in the United States is breathtaking — and perhaps unprecedented — in its ideological diversity. The observations of "liberal" Catholics like editorialist Anna Quindlen, long tired of what she has described as the Vatican's double standard in dealing with Catholic women (and long loudly vocal about it) might be expected. For Richard John Neuhaus, a Catholic priest, editor of the "conservative" journal *First Things,* and one of the most vocal supporters of Vatican policy in the United States, to describe the hierarchy's handling of the case as "inexcusable" is something else again. "Those responsible can be forgiven, but they cannot be excused" is how Neuhaus's editorial put it. Strong stuff, especially from a Vatican friendly Catholic conservative describing the activities of the pope's chief point men in the United States.[2]

Balancing this word in describing the mess that broke onto the public stage in Boston in January 2002, however, is another word: "irony." Andrew Greeley's May 7, 2002, editorial in the *Daily News* ("New York's Hometown Newspaper," as it proudly describes itself, unapologetically read more often on subways than in corporate board rooms) luxuriated in it. Greeley observed that it was not those liberals dismissed by Rome as "cafeteria Catholics" who created the mess in the first place, or who exacerbated it in cover-ups and in what the post-Watergate world calls "nondenial denials." It was not those ostensible liberals regularly accused by both Rome and its most loyal spokespersons in the United States of being more American than Catholic who were responsible for what was immediately perceived as a crisis within American Catholicism of unprecedented proportions. Those responsible were, rather, conservative clerics "who are, in the parlance of the curia, safe men" — that is, churchmen who loyally and regularly reinforce the Vatican positions on birth control, homosexuality, and the role of women in the church. It was the Vatican's own hand-picked team of papal supporters who are responsible for the mess. Greeley drove it home in some of the strongest language ever printed by a Catholic priest in good standing against the leaders of his own church:

> It turns out that in times of ongoing crisis, safe men are not safe at all. The leadership blighted the hopes of my generation of priests, a small fact, doubtless, from their viewpoint. What right did we have to hope, anyway? But by their rigidity, they created the climate of insensitivity — I almost said stupid insensitivity — that now blights the whole church. God forgive them for losing their nerve.[3]

Greeley's recognition of that irony must balance "inexcusable" in accounting for what I would term the dark underside of the Catholic worldview that has formed the foil for much of the anti-Catholicism narrated in previous chapters. It is crucially necessary, given the interesting times in which the American Catholic Church now finds itself, to explore how the Catholic worldview itself contributed to this situation.

The tragedy narrated here focuses only secondarily on those predatory priests who sexually molested hundreds of children entrusted to their care. Words like "inexcusable" and "ironic" hardly do justice to their behavior. Rather, words like "sociopathological," "gravely sinful," and (given the location of some of the sexual attacks in confessionals and church sanctuaries) even "blasphemous" are better suited to describe the searing betrayal of parental and churchly trust. Primarily, questions will be raised about the culture of church leadership that abetted the "extraordinary cloak of secrecy" at the heart of the tragedy.[4]

The chief players contributing to the scandal that unraveled after January of 2002 were not themselves personally malicious or evil; nor did they consciously seek harm to be done to children, although their administrative decisions did, in fact, allow that over decades. But just as important in understanding the story is an appreciation of the fact that Catholic bishops were participants and abettors of a culture in which the good name and reputation of the institutional church and its representatives outranked all other considerations, even the safety of children. Thus, in the name of protecting what they perceived to be the good name and respected status of Catholicism as an institution, a number of sexually abusive priests were dealt with, or not dealt with, in secrecy.

Church leaders are always called to be pastors first and administrators second. A good English translation of the Greek word *episcopoi*, from which the term "episcopal" derives, might be rendered as "shepherds" or "pastors." The very efforts to smooth over the tawdry trail of clergy child molestation, in the face of consistent and reliable reports that something was very wrong, has brought the institution that they sought to protect into a public disrepute unparalleled in the history of U.S. Catholicism.

As Fr. Neuhaus has observed, Catholics simply can't dismiss all of the shocked — and shocking — press coverage of the Boston scandal as further evidence of the anti-Catholicism of the press. "The *Globe,* like its owner the *New York Times,* is no friend of the Church. All of that is true; but it is of limited pertinence," he said, for "the leaders of the Church are guilty of giving ammunition to those who would attack her." Neuhaus is exactly right. The observations of Catholic leaders like Archbishop Julian Herranz of the Roman Curia, who dismissed much of the coverage as due to the "tenacious, scandalistic style" of the U.S. press, or Oscar Cardinal Maradiaga of Honduras, who declared that the "church should be free of this kind of ... fury which reminds me of the times of Diocletian and Nero, and more recently, Stalin and Hitler," are embarrassing for U.S. Catholics. The North American press has been almost gleeful at times in uncovering the scandalous trails of serial child abuse by scores of priests: "all of that is true; but it is of limited pertinence." The story is ultimately about the culture within the church that made it possible rather than about the hostile press that uncovered and reported it.[5]

Child psychologist Carolyn Newberger — called in by Cardinal Law at one stage to advise him on how to handle cases of clerical sexual abuse — testified to her first glimpse of that culture at lunch with the cardinal in his own residence in Brighton, Massachusetts. When she and her colleagues advised the cardinal that priests accused of such acts should be removed from their parochial assignments without delay and kept as far from contact with children as possible, the cardinal observed that "canon law had to be considered." She later recalled,

> Whatever we had just told him didn't seem to be registering. Canon law was irrelevant to us. Children were being abused. Sexual predators were being protected. Canon law should have nothing to do with it. But they were determined to keep this problem, and their response to it, within their culture.[6]

What Dr. Newberger saw was an entire worldview and language of discourse with revered and ancient roots in the Catholic past. But it would betray many children entrusted to it for spiritual formation, and church leaders, blameless in terms of personal culpability, were themselves betrayed by that worldview and language. Many of the bishops now being demonized as one step removed from child molesters themselves were dedicated churchmen attempting to do the best they could in very difficult circumstances, operating within a clerical culture that had official sanction and blessing. To vilify these men personally as the bad guys behind the affair simply compounds the tragedy, given their records on other issues — like Cardinal Law's as a valiant and progressive champion of the rights of immigrants and illegal aliens. Such a portrayal also ignores the fact that most of these men inherited a crisis that was not of their making.[7]

In the Catholic tradition, the importance of the community in which the encounters with the Holy take place in sacraments invariably gives rise to a temptation to sacralize the institution itself. The rights of individuals over the community's prerogatives were expendable for larger goods — like the reputation of the community. Among the tendencies inherent in this sinful underside is the potentially idolatrous impulse (always prophetically — and correctly — denounced by spokespersons for the Protestant tradition like Martin Luther and Karl Barth) to celebrate the human authority structures of the church as a perfect society, untouched by the sinful complicities of history and human decision making. In this reading of the authority of church leaders, decisions once made must be defended at almost any cost to avoid the appearance of mistakes that would reveal that society as less than perfect. Further, the emphasis on loyalty to institutional decisions as an almost religious duty risks forgetting that the entire tradition rests on analogy. God's purposes and those of the human institution commissioned to preach and bind in God's name are alike, but also different. Loyalty to one is not always and everywhere loyalty to the Other.

Betrayal

The betrayal, or more correctly its revelation, began with a deceptively mundane court filing. On June 8, 2001, Bernard Cardinal Law submitted to the Suffolk Superior Court, in response to a lawsuit against the Reverend John Geoghan in which the archdiocese was named as a party, a document in which he admitted that in 1984 — just months after his installation as the new archbishop of Boston — he had reassigned Geoghan to St. Julia's Church, a cushy suburban parish in affluent Weston, Massachusetts. Law admitted to having been notified two months earlier that Geoghan was alleged to have sexually molested seven boys. To several investigative reporters on the staff of the *Boston Globe* that balmy June day, both the court filing and the admission that it contained constituted a turning point. As they would later report it, "a story about a priest who was accused of molesting children was now a story about a bishop who protected that priest." The public perception of Law's court filing, despite being proffered as full disclosure, was not helped when a month later the archbishop's legal counsel submitted a copy of a letter from Geoghan's doctor, dated October 20, 1984. That letter said that, despite an "unfortunate traumatic experience" at a previous parish, and following a "brief but beneficial respite," Geoghan was now fit for reassignment to another parish. The reporters at the *Globe* were uncomfortable with the doctor's

description of the sexual molestation of children as an "unfortunate traumatic experience," and decided that further investigation was necessary.
(It was only much later that they discovered that the physician writing
that memo was a Geoghan family friend.)[8]

The *Globe* decided to let the newspaper's Spotlight Team begin a much
broader investigation into whether the Geoghan case (as it was now being
called) was an anomaly or part of a broader pattern of clergy sexual abuse
involving children. The tawdry and shocking history that was uncovered
as a result of that decision was revealed on the newspaper's front page six
months later. Under the headline "SCORES OF PRIESTS INVOLVED IN SEX
ABUSE CASES," was a story that announced that

> under an extraordinary cloak of secrecy, the Archdiocese of Boston
> in the last 10 years has quietly settled child molestation claims against
> at least 70 priests. In the public arena alone, the *Globe* found court
> records and other documents that identify 19 present and former
> priests as accused pedophiles. Four have been convicted of criminal
> charges of sex abuse, including former priest John Geoghan. Two
> others face criminal charges. But those public cases represent just
> a fraction of the priests whose cases have been disposed of in pri-
> vate negotiations that never brought the parties near a courthouse,
> according to interviews with many of the attorneys involved.[9]

The shocking phrases peppered throughout that morning's front-page
story would soon become heartrending breakfast fare for the next six
months. The headline would soon be followed by others equally unset-
tling: "CARDINAL PROMOTED ALLEGED SEX ABUSER," "PRIEST ABUSE CASES
SEALED BY JUDGES," and "MORE ARE CALLING FOR CARDINAL TO RESIGN."[10]

The Spotlight Team encountered stiff resistance from the Archdiocese
of Boston and its legal representatives even as they began their efforts to
unseal court documents and talk to victims of clerical abuse. The reporters
discovered within days of beginning their investigation that in scores of
civil lawsuits pending against Catholic clergy, judges had placed a confidentiality seal on all court documents relevant to the cases, including
depositions and personnel records. The new editor of the *Globe,* Martin
Baron, decided that his paper should legally challenge those confidentiality orders on the grounds that public interest outweighed the privacy

of the litigants involved, and in August 2001 the *Globe*'s lawyers filed a court motion seeking to unseal court records. Superior Court judge Constance Sweeney (herself a practicing Catholic) ruled in the *Globe*'s favor in November 2001, a decision immediately appealed by the Archdiocese of Boston. A month later a state appeals court judge upheld Sweeney's ruling and announced that the documents would be released in January 2002. But on December 17, 2001, Wilson D. Rogers, legal counsel for Cardinal Law, sent the *Globe* a letter threatening legal action against the newspaper and its law firm if the paper published any information from the personnel records of the archdiocese, and warned that the Cardinal would seek a court-imposed sanction against reporters seeking interviews with priests involved in the unsealed documents.[11]

While these operatic courtroom dramas were being enacted the *Globe*'s reporters turned to other sources to track the information they sought. They discovered a wealth of information in the archdiocesan annual directories, which listed the assignments of priests serving the Boston church, and developed a computerized database that focused on clerical reassignment, sick leave, or removal. Among the interesting statistics that emerged, the database showed that the number of priests listed as being on "sick leave," "absent on leave," or "awaiting assignment" had grown to 107 in 1994 (out of a population of about 650 diocesan and 700 order priests in the diocese), three times the number placed in similar categories just a decade earlier. The reporters began making inquiries — in parishes and in court records — about why such a large increase occurred in the course of a decade.

They found that the number of priests listed in these holding categories had exploded after 1992, in the aftermath, it would turn out, of sex abuse allegations against a priest in the neighboring Diocese of Fall River, Massachusetts. The allegations against James Porter had been described in newspapers throughout New England as "horrific" in both kind and number. The shocking nature of Porter's abuse made 1992 a marker in the consciousness of Catholic bishops throughout the United States. One Boston attorney tracked down by the *Globe* team was quoted on condition of anonymity as saying that "the cardinal was running scared after the Porter case, so the archdiocese paid what amounted to 'hush money' to settle cases. Their motive was to avoid scandal and hope it would all go away."[12]

The team discovered that the archdiocese had quietly settled in court claims of sexual abuse against at least seventy other Boston priests. The January 31 article observed that that number was conservative, because a number of cases had been settled out of court, and the records of another twenty suits had been impounded by the court for undisclosed reasons.[13]

Those reasons — and the names of the priests involved — would be on the front page of the *Globe* in the following months. But the one name that became indelibly burned into the public consciousness and the name that would be hurled at Cardinal Law by an increasingly enraged part of his flock was the one that had led to the cardinal's court filing on June 8, 2001, and had started the *Globe's* Spotlight Team on their investigation.[14]

John Geoghan has been described (even by the families of his victims) as a man with a "disarming smile that, from a distance, gave him the gentle bearing of a kindly uncle." It was difficult to detect "the darkness behind John Geoghan's bright eyes." Maryetta Dussourd, herself to become a major player in sending Geoghan to jail, noted in the course of her court-room deposition that "he looked like a little altar boy." But when Geoghan entered the seminary in 1954, the faculty at the archdiocese's preparatory seminary in Jamaica Plain found him "decidedly immature." The prep seminary's rector, Monsignor John J. Murray, observed that "scholastically he is a problem. To be sure he received passing grades in most subjects, but I still have serious doubts about his ability to do satisfactory work in future studies."[15]

Geoghan did move on to major seminary, not least because of the intervention of his uncle, Monsignor Mark Keohane. Keohane was the brother of Geoghan's mother, a prelate whom Geoghan later described as the "perfect substitute father," but whom others have described as a "formidable figure — autocratic, old-school, domineering, and, some would say, mean." The pastor of a sprawling suburban parish in Needham, Massachusetts, Keohane consistently went to bat for his sister's boy, especially in the face of reservations on the part of the preparatory seminary's rector about allowing Geoghan to continue there. Keohane's efforts on his nephew's behalf continued when Geoghan was accepted into St. John's in Brighton. The correspondence between the rector, Thomas J. Riley, and Keohane continues the discussion of "problematic tendencies." In one such letter, Riley told Keohane that he was pressing for too much leniency toward "the lad's" shortcomings, and reminded Keohane that he should be the last to press for "exceptions" in accepting candidates for the priesthood, that it was crucially important "to deal with matters such as this on a completely objective basis, since unauthorized concessions made to one student so easily set a precedent which would lead others to seek favors." But Keohane would have none of this and wrote back immediately that "I resent your implication that I sought favors or preferment for John" — even while confessing that his nephew was "now sick, unhappy, and appears to be wrestling with his soul." Shortly thereafter, Geoghan withdrew from the seminary and enrolled at the College of the Holy Cross in Worcester, Massachusetts. There, apparently, his soul wrestling was resolved, for he reapplied to St. John's Seminary, was accepted, and was ordained as a Catholic priest in 1962.[16]

Whether Geoghan's unhappy early career as a seminarian was a result of psychological immaturity, sexual dysfunction, or clinical depression was much discussed in the papers after January 2002, although anything like a conclusive diagnosis is beyond reach. Geoghan himself later asserted that he was a heterosexual raised in a home free of physical, sexual, or verbal abuse. The 1989 report of a therapist at St. Luke's Institute, a Catholic psychiatric hospital in Maryland that had developed a treatment program for priests with sexual disorders, reported that "after ordination, Father Geoghan says he consciously repressed his enjoyment of the company of women for fear of conflict with his desire for celibacy."

Whatever set of impulses drove Geoghan in his predatory acts on children, he later confessed to a psychiatrist that almost immediately upon his arrival at his first parish assignment after ordination — Blessed Sacrament Church in blue-collar Saugus, Massachusetts, in 1962 — he grew sexually aroused in the company of boys. For the next three decades, Geoghan acted out a shocking pattern of serial sexual abuse on prepubescent and teenage boys, inviting them to sit on his lap, fondling them over their clothing, and in some cases even reaching inside their underclothes to masturbate them. In 1995 Geoghan admitted to having molested four boys from the same family, aged nine, ten, and eleven, and "on rare occasions" the seven-year-old as well. He also protested in that same deposition that he was very "careful never to touch the one girl in the family."[17]

It is not clear now how much, if anything, chancery officials knew about these early attacks, although Anthony Benzevich, a former priest who shared the Saugus rectory with Geoghan, recalled witnessing the newly ordained priest escorting young boys into his bedroom and alerting church higher-ups about it at the time. But Benzevich admitted at a pretrial deposition in 2000 that his memory was "foggy." If anyone had been informed of this, the pastor of Geoghan's second assignment, the Reverend Thomas W. Moriarity, knew nothing about it. Recalling Geoghan's record at St. Paul's parish in Hingham, Massachusetts, from 1967 to 1974, Moriarity recalls that "I found him different, I must say. I just didn't know how to react to him." And while he asserted that he didn't know what that "difference" might be, he recalls thinking that "something is wrong.... Something is not right here, but you can't put your finger on it."[18]

During those seven years in Hingham, Geoghan befriended Joanne Mueller, a single mother of four boys, whom the priest read stories to, took out for ice cream, and "helped in and out of the bathtub." Ms. Mueller, at the time of her heartbreaking deposition, said of Geoghan that "he was our friend." She considered the priest's care for her sons exemplary until one night in 1973, when her third son (then seven years old) grew very upset after she said that the priest was on his way over for a visit. When she pressed him, her son sobbed that he didn't want Geoghan "touching my wee-wee." Her five-year-old son likewise dissolved into tears, and Mueller summoned the two older boys, who likewise began to cry. Finally her oldest son said that "Father said we couldn't talk about it and tell you, never to tell you because it was a confessional [*sic*]." She immediately took the boys to see Fr. Paul Miceli, a parish priest who knew both Geoghan and her family as well. Mueller stated in her court deposition on August 17, 2000, that Miceli's advice to her and her sons that traumatic evening was "to try to not think about this; to forget about it. 'Bad as it is,' he said, 'just try.' Don't think about it. It will never happen again.' He said, 'He will never be a priest again. It will never happen again,' he reassured me."[19]

Miceli later took issue with Mueller's account in his own court deposition, stating that he did not recall Mueller's name and had never received the visit from her and her sons that she described. He did acknowledge receiving a phone call from a woman claiming that Geoghan was spending too much time with her children, but he claimed that the phrase "sexual abuse" was never mentioned in that conversation. But Miceli did say that the phone conversation had so disturbed him that he drove over to confront Geoghan face-to-face. Geoghan's absolute denial of Mueller's account apparently convinced Miceli. The tawdry tale ended there. No diocesan action was taken by Miceli or evidently recorded at the time.[20]

From the affluent south shore of Boston, Geoghan was next sent to St. Andrew's parish in hardscrabble Jamaica Plain in 1974 — an unremarkable reassignment for an assistant pastor — where he would be stationed for six years. It was in this working-class parish that Maryetta Dussourd was raising her four children — three boys and a girl — as well as her niece's four boys. Geoghan had been assigned responsibility for the Boy Scout troop that met at St. Andrew's, as well as the training of new altar boys, most of whom were younger than fourteen. Geoghan quickly befriended Dussourd and her sons and nephews, visiting her apartment almost every evening "to put the boys to bed." As it turned out, Geoghan was sexually molesting all seven boys in Dussourd's own apartment, in some cases performing oral sex on them. An archdiocesan memo dated December 30, 1994 (labeled "PERSONAL AND CONFIDENTIAL"), reported that Geoghan later confessed to actually staying in the Dussourd home while on a three-day retreat, "because he missed the children so much." The memo also noted that Geoghan "would touch them while they were sleeping and waken them by playing with their penises."[21]

Dussourd discovered what was happening only after the seven boys told her sister, Margaret Gallant. Horrified at what had been happening in her own home for several years, Dussourd told Fr. John E. Thomas in the neighboring parish of St. Thomas Aquinas, who confronted Geoghan directly. Thomas later confessed to being taken aback by what he termed Geoghan's casual admission that "yes, that's all true." Thomas promptly drove to the chancery (the archdiocese's offices in Brighton) that very afternoon — February 9, 1980 — to notify the administrator of the diocese, Bishop Thomas V. Daley. As later reported, Bishop Daley telephoned Geoghan at St. Andrew's rectory, in John Thomas's presence, that same day, curtly telling him to "go home." Geoghan left the rectory. Several weeks later, Fr. Thomas appeared at Maryetta Dussourd's doorstep, pleading with the distraught mother and aunt not to go public about Geoghan's activity. "Do you realize what you're taking from him?" Dussourd later reported Thomas as saying. And she did not go public.[22]

After being listed as "on sick leave" for almost a year (during which time he lived with his mother in West Roxbury, Massachusetts), Geoghan was assigned in February 1981 to St. Brendan's parish in Dorchester.[23]

The Bishops and the Conflagration after 1985

Any evaluation of the responsibility of Catholic bishops in abetting a culture that allowed sexual predators like Geoghan to be moved from one pastoral assignment to another, even after reports that inappropriate behavior with young boys had begun to be received by diocesan officials, must balance two sources of information available to church leaders in the 1980s.

One source can be dated quite specifically — to May 1985. That date represents something of a legal (and, possibly, moral) watershed in the story. A ninety-two-page confidential report (commonly referred to as "the Manual") on clergy sexual abuse of children was prepared for and delivered to the National Conference of Catholic Bishops for their meeting at St. John's Abbey in Collegeville, Minnesota. The report, entitled "The Problem of Sexual Molestation by Roman Catholic Clergy: Meeting the Problem in a Comprehensive and Responsible Manner," informed the assembled U.S. bishops that while treatment could "help rehabilitate clerics so that they could return to active ministry," it tempered that optimistic evaluation with the sober warning that strict conditions and lifelong treatment must also be imposed. Such treatment should include a minimum six-month stay in a treatment facility, six months to a year of residence in a half-way house overseen by mental health professionals, and continuous treatment in outpatient therapy. The report also noted that "recidivism is so high with pedophilia ... that all controlled studies have shown that traditional outpatient psychiatric or psychological models alone *do not work.*" It advised the bishops that they should immediately suspend any priest accused of sexual child abuse when the "allegation has *any* possible merit or truth" and send such clerics for treatment in a closed environment for at least six months. Further, the report quite presciently advised the bishops to abandon their strategy of staying away from the media when such cases were discovered among the clergy, for "in this sophisticated society a media policy of silence implies either necessary secrecy or cover-up. Cliches such as 'no comment' must be cast away" as a misunderstanding of communication politics in a democratic society.[24]

The report had been assembled by Michael Peterson, a Catholic priest and founder/director of St. Luke's Institute in Suitland, Maryland, Thomas Doyle, a Dominican priest and canon (church) lawyer working at the office of the papal nuncio in Washington, D.C., and Ray Mouton, a civil attorney representing a Catholic priest, Gilbert Gauthe, then charged with the sexual abuse of dozens of small children in Lafayette, Louisiana. Beginning in January 1985, these three began work, supported with testimony from psychiatrists, social workers, and attorneys, on the medical, legal, insurance, and pastoral aspects of clerical child abuse. Their document included the information that as of May 1985 more than $100 million in claims had been made against just one diocese as a result of sexual abuse by one priest against a number of minors, while the "total projected losses for the decade could rise to $1 billion."[25]

In summing up this data, the three noted — in words that the bishops at the time might have thought extreme — that the Catholic Church in the United Stated faced "extremely serious financial consequences," as well as "significant injury to its image as a result of the sexual molestation of children by clerics, priests, permanent deacons, nonordained religious, lay employees, and seminarians." Chilling warnings offered in the Executive Summary are particularly pertinent in grappling with episcopal responsibility in overseeing the Geoghan case. Those warnings were: "Failure to report the child abuse suspicion by a cleric by the Diocese is probably the most common error, and the greatest vulnerability in the long term"; and "It is important to know what matter should be contained in a priest's personnel file, considering the very probable discoverability of these files."[26]

Thomas Doyle, O.P., later claimed that Cardinal Law was nothing if not supportive of the report and of his own efforts to get the report to the U.S. bishops prior to the Collegeville meeting. Doyle said that the report would rely heavily on the support of John Cardinal Krol (then archbishop of Philadelphia) "and, primarily, Law" if it was to have any success in warning North American bishops about the dangers they faced by the increasing number of clergy abuse cases being reported in the press. Bernard Law, as head of an NCCB committee on "research and pastoral practices," was an especially important player in the dissemination of the Manual among fellow bishops. As Doyle later reported it, "Cardinal Law (Boston) stated that he would get the project into the NCCB by creating a special ad hoc committee of his own committee."[27]

When Doyle had first met Law, before he was made archbishop of Boston, Doyle claimed that "I liked him because he seemed to be a thinker, and not somebody primarily concerned with church politics." Doyle fondly remembered chatting with the socially activist bishop whenever Law visited Washington. Up until May 1985, Doyle considered Law one of the most sympathetic ears among the U.S. bishops to Doyle's efforts to alert them about the potentially devastating issue of clergy sexual abuse. Doyle remembers that in early 1985, "I told Bernie, this is our report. These are our recommendations. We need to get the conference to study this," and remembers that Law "was very supportive" of both the report and its recommendations.[28]

But at the meeting of the NCCB, Doyle claimed that Law changed his stance toward the Manual. The assembled bishops were quietly briefed on the report's contents, but no formal motion to study it was introduced by Law or by anyone else. The *National Catholic Reporter* later quoted Doyle as saying that Law failed to follow through on his promise to create an ad-hoc committee of the NCCB to study how the document might be implemented by the U.S. bishops in the years after 1985. But whatever the promises made or broken between Doyle and Law in 1985, the very existence of such a report prepared for the Catholic bishops of the United States must in fact play some role in evaluating the culpability of bishops in abetting a culture that shielded predators like Geoghan. It would bear on two very important questions: "What did the bishops know?" and "When did they know it?"[29]

There existed another set of professional sources offering advice to bishops on clergy sex abuse in the 1980s, which bishops later claimed offered opposing — or at least conflicting — advice from that contained in the

Manual. This set of evaluations for treatment was read by church leaders like Cardinal Law to be at least as trustworthy as the Manual. It was produced by health-care professionals and physicians trained in the field of abnormal psychology.

A well-organized network of psychiatric centers — the Institute of Living in Hartford, Connecticut, St. Luke's Institute in Maryland, the Southdown Institute outside of Toronto — issued reports to bishops which, however tragically misworded or misread, appeared to promise more sanguine prognoses for the effective treatment and rehabilitation of clergy with sexual abuse disorders. These specially designed treatment centers for Catholic clergy and religious in the United States were established after World War II. As one canny observer has noted:

> For several decades before priests like Geoghan propelled clergy sexual abuse into a crisis, the Catholic Church saw places like St. Luke's as one of their best defenses against recidivist priests.... The bishops shipped them their most troubled priests. Psychiatrists evaluated the priests, sent reports estimating the risk of relapse to supervising bishops, and then frequently returned them to their ministry.[30]

Geoghan himself was an alumnus of two of these treatment centers, St. Luke's and the Institute of Living, and returned to parish duties after stays of varying lengths (from ten days to three months) at each. Boston diocesan officials read the diagnostic evaluations produced by these treatment centers as being sanguine enough to warrant Geoghan's return to parish ministry after fairly brief visits to these centers.

But the psychiatric prognosis for recovery in cases of pedophilia and ebophilia changed dramatically in the course of the 1980s — more quickly than Catholic officials (for whatever reasons) understood or recognized. It was precisely this point that journalist Peter Steinfels made in a piece entitled "Abused by the Media," one of the most balanced and fair pieces written about evaluating episcopal culpability in moving sexual predators from one assignment to another:

> What was involved in the American clerical sex abuse crisis was the behavior of some 1.5 per cent of the roughly 150,000 priests

who served under hundreds of bishops in the course of half a century. During that time psychological understanding, social attitudes, and legal expectations and practices regarding molestation of minors changed markedly. So did the Church's attitudes and policies — although often with a distressing lag. The reasons for that lag, which in some respects I consider morally culpable, deserve investigation. It is quite another matter, however, implicitly to measure bishops' decisions, as has been frequently done, as though the bishops possessed — and deliberately and perversely ignored — knowledge and attitudes that were decades later in coming.[31]

Steinfels, of course, is right: church leaders cannot be held legally accountable for medical information about the treatability and recovery of sexual predators that even health care professionals did not possess in the 1970s and early 1980s (although the question of their moral accountability still remains an open one).

But granted this, what of complaints made by health providers after the 1980s — like the March 2002 statement issued by the psychiatrists at Hartford's Institute of Living, charging that church leaders had "intentionally disregarded their clinical advice — with sometimes disastrous results." In response to Edward Cardinal Egan's claim earlier that year that the Institute's own reports had been used as justification for returning priests to the ministry, Leslie M. Lothstein, director of psychology at the Institute in 2002, told the *Hartford Courant* that "I found that they rarely followed our recommendations. They would put [priests] back into work where they still had access to vulnerable populations."[32]

Given the often dramatic changes that marked the psychiatric profession's diagnosis and treatment of psychological pathologies like sexual molestation in the period from 1975 to 1990, Catholic bishops can — and, at least for the sake of argument, probably should — be given the benefit of the doubt in claiming that they simply weren't up to speed regarding the increasingly dark prognosis for the recoverability of sexual abuse predators that marked the professional literature after the mid-1980s. If such a benefit of the doubt is granted, there did appear to be more leeway in interpreting the prognosis for treatment and eventual recovery of sexual predators during the first decade and a half of Geoghan's terrible trail of betrayal and gravely disordered acts. Evidence can be gleaned from a memo from the highly respected psychiatrist John H. Brennan, of Boston Clinical Associates, to Bishop Thomas Daley, dated January 13, 1981, in which he informed the bishop that "it was mutually agreed that he [Geoghan] was now able to resume his priestly duties."[33]

Far more problematic, however, was the reliance of diocesan leaders on reports issued by physicians completely untrained in the field of psychiatry, abnormal or otherwise. What to make of the prognosis of Dr. Robert W. Mullins, Geoghan family doctor and friend? What role did this kind of evidence play vis-à-vis more relevant psychiatric prognoses, and why was Mullins even approached for such an evaluation in the first place?[34]

How is one to explain the decision of the Boston archdiocese to ignore the rather sobering directives of the 1985 Manual as well as the mounting record of disturbing accusations sent to diocesan officials over a number of years by distraught parents and families, charging John Geoghan with crimes against children of the most serious moral and legal nature — in favor of Geoghan's repeated denials of wrongdoing and reports from psychiatric professionals and medical doctors with no training in psychological pathology at all? Why was quite alarming evidence — pressed by Geoghan's victims and by three professionals well-versed in the issues involved and quite committed to the church's well-being — so regularly ignored, downplayed, or written off as duly addressed, while other evidence was regularly used to justify placing Geoghan in pastoral contexts in which his sexual abuse of children could continue? What was it in the culture of the Catholic Church in Boston that made such tragically incorrect reading of the evidence possible?

"A Morally Culpable" Lag

With his arrival at St. Brendan's, Dorchester, in February 1981, John Geoghan was assigned (among other parochial duties) the preparation of the seven- and eight-year-olds of the parish for their First Communion. Once established in his new assignment, Geoghan began taking some of the young boys from his First Communion class to his family's summer home in the north shore beach community of Scituate, where he continued his by-now ritualized pattern of sexual attacks on prepubescent boys.[35]

In a letter dated August 16, 1982 — that is, about a year and a half after Geoghan's arrival in St. Brendan's — Margaret Gallant, the sister of Maryetta Dussourd in Geoghan's previous parish in Jamaica Plain — sent an anguished, handwritten letter to Bernard Law's predecessor as archbishop of Boston, Humberto Cardinal Medeiros. This missive opened with a reference to a meeting which Dussourd and her family had had two weeks previously with Bishop Thomas Daley — the diocesan official who had ordered Geoghan to leave St. Andrew's rectory at once after hearing the accusations against him two years before. Margaret Gallant recounted to Medeiros how she and her family had informed Daley at that meeting about Geoghan's alleged sexual attacks on seven young boys of her extended family in St. Andrew's parish. Her barely controlled anger flashed out at diocesan officials. Gallant voiced astonishment that Geoghan "is still in his parish. It appears that no action has been taken. Am I to assume now that we were patronized?" Gallant's letter, at that point, erupts into the kind of emotion that we can safely assume the archbishops of Boston rarely had directed at them by their own faithful:

> It was suggested that we keep silent to protect the boys — that is absurd since minors are protected under the law, and I do not wish to hear that remark again, since it is insulting to our intelligence. . . . I am very angry with you now, and do not understand this. His actions are not only destructive to the emotional well-being of children, but hits at the very core of our being in our love for the Church — he would not gain access to the homes of fallen away Catholics[!]. Regardless of what he says, or the doctor who treated him, I do not believe he is cured; his actions strongly suggest that he is not, and there is no guarantee that persons with these obsessions are ever cured.[36]

Having spent her fury, Gallant said at the end of her letter that "my heart is broken over this whole mess — and to address my cardinal in this manner has taken its toll on me too." Medeiros's answer to Gallant was written four days later — on August 20, 1982 — and opened by thanking Gallant for her "candid expression of opinion" about a priest who had "caused hardship" to her family, and "most especially to several of the boys." But at the same time Medeiros observed that both she and the others involved in this case "must be very sensitive to a very delicate situation, and one that has caused great scandal." While he understood the pain of both Gallant and her family, Cardinal Medeiros said,

> I must at the same time invoke the mercy of God and share in that mercy in the knowledge that God forgives sins and that sinners indeed can be forgiven. To be sure, we cannot accept sin, but we know well that we must love the sinner and pray for him.[37]

Besides counseling the Gallant family to love the sinner but hate the sin, Medeiros recognized that something had to be done to defuse a potentially explosive situation. But the method settled upon must have enraged both the Gallants and other families of Geoghan's victims when it was revealed a decade later — after diocesan personnel records were subpoenaed by the courts. Medeiros decided to ship the accused priest off to a scholarly renewal program in Rome for three months — a Roman holiday at the archdiocese's expense. "I am happy to inform you that you will receive a grant of $2,000 to help you with expenses," Medeiros wrote in his letter to Geoghan:

> These funds will be sent to you when they become available as a result of the generosity of your fellow priests. It is my hope that the three months will provide the opportunity for the kind of renewal of mind, body and spirit that will enable you to return to parish work refreshed and strengthened in the Lord.[38]

Almost exactly two years, later the archbishop of Boston, now Bernard Law, received a similar letter from Margaret Gallant, dated September 6, 1984. This letter began by noting that "it is with deep regret that I impart the following information. There is a priest at St. Brendan's in Dorchester who has been known in the past to molest boys." Gallant reported that she knew that Medeiros had "sent father away . . . and after returning to parish duties he maintained a low profile for a while." As in the previous letter, Gallant noted that "my heart is broken over the whole situation and it is a burden to my conscience."

But the fact that the archdiocese had seen fit to return Geoghan to the very parish from which he had been removed after his three months in Rome, and then to entrust him with the self-same duties he had previously carried (including the training of altar boys and first communicants) now led Gallant to raise a chilling specter to the new archbishop of Boston: while never threatening anything explicit in her second letter to a Boston archbishop in two years, she nonetheless speculated (in language that, like the prospect of hanging in the morning, must have focused the attention of chancery officials) on the "disgrace this would bring to the Church, to all good priests and finally, but most importantly, my fellow members in this Body of Christ, who are left in the dark as to the dangers their children are in, while I have knowledge of this truth."[39]

Law's response to Gallant on chancery letterhead two weeks later, September 21, 1984, assured her that the "matter of your concern is being investigated and appropriate pastoral decisions will be made both for the priest and God's people." After thanking Gallant for her concern, the new bishop asked her (undoubtedly sincerely, given the circumstances in which he now found himself) to "please pray for me." Well before the letter was sent Law had consulted Bishop Thomas Daley (the diocesan administrator for Medeiros, and now for Law himself), and removed Geoghan from St. Brendan's, Dorchester, listing the priest as "in between assignments" (the red flag later picked up by the *Boston Globe*). Law had likewise heard from St. Brendan's pastor, the Reverend James Lane, who was so devastated by the news of what Geoghan had been doing in his own parish that he broke down in relaying the news to one of the teachers in his parish school. "Father Lane was almost destroyed by this," the teacher recalled years later, after Lane's retirement. Everyone agreed that Geoghan had to be removed from St. Brendan's immediately.[40]

It was then — in September of 1984 — that the distressing gulf between Geoghan's personnel record and first-hand reports of his treachery by distraught families and decisions made by church officials becomes disconcerting. Although Geoghan was removed from St. Brendan's parish after Gallant's letter to Archbishop Law, he was assigned to yet another parish several months later rather than being permanently removed from situations in which he might have contact with children. As we have seen, this came after a consultation with Dr. Robert Mullins. He was sent to St. Julia's Church in suburban Weston, Massachusetts. There is some dispute as to whether St. Julia's pastor was informed of Geoghan's previous parochial history, but the parishioners of St. Julia's were not. This caused a deep feeling of betrayal in a significant portion of that parish as events unfolded.[41]

Geoghan's reassignment did not go uncontested among the higher ups of the diocese, however. On December 7, 1984, shortly after he moved to St. Julia's, auxiliary bishop John M. D'Arcy (soon to be named bishop of Fort Wayne–South Bend, Indiana) sent a letter to Archbishop Law protesting Geoghan's placement in what he noted had been "for some time a divided and troubled parish." D'Arcy told Law there were "two things that give me concern," the first and most important being that "Fr. Geoghan has a history of homosexual involvement with young boys." D'Arcy said, "I understand his recent abrupt departure from St. Brendan's, Dorchester, may be related to this problem." D'Arcy then noted:

> I am afraid that this assignment has complicated a difficult situation. If something happens, the parishioners already angry and divided will be convinced that the Archdiocese has no concern for their welfare and simply sends them priests with problems. . . . I am anxious to help you in any way I can to relieve the difficult pastoral situation there, and it is my obligation to keep you fully informed at this time so [that] you would not be "blindsided" later on.[42]

Geoghan would not be removed from parish ministry until January 1993, almost a decade later. It becomes increasingly difficult to understand the passivity of diocesan oversight after Bernard Law returned from that Minnesota meeting: Why was the quite sobering information offered to the U.S. bishops not utilized in a timely way after that Collegeville meeting when such a startling instance was right in front of him?

Cardinal Law himself would later admit that "judgments were made regarding the assignment of John Geoghan which, in retrospect, were tragically incorrect." It was subsequently learned that not only had Geoghan molested a number of young boys after his assignment to St. Julia's, many of whom were serving as altar boys for his masses, but that his activities during his years at St. Julia's extended beyond the parish: He began hanging out at the Boys & Girls Club of nearby Waltham (a working-class Boston suburb not far from Weston), where he molested yet more young boys. This infuriating and preventable trail of sexual abuse would continue for another five years, until 1989, when Boston's cardinal finally sent Geoghan to St. Luke's Institute after a growing outcry against him in the parish. St. Luke's diagnosed Geoghan as being a "high risk" to children, and he was forthwith sent to Hartford's Institute of Living for "treatment." After just three months, in November 1989, Geoghan was yet again reassigned to St. Julia's, Weston, where he stayed until January 1993. In a letter of June 29, 1990, to Cardinal Law, Geoghan had the temerity to formally request designation as pastor of St. Julia's, after the incumbent pastor had announced his retirement. This request was not granted.[43]

On December 30, 1994, Bernard Cardinal Law sent a letter to Geoghan in which he announced that he "was sorry to learn of the recent allegations made against you," in light of which the cardinal felt obliged to place Geoghan on administrative leave from public ministry. But Law noted in that same letter that "I realize that this is a difficult time for you and for those close to you. If I can be of help to you in some way, please contact me. Be assured you are remembered in my prayers."

Geoghan angrily denied the growing number of allegations against him — both in Weston and from earlier parishes. He refused to resign as associate director of the Office for Senior Priests (an assignment he had been given after leaving St. Julia's). "I have been falsely accused and feel alienated from my ministry and fellowship with my brother priests," he wrote to Monsignor William Murphy of the archdiocese's Office for Senior Priests. "I cannot believe that one should be considered guilty on an accusation. Where is there justice or due process?"

On May 8, 1998, Geoghan was defrocked, and a year and a half later, on December 9, 1999, — a formal complaint was filed against Geoghan in Middlesex Superior Court by the Commonwealth of Massachusetts on behalf of what would soon become dozens of plaintiffs.[44]

"Tragically Incorrect" Judgments

What the Spotlight Team of the *Boston Globe* discovered in the months after their bombshell headline on January 31, 2002, of course, was that the terrible and shocking swathe of betrayal, pathology, and shattered lives left by John Geoghan was not a singular event, as many Boston Catholics hoped. Indeed, cases of dozens of other priests in the Archdiocese of Boston — especially that of Paul Shanley — soon came to light in almost-daily revelations. There were regular protests outside the cardinal's residence and his cathedral, and bodyguards were hired to protect him from death threats. The word "crisis" began to be used by Catholics.

There was, as well, something of an orgy of blame within the Catholic Church in the following months. The subtitle of Michael Rose's book, *Goodbye, Good Men,* was "How Liberals Brought Corruption into the Catholic Church," the explanation favored by many conservative Catholics. Those on the other end of the ideological spectrum blamed what they termed the repressive sexual culture of the institutional church (especially regarding celibacy). "Bishops Should Marry," Professor Rodger Van Allen opined in *Commonweal,* a response he felt would "help put to rest [Catholicism's] historical negativity about sexuality," which had provided the context for the whole mess. Still others accused the U.S. Catholic bishops themselves, and most especially Bernard Cardinal Law of Boston, for sloppy or indifferent pastoral oversight and careerism. There was also the accusation, pressed by a surprising number of Catholic priests as well as by Catholic lay groups like Voice of the Faithful, that the entire sad imbroglio had been presided over, and was to some extent the product of, "safe men" appointed by a Roman bureaucracy. For these groups, the long-term answer was a progressive application of the changes begun by the Second Vatican Council: "Keep the Faith. Change the Church."[45]

This disaster cannot be explained by any one set of cultural and historical components. The particular cultural factors of Boston Catholicism itself, the most Catholic metropolitan area in the United States — where the grandchildren of Irish immigrants daily fought a culture war against Yankees long after that group had lost cultural and political hegemony in that city, provided tinder for the bonfire by making the good name of the church paramount in the face of hostility. The cultural demons unleashed in the 1960s — the decade when most of the priest abusers either came of age or first began their priestly ministry — likewise contributed to the conflagration by encouraging clerics to explore their sexuality. The sheer amount of bureaucratic paperwork for which the leaders of immense dioceses like that of Boston were responsible further complicates the story.

But even when allowances are made for all of that — and many other factors as well — the question remains of how such tragically incorrect decisions could have been made by church leaders who themselves abhorred the kind of activities that Geoghan and dozens of others perpetrated on children.

Bishops, themselves talented, devoted, and arguably even holy individuals, who had been warned by other bishops and by canon lawyers about the terrible price to be paid if the accusations of such abuse information were ever made public, later claim to be blindsided by such stories in newspaper headlines. Such claims are very difficult to understand. "Scandals will come," Jesus told his disciples, "but woe to those by whom they come" — a New Testament prophecy that must keep at least some bishops awake at night.

The bureaucratic explanation made in cases like that of John Geoghan does not go far enough by half. From a theological point of view, the devastating swathe of destruction wreaked by predators like Geoghan is better explained by the *mysterium iniquitatis* — that demonic "mystery of iniquity" foretold in scripture as part of the devil's work and lamented by Pope John Paul II in his 2002 Holy Week exhortation to priests — than by bad bookkeeping.

First, and most tragically, the children entrusted to the safekeeping of the Catholic Church for spiritual and psychological formation were betrayed by official representatives of that very institution. The parents of those children, who served as altar boys or participated in C.Y.O., were likewise betrayed. Mental health professionals were betrayed by the episcopal use — or, as they now claim, mis-use — of their clinical advice. The 97.5 percent of Catholic priests in the United States who, by and large, live lives of dedicated service to their flocks were betrayed as well by fellow priests who engaged in such enormities; by portrayal of themselves as potential predators in the press, and by their bishops, who at the June 2002 meeting of the NCCB in Dallas overwhelmingly passed a resolution that warned that any "reasonable" accusation of sexual abuse against a cleric would lead to immediate removal from their ministry without any kind of due process protocol to look into the reliability of such charges.

However distasteful such an admission might be to the many Catholics (including priests) who are furious at their bishops in the wake of the shocking amount of prior episcopal knowledge of abuse — the bishops who passed that Dallas resolution, too, must feel betrayed by a tradition of church government that had served the American Catholic community well for over two centuries. That tradition, defined by attention to, and care of, the reputation and smooth running of the institution, had helped to make the Roman Catholic Church the largest single community of religious believers in the United States. Bishops like Bernard Cardinal Law no doubt made pastoral decisions that violated both the rights of individuals and their own responsibility in the name of the good of the church. Whatever personal sin does or does not result from such decisions, their choices led to a profoundly immoral and unchristian corporate culture for which Catholics (especially bishops) must atone. Even the staunchest critics of the bishops' behavior in this mess of scandal and betrayal might find some compassion for those who will be held accountable to an even higher authority than the Suffolk Superior Court.

To describe the mess, however, as resulting from tragically incorrect decisions on an administrative level is both more and less than the truth: the betrayals resulted from decisions made in the context of a deeply flawed corporate culture, and it is to that analogical culture itself that Catholics should now turn their attention. To even think that better administrative protocols dictating procedures will forestall future scandals, if such book-keeping or protocols still operate in the same context of "their culture," is insulting to those who suffered unspeakable violations by their pastors. Individual diocesan decisions, however tragically made, can hardly account for the multiple levels of "scandal" (*scandalion,* "stumbling blocks to faith" according to the original meaning of the Greek word used in the New Testament) that arose as a result. On the other hand, for bishops even to attempt to exculpate their behavior as simply a result of wrong but understandably human decisions is inexcusable to the faithful to whom they must render an account of their stewardship. They can be forgiven. They cannot be excused.

The betrayals that resulted from this scandal were the result of complex psychological, sociological, cultural, and religious factors and the personal decisions of bishops; they were likewise the result of the underside of the worldview that had provided the spiritual glue for U.S. Catholics in the first place. Carolyn Newberger had recognized "their culture" as the very heart of the issue, the epicenter of the crisis. "Their culture" was that knotted complex of loyalties and beliefs that shaped U.S. Catholicism in hundreds of discreet ways — who is rendered respect and who is not, what is an important issue and what can be ignored, which values are crucial to the institution's health and which are secondary.[46]

But the hierarchically defined, institutionally centered culture based on order and reputation as primary institutional values and on an almost pathological concern with privacy in accounting for (or, rather, not accounting for) leadership decisions has an uncertain future among U.S. Catholics, even among devout and loyal ones. There is a sense that North American values like accountability and reciprocity must now be incorporated into the Catholic imagination — something that seems to make curial officials in Rome very nervous indeed.

David Tracy often calls himself an ecumenical theologian, not to distance himself from Catholicism or to imply that Catholic Christianity itself is somehow inferior to the Protestant tradition but rather because, as a loyal Roman Catholic, he recognizes that the Catholic analogical language of sacramentality and community is itself incomplete if it is not complemented and balanced by other rich insights. Church leaders must be respected primarily, or perhaps only, because, as Jesus reminded his disciples, they are the "servants of all." A Christian leadership that is, or is perceived to be, unaccountable to the People of God is a contradiction in terms.

Several decades ago, Tracy pointed out that the very strengths of what he designated as the analogical imagination — the vibrant sense of communal cohesion and loyalty; the celebratory sense of God's nearness and presence in the church's sacraments and structures; the profound respect for institutional protocols as "holy" — can also contribute to sinful situations in which the rights of individuals might be undervalued in the name of community safety, or create institutional loyalties that can tend toward confusing the good name of the church with fidelity to the Gospel. Such crude and uncomplemented readings of the tradition, Tracy warned his readers, can reduce the Holy to the beck and call of human beings, and make the purposes of the very human institutional church indistinguishable from the demands of the Kingdom of God itself. The Catholic

tradition has always asserted (in good dialectical fashion) that the Kingdom of God — while glimpsed in its beginnings in the Church Militant
on earth, and as organically related to that church in history as fruit is
to seed — finally stands beyond history and judges the good-intentioned
but always incomplete purposes of all human institutions (including and
most especially the church itself) as falling short of the demands of the
Kingdom. "No man born of woman is greater than John the Baptizer,"
Jesus told his disciples, "yet the least in the Kingdom of Heaven is greater
than he."

The down side of the grace-filled analogical tradition imperceptibly but
palpably contributed to a congeries of decisions in which the meanings
of community and institution, church and clergy, sinful and discredited
were collapsed into each other in a way that seemed to mirror Catholic
sacramental theology. The best Catholic theologians always warned that
the similarities that define the divine presence in the material forms evap-
orate if the tension between Divine and material realities is collapsed into
one: the Kingdom is not just the church; Jesus is not just the Bread; being
born again is not just being baptized; repentance is not just going to confession. Loyalty to the church and its institutional needs is not always, in
every case, loyalty to Christ and the Gospel. The church itself mediates
real divine authority and presence precisely because it does not do so on
its own authority, but on God's. It was precisely these kinds of unchecked
Catholic loyalties that made Protestants like Paul Blanshard, Norman Vincent Peale, and Kenneth Hardy uncomfortable in the first place. The lack
of accountability, recourse to institutional secrecy, and misplaced trust
in hierarchical leadership that so defines the tawdry story of the Boston
sex abuse scandals represents, on one level, the legitimization of their
worst fears.

The Boston clergy abuse scandal has multiple morals: first, that North
American Catholics can and should hold their church leaders account-
able for what occurred while also raising more long-term questions about
Catholic culture. Second, the vibrant set of loyalties that has served the
U.S. Catholic Church so well must now be balanced by another (equally
Christian) set of loyalties more often pressed by their Protestant broth-
ers and sisters. Third, personal responsibility and attention to individual

persons are Christian, and not just North American, cultural, values — values for which bishops, like all Christians, are accountable. But perhaps the chief moral of the affair is that some kinds of distrust of the Catholic Church's analogical culture is not the last prejudice in the United States, but an acceptable one if pressed by Catholics themselves for more accountability on the part of church leaders in governing their community.

Chapter Eleven

The Last Acceptable Prejudice?

Sic et Non

"Yes and no." That is my answer to the question posed by the title of this chapter. *Sic et Non* is the title of one of the most perceptive works of medieval theology, written by the famous University of Paris theologian Peter Abelard in the twelfth century. It consisted of a series of contradictory statements made by various Fathers of the Church, placed opposite each other in order to tease out a nuanced "middle course" between polar positions in theology. It was also one of the classic works of dialectical Catholic theology, searching for a synthesis that transcended trenchant opposing positions.

Though not as well known as other works of medieval theology like the *Summa Theologiae* of St. Thomas Aquinas or the works of St. Bernard of Clairveaux, *Sic et Non* offers a compelling model for contemporary theologians attempting to understand the relation of the Holy to the complex cultures of the United States. It argued that the truth was most likely not to be found in either pole of a contested theological question, but in the conflicted middle ground. A similar dialectical interpretation of the anti-Catholic impulse can be instructively made.

On the "no" side, the theological roots of new anti-Catholicism are actually quite old — certainly older than the late twentieth-century origins proposed by some Catholic cultural commentators in the United States. Popular anti-Catholicism (consciously or not) is in fact rooted in a profound intellectual tradition of Christian theology. This language formed part of the high tradition of theology but was and is played out even in popular forms like comic books. This form of the Christian religious imagination considerably predates the Reformation of the sixteenth century; it found classic expression during the High Middle Ages in the negative mysticism of the Rhineland mystics and in works of Catholic medieval theologians like Peter Abelard. It is a complementary impulse to the analogical principle informing sacramental and communal theology and informs all Christian, including Catholic, theology.

But this conceptual language found its most dramatic post–sixteenth-century form in the works of Protestant theologians like John Calvin and his English Reformed disciples. While a significant number of Protestant Christians tracing their modern identity to the Reformation (like Anglicans and Lutherans) retained significant analogical loyalties in their worship and ecclesiology, those groups of Calvinists that cast the broadest shadow in what would become the United States were resolutely and identifiably dialectical in both theology and in political philosophy. Because of the sheer numbers and intellectual authority of these Christians during the first century and a half of the North American colonization (even granting the presence of sacramental religious culture in Anglican Virginia and Catholic Maryland, and of laissez-faire cultural pluralism in Dutch New Amsterdam and Quaker Philadelphia), the founding structures and documents of the secular culture of the United States were saturated with dialectical loyalties. The Reformed Protestant foundation of our now multicultural society is self-evident.

The American cultural circumstance, as Greeley observed, shows that the old distrust of loyalties that so defined anti-Catholic nativism — to the extent that it is embedded in the very structures of our democratic culture — never really went away. In that sense, too, the new anti-Catholicism isn't new at all.

The cultural location of some of the more recent players working out the implications of these revered Protestant loyalties — with resolutely secular and sometimes even anti-religious loyalties — is new. Therefore, on the "yes" side, certain manifestations of the "new" anti-Catholicism are new. In the years following World War II, when Will Herberg and other cultural pundits were perhaps too ebulliently announcing the end of the old distrust of others in works like *Protestant, Catholic, Jew,* a number of self-proclaimed secular intellectuals like Paul Blanshard and John Dewey took up the mantle of the prophets to warn democracy-loving North Americans of the threat posed by the totalitarianism of Catholicism.

Some late-twentieth-century expressions of dis-ease with Catholic authoritarianism, expressed by books like *American Freedom and Catholic Power*, in ostensibly scientific analyses published in academic journals, and in tax-supported public art projects, manifest a new type of secular or post-Christian distrust of Catholicism. This dis-ease (at least on a conscious level) has little or nothing to do with theology, and supposedly everything to do with cultural values. But despite the purported secular agenda, it has deep theological roots.

U.S. Catholics have not always responded to this secular distrust well, or in the smartest way. One of the many tragedies of the Boston clergy sexual abuse case is its handy availability as proof positive for those citizens already uneasy with Catholicism that their fears were well placed after all: "See," critics are now able to say, "see what happens to the powerless in a corrupt system like this?"

It is indeed true that at least some prejudice in the United States — including religious bias against Catholicism — is an irrational (and anti-democratic) bias against other citizens based solely on their race or religious affiliation. Such discrimination is both ethically repugnant and illegal, and must be answered point-for-point and issue-by-issue without apology in very public ways in a society formally pledged to equal opportunity and freedom of religion. Some anti-Catholic prejudice, like the crusade launched by the Reverend Mr. Peale in 1960, is indeed related to old nativist fears about "papists," "micks," and "mackerel snappers" and represents a betrayal of the very principles ostensibly being defended by these cultural guardians. The effort to keep the Catholic candidate out of the White House in 1960 represents this kind of prejudice. There are pockets of this very tired brand of religious discrimination still present in the United States, and these pockets should be taken more seriously than they are.

But not all prejudice is necessarily based in ignorance or unethical discrimination, and not all forms of critical pre-judgment directed against Catholic Christianity are unhealthy. Some dialectical suspicion of uncritical analogical loyalties serves the best interests of the Catholic tradition itself. The absence of a healthy distrust of uncritical devotion to the reputation and standing of the institutional church betrayed so many people in the Archdiocese of Boston and allowed the pattern of clergy sexual abuse to spiral out of control. The dismissal of criticisms as Catholic bashing or the work of a church-hating secular press expresses a misplaced devotion to institutional solidarity or a profoundly unchristian understanding of what loyalty to the church means. To anyone on any side of this debate, a church culture that places the reputation of the church above the safety of children is a church culture that must be seriously reexamined.

Anti-Catholicism is hardly the last bias in the United States, nor is "Catholic bashing" acceptable in most middle-class cultures in North America. Given the resiliency of anti-Semitism in the United States — at least as evinced in hate messages still spray-painted on the walls of suburban synagogues and yeshivas — as well as the deeply problematic statistics linking race and class in the United States, it would be risible to insist that bias against Catholics alone remained after other forms of discrimination had now disappeared. Further, the troubling homophobic impulses manifested in the Laramie, Wyoming, murder of gay college student Matthew Shepard (with some incendiary justifications even pressed by several Christian ministers) make any claim of Catholic uniqueness on the topic of cultural derision or violence deeply problematic: violence against Catholic Americans based on religious prejudice is extremely rare, if not now largely absent in the various North American regional cultures.

The discussion of convent burnings and of signs reading "No Catholics Need Apply" is now covered in history books, not in newspapers. The most publicized recent case of destruction of Catholic church property in New York City — the decapitations of religious statues outside several parishes in the boroughs of Brooklyn and Queens in 2000 — was perpetrated by a mentally unstable immigrant to the United States, whose moral accountability for the desecrations was much debated, even in the Catholic press. Physical violence and destruction of Catholic church property is hardly acceptable, even by the most militant Protestant fundamentalist groups. Bob Jones University, for example — arguably the most visible anti-Catholic institution in the North American educational world — doesn't admit Catholic students on principle; but neither does it send students out to spray-paint or burn down Catholic churches. Further, the anti-Catholic admissions policies of Bob Jones are itself the object of widespread derision, as the press coverage of the campaign visit of presidential candidate George W. Bush to that campus demonstrated.

But again, on the "yes" side, the description of anti-Catholicism as the last acceptable prejudice rings true for many U.S. Catholics; few would dismiss it as groundless. While most Americans would hardly dare voice any kind of overt prejudice against political candidates, job applicants, or potential spouses for their children on the basis of Catholic affiliation, there are regular depictions of Catholic belief and practice in the press and popular entertainment that are deeply offensive to practicing Catholics. It would be highly unlikely that any depiction of an other-than-Catholic house of worship as a "house of walking swastikas" would be defended by the *New York Times* as simply a "matter of personal opinion" — even if its teaching on abortion, women clergy, or homosexuality were exactly the same as that of the Roman Church. The unlikelihood of such an offensive ascription being applied to any other house of worship in New York was first observed by the Catholic League for Civil and Religious Rights. Whatever one thinks of its often pugnacious stance toward the New York press, the League's observation was probably correct: both the NEH and the *Times* could get away with it only because the slur was made against St. Patrick's Cathedral.

Reporters questioned about this unique status of Catholicism as target of ridicule and denunciation say that American Catholicism's power, size, organization, and unity make it fair game. So this very singular argument goes. This justification contains an argument about church-state relations that few believers in the United States of whatever denominational stripe would accept: the belief that religion in democratic societies is safe as long as it is marginal, disorganized, and relatively powerless to affect public discourse. If religious institutions are large, well organized, and take ethical stands on public and political issues that actually influences people's voting behavior, then they must be stopped — even in sacrilegious, prejudicial, and insulting ways. Such a secularist creed must be opposed not only by Catholics, but by all religious believers as a profound betrayal of the liberties ensured to religious groups in the First Amendment.

"Wise and Blameless"

"Be as wise as serpents, but as blameless as doves," Jesus advised his first-century followers, offering a complex cultural stance for believers. His advice is as timely to his Catholic disciples in the United States in the twenty-first century as it was to his followers two thousand years ago. It is difficult to be consistently blameless and always wise.

The intellectual and political cultures of North American democracy are rooted in concerns for individual rights, freedom of belief and expression, and political balance of power that derive from both the Protestant religious imagination and the Western philosophical Enlightenment. The cultural impulses deriving from these roots have served the United States exceedingly well for over two centuries, and Catholic citizens of the republic (like all other citizens) are grateful for the political, economic, and social results. Recognizing these Protestant Reformed and Scottish Enlightenment roots of American loyalties should in no way lessen the respect and devotion Catholics should have for them. Indeed, a number of Catholic citizens in the early Republic and since have endeavored to prove that those impulses originated within the Catholic tradition. Such impulses are a testimonial to Catholic devotion to what are now perceived to be simply American values shared by all citizens regardless of religious belief. To the extent that Catholic citizens of the United States accept and cherish these values, then they too can be said to share in dialectical loyalties, like every other citizen.

Catholic citizens of the United States were, and are, outsiders, "others" in a culture shaped and still powerfully influenced by Protestant language and presuppositions. This is neither a bad thing in itself, nor a retreat to victimization language. Religious outsiders have a revered place in North American religion, beginning with the New England Puritans themselves, then with their outsider saints like Roger Williams and Anne Hutchinson, right down to Ralph Waldo Emerson. It is disingenuous for Catholics to feign surprise, anger, or grief to learn that they are not in the mainstream of their culture, or that they are perceived as such by a number of their fellow citizens who shape cultural tastes. Such has always been the (blessed) lot of the saints in every age. As St. Paul was at pains to remind them, "We have here no lasting city, but seek the one that is above." This in no way lessens the urgency of Jesus' command to be both wise and blameless in our age; but perhaps it offers some peace to those who are aware that Catholicism doesn't completely fit into the lively experiment that is the United States, and probably never will.

That's the good news.

Notes

Chapter One / Catholic Otherness

1. The Arthur Schlesinger quote comes from James Martin, "The Last Acceptable Prejudice?" *America* 182 (March 25, 2000): 9. "Last acceptable prejudice" from Andrew Greeley, *An Ugly Little Secret: Anti-Catholicism in North America* (Kansas City, Mo.: Sheed, Andrews & McMeel, 1977). See also William A. Donohue, *The Deepest Bias: Anti-Catholicism in American Life,* one-hour video cassette (New York: Catholic League, 1996).

2. Ray Allen Billington, *The Protestant Crusade, 1800–1860: A Study of the Origins of American Nativism* (New York: Macmillan, 1938). See especially chapter 1, entitled "The Roots of Anti-Catholic Prejudice" for an excellent historical overview of the cultural traditions of colonial anti-Catholicism. This essay will refer to a more recent printing of this work under the same title, published by Quadrangle Books of Chicago in 1964. In the study of U.S. history and culture, New England (until the past three decades) has loomed large as in some sense the birthplace of the later culture. This "myth of New England founding" achieved magisterial form in Perry Miller's "Errand into the Wilderness," chapter 1 in *Errand into the Wilderness* (Cambridge, Mass.: Harvard University Press, 1956). See also Sacvan Bercovitch's *The Puritan Origins of the American Self* (New Haven, Conn.: Yale University Press, 1975) for a more contemporary critical "read" of this myth. On Foxe's *Book of Martyrs,* see William Haller, "John Foxe and the Puritan Revolution," in *The Seventeenth Century,* ed. Richard F. Jones (Stanford: Stanford University Press, 1951), 213–19. On Foxe's interpretation of the Church of Rome as the Anti-Christ himself, see Robert C. Fuller, *Naming the Antichrist: The History of an American Obsession* (New York: Oxford University Press, 1995), 41ff. Thomas Brown, "The Image of the Beast: Anti-Papal Rhetoric in Colonial America," in *Conspiracy: The Fear of Subversion in American History,* ed. Richard Curry and Thomas Brown (New York: Holt, Rinehart and Winston, 1972), 4ff.

3. On the "Augustinian Strain of Piety," see Perry Miller, *The New England Mind: The Seventeenth Century* (Cambridge, Mass.: Belknap Press, 1982 [1939]), chapter 1, "The Augustinian Strain of Piety," 3–34. By this "Augustinian strain" Miller meant a brand of piety derived from a Reformation-era reading of St. Augustine that stressed moral seriousness, experiential piety, sobriety, and a profound distrust of human intentions and power based in the Christian doctrine of original sin. On the "Protestant work ethic," see Max Weber, *The Protestant Ethic and the Spirit of Capitalism,* trans. Talcott Parsons (New York: Scribners, 1930); on the Puritan roots of modern political radicalism, Michael Walzer, *The Revolution of the Saints: A Study in the Origins of Radical Politics* (New York: Atheneum, 1976 [1965]).

4. On the essentially Durkheimian sociological interpretation of the uses of "otherness," see Mary Douglas, *Natural Symbols* (London: Barrie & Rockliff, 1970). On an

application of (Puritan) biblical interpretation to Catholic alterity, see Fuller, *Naming the Antichrist*, chapter 2 ("Thwarting the Errand," 40–73).

5. By "evangelical" here I mean the pan-Protestant belief that achieved something like canonical status among many nineteenth-century Protestant Christians that a personal conversion, and not sacramental baptism or a belief in certain doctrines, was the real basis for Christian identity and (in groups like the Baptists) church membership. See William McLoughlin, ed., *The American Evangelicals, 1800–1900: An Anthology* (New York: Harper & Row, 1968). James Findlay's very fine bibliographic essay in the foreword to *Dwight L. Moody: American Evangelist, 1837–1899* (Chicago: University of Chicago Press, 1969) offers a superb historiographic essay on the history of evangelicalism in the United States.

6. William McLoughlin, *Revivals, Awakenings, and Reform: An Essay on Religion and Social Change, 1607–1977* (Chicago: University of Chicago Press, 1978); *Modern Revivalism: Charles Grandison Finney to Billy Graham* (New York: Ronald Press, 1959).

7. Donald Mathews, "The Second Great Awakening as an Organizing Process, 1780–1830," *American Quarterly* 21 (1969): 23–43, and *Religion in the Old South* (Chicago: University of Chicago Press, 1977).

8. Talcott Parsons, "Memorandum for the Council on Democracy" [1940], box 2, Parsons Papers. Robert K. Merton, *Science, Technology, and Society in Seventeenth Century England* (New York: Fertig, 1970; orig. ed. 1938), 99. Both of these quotes are taken from John McGreevy's very fine article, "Thinking on One's Own: Catholicism in the American Intellectual Imagination, 1928–1960," *Journal of American History* 84 (June 1997): 116.

9. Merle E. Curti, *The Growth of American Thought*, 3d ed. (New York: Harper & Row, 1964); Stow Persons, *American Minds: A History of Ideas* (New York: Henry Holt, 1958); G. Adolf Koch, *Republican Religion: The American Revolution and the Cult of Reason* (New York: Henry Holt, 1933).

10. Ralph Henry Gabriel, *The Course of American Democratic Thought: An Intellectual History since 1815* (New York: Ronald Press, 1940), chapter 2: "The Doctrines of the American Democratic Faith," 14–16.

11. Ibid., 22–23.

12. Ibid., chapter 3: "Christianity and the Democratic Faith," 28, 37. Generally accepted as the first modern history of religion in the United States, Robert Baird's *Religion in America*, published in 1844, divided all of American religion into "evangelical" and "nonevangelical" groups, with the former receiving three-quarters of the page space; the groups listed under the latter designation included Catholics, Jews, Unitarians, and free thinkers. See Robert Baird, *Religion in America* (New York: Harper & Row, 1970) [1844], Table of Contents; Winthrop Hudson, *The Great Tradition of the American Churches* (New York: Harper and Brothers, 1953); Francis Weisenberger, *Triumph of Faith: Contributions of the Church to American Life, 1865–1900* (Richmond, Va.: William Byrd Press, 1962). Among the latter scholarly studies, see Ernest Lee Tuveson, *Redeemer Nation: The Idea of America's Millennial Role* (Chicago: University of Chicago Press, 1968); Nathan Hatch, *The Sacred Cause of Liberty: Republican Thought and the Millennium in Revolutionary New England* (New Haven, Conn.: Yale University Press, 1977); Catherine Albanese, *America: Religions and Religion* (Belmont, Calif.: Wadsworth, 1981); see especially part 2 of her study "The Oneness of Religion in America."

13. Sidney Mead, "From Coercion to Persuasion: Another Look at the Rise of Religious Liberty and the Emergence of Denominationalism," in *The Lively Experiment: The Shaping*

of Christianity in America (New York: Harper & Row, 1963), 18; *The Nation with the Soul of a Church* (New York: Harper & Row, 1975).

14. Daniel Boorstin, *The Lost World of Thomas Jefferson* (New York: Henry Holt, 1948); Eric Foner, *Tom Paine and Revolutionary America* (New York: Oxford University Press, 1976); Bernard Bailyn, *The Ideological Origins of the American Revolution* (Cambridge, Mass.: Harvard University Press, 1967); Gordon Wood, *The Creation of the Republic, 1776–1787* (Chapel Hill: University of North Carolina Press, 1969). The most intellectually elegant of all of these studies is Henry May's *The Enlightenment in America* (New York: Oxford University Press, 1976).

15. John Dewey, *A Common Faith* (New Haven, Conn.: Yale University Press, 1934), 26; Harold Laski, "America — 1947," *Nation* (December 13, 1947): 643; *Present Day Thinkers and the New Scholasticism: An International Symposium*, ed. John S. Zybura (St. Louis: B. Herder, 1926), 29–30; Walter Lippmann, *Drift and Mastery: An Attempt to Diagnose the Present Unrest* (New York: M. Kennersley, 1914), 115. All of these quotes are taken from McGreevy, "Thinking on One's Own," respectively 101, 105, 102.

16. Lippmann quoted in McGreevy, "Thinking on One's Own," 100. Abraham Maslow, *Motivation and Personality* (New York: Harper, 1954), 221; quoted in McGreevy, "Thinking on One's Own," 118.

17. George M. Marsden, *The Outrageous Idea of Christian Scholarship* (New York: Oxford University Press, 1997), 14, 18. See also Marsden's *The Soul of the American University: From Protestant Establishment to Established Nonbelief* (New York: Oxford University Press, 1994), and George Marsden and Bradley Longfield, eds., *The Secularization of the Academy* (New York: Oxford University Press, 1992).

18. Sigmund Freud, *Moses and Monotheism*, trans. Katherine Jones (New York, 1939), 85; Julie A. Reuben, *The Making of the Modern University: Intellectual Transformation and the Marginalization of Morality* (Chicago: University of Chicago Press, 1996), 87. Both quotes from McGreevy, "Thinking on One's Own," 101. The *disputatio* — a public debate between at least two opposing scholars, which formed a central component of medieval university life, has been presented by Catholic historians as the historical basis for later models of debate and free exchange of ideas in academic culture.

19. In this study, "alterity" ("otherness") is understood axiomatically as the reason for the social expressions of anti-Catholic nativism discussed here. I have argued this point at some length in *Catholics and American Culture: Fulton Sheen, Dorothy Day, and the Notre Dame Football Team* (New York: Crossroad, 1999), 23ff.

20. Emile Durkheim, *The Division of Labor in Society*, trans. George Simpson (Glencoe, Ill.: Free Press, 1947), 102. This paragraph has been largely taken from my *Catholics and American Culture*, 23. For a brilliant application of this Durkheimian theory to American religious history, see Kai Erikson, *Wayward Puritans: A Study in the Sociology of Deviance* (New York: Wiley, 1966), 4–12.

21. John Higham, *Strangers in the Land: Patterns of American Nativism, 1850–1925* (New Brunswick, N.J.: Rutgers University Press, 1958), 3, 4. Other scholarly works utilizing this approach include David Brion Davis, *The Fear of Conspiracy: Images of Un-American Subversion from the Revolution to the Present* (Ithaca, N.Y.: Cornell University Press, 1971), and Richard Hofstadter, *The Paranoid Style in American Politics and Other Essays* (New York: Random House, 1967). More recent scholarly studies in this genre include Jenny

Franchot, *Roads to Rome: The Antebellum Protestant Encounter with Catholicism* (Berkeley: University of California Press, 1994), 38–42, 154–61, 172–73.

22. John Tracy Ellis, *American Catholicism*, rev. ed. (Chicago: University of Chicago Press, 1969); Thomas McAvoy, "The Formation of the Catholic Minority," in *Catholicism in America*, ed. Philip Gleason (New York: Harper & Row, 1970); Charles Morris, *American Catholic: The Saints and Sinners Who Built America's Most Powerful Church* (New York: Times Books, 1997).

23. Among Peter Berger's works studying the process of secularization are *The Sacred Canopy: Elements of a Sociological Theory of Religion* (New York: Doubleday, 1967) and *The Heretical Imperative: Contemporary Possibilities of Religious Affirmation* (Garden City, N.Y.: Anchor Press, 1970).

24. Berger, *The Sacred Canopy*, 133–34.

25. Ibid., 151–52, 147.

Chapter Two / The Varieties of Anti-Catholicism in the United States

1. Ray Allen Billington, *The Protestant Crusade, 1800–1860: A Study of the Origins of American Nativism* (New York: Macmillan, 1938), 1.

2. Ibid., 2, 18–19. The "Gunpowder Plot" is the designation given to the plan to blow up both houses of Parliament and King James I on November 5, 1605. A group of thirteen Catholic conspirators, led by the redoubtable Guy Fawkes and touted as promoted by the Jesuits, were accused of placing barrels of gunpowder in the cellar of the hall where the monarch would be addressing Parliament; the resulting unbalance of power was supposedly going to lead to a Catholic uprising that would place a Catholic monarch on the English throne. Fawkes and the other conspirators were convicted and then drawn and quartered in an event celebrated annually to mark the victory of English government and Reformed Protestantism against the machinations of Catholic "recusants" and foreign authoritarianism. See Hugh Ross Williamson, *The Gunpowder Plot* (New York: Macmillan, 1952), and especially Mark Nicholls, *Investigating the Gunpowder Plot* (Manchester [England]: Manchester University Press, 1991). Nicholls's book raises a number of provocative historical and interpretive questions about exactly what happened on November 5, 1605. William Haller, "John Foxe and the Puritan Revolution," in *The Seventeenth Century: Studies in the History of English Thought and Literature from Bacon to Pope*, ed. Richard F. Jones (Stanford, Calif.: Stanford University Press, 1951), 122ff.

3. Billington, *Protestant Crusade*, 6, 7–8.

4. Ibid., 7–8, 16.

5. Carl Bridenbaugh, *Mitre and Sceptre: Transatlantic Faiths, Ideas, Personalities, and Politics, 1689–1775* (New York: Oxford University Press, 1962); Alan Heimert, *Religion and the American Mind from the Great Awakening to the Revolution* (Cambridge, Mass.: Harvard University Press, 1966); Nathan Hatch, *The Sacred Cause of Liberty: Republican Thought and the Millennium in Revolutionary New England* (New Haven, Conn.: Yale University Press, 1977).

6. Bridenbaugh, *Mitre and Sceptre*, 333. The "Intolerable Acts" was the collective phrase used by the North American "patriots" to describe the successive acts passed by

the British Parliament placing high taxes on tea, sugar, and printed matter, as well as demanding the sequestering of British troops in the homes of colonial citizens.

7. Heimert, *Religion and the American Mind.* James West Davidson, *The Logic of Millennial Thought: Eighteenth Century New England* (New Haven, Conn.: Yale University Press, 1977). Davidson builds on the brilliant work of Tuveson in *Redeemer Nation* to show how the New England Puritan tradition of reading the Book of Revelation — with its "millennial" understanding of history working toward the thousand-year reign of Christ on earth (the "millennium") — as a "blueprint for history" profoundly shaped the preaching and political ideology of colonial supporters of the Revolution.

8. Robert T. Handy, *A Christian America: Protestant Hopes and Historical Realities* (New York: Oxford University Press, 1971), 56, 58. For a smart application of the Handy thesis, see Ryan K. Smith, "The Cross: Church Symbol and Contest in Nineteenth-Century America," *Church History* 70 (December 2001): 705–34.

9. Maria Monk, *Awful Disclosures of the Hotel Dieu Monastery of Montreal* (New York: Howe and Bates, 1836). For an excellent collection of this "convent literature," see Nancy Lusignan Schultz, ed., *Veil of Fear: Nineteenth-Century Convent Tales* (West Lafayette, Ind.: Purdue University Press, 1999). For a description of the machinations that led to its publication by the "dummy firm," see Billington, *Protestant Crusade,* 101–2.

10. Monk, *Awful Disclosures,* 47, 49. This narration is found in Billington, *Protestant Crusade,* 99.

11. Rebecca Theresa Reed, *Six Months in a Convent* (Boston, 1835). Josephine M. Bunkley, *The Testimony of an Escaped Novice from the Sisters of St. Joseph, Emmitsburg, Maryland* (New York: Harper & Brothers, 1855). See also the responses to these works, for example, Mary Edmund Saint George, *An Answer to "Six Months in a Convent," Exposing Its Falsehoods and Manifold Absurdities* (Boston, 1835). Rosamond Culbertson, *Rosamond, or, A Narrative of the Captivity and Sufferings of an American Female Under the Popish Priests in the Island of Cuba, with a Full Disclosure of Their Manners and Customs, Written by Herself* (New York, 1846).

12. On the vast network of voluntary associations operating in the "Evangelical Empire" in the first half of the nineteenth century, see chapter 1 ("The Evangelical Basis") in Perry Miller, *The Life of the Mind in America: From the Revolution to the Civil War* (New York: Harcourt, Brace, and World, 1965); Samuel F. B. Morse, *Foreign Conspiracy against the Liberties of the United States,* 5th ed. (New York, 1841); *Imminent Dangers to the Free Institutions of the United States through Foreign Immigration* (New York, 1835). My interpretation of both of these works is shaped by Billington, *The Protestant Crusade,* 123–24.

13. Lyman Beecher, *A Plea for the West* (Cincinnati, 1835), quoted in Billington, *The Protestant Crusade,* 126. On the impressive familial network of evangelical impulses sired by Beecher, see Stuart Henry, *Unvanquished Puritan: A Portrait of Lyman Beecher* (Grand Rapids, Mich.: William B. Eerdmans, 1972).

14. Jenny Franchot, *Roads to Rome: The Antebellum Protestant Encounter with Catholicism* (Berkeley: University of California Press, 1994), 136.

15. "Dr. Beecher's Sermon at Park Street Church, August 11 [sic], 1834," in *Christian Watchman* (Boston), August 15, 1834, quoted in Nancy Lusignan Schultz, *Fire and Roses: The Burning of the Charlestown Convent, 1834* (New York: Free Press, 2000), 166. On Beecher's role in the riot, see Jeanne Hamilton, O.S.U., "The Nunnery as Menace: The

Burning of the Charlestown Convent, 1834," *U.S. Catholic Historian* 14 (winter 1996): 35–65.

16. Schultz, *Fire and Roses*, 165–82. On the vulgar language of the ringleader of the mob, see "Statement by the Leader of the Knownothing Mob, Destruction of the Charlestown Convent," *U.S. Catholic Historical Society, Historical Records and Studies* 12 (1918): 66ff. See also Wilfred J. Bisson, *Countdown to Violence: The Charlestown Convent Riot of 1834* (New York: Garland, 1989). Both of these accounts rely on a memoir published later by a student at the convent, Louisa G. Whitney (*The Burning of the Convent: A Narrative of the Destruction, by a Mob, of the Ursuline Convent on Mount Benedict. As Remembered by One of Her Pupils* [Cambridge, Mass., 1877]); on Isaac Frye, *The Charlestown Convent; Its Destruction by a Mob, on the Night of August 11, 1834* (Boston: Patrick Donohoe, 1870). This paragraph follows closely the interpretation offered by Franchot in *Roads to Rome*, 136.

17. *Trial of John R. Buzzell, the Leader of the Convent Rioters, for Arson and Buglary Committed... By the Destruction of the Convent on Mount Benedict, in Charlestown, Massachusetts* (Boston, 1834), 15–16. Billington, *Protestant Crusade*, 88, 226–28.

18. "Address of the American and Foreign Christian Union to the Public," in the *New York Observer*, June 30, 1849; American and Foreign Christian Union, *Second Annual Report* (New York, 1851), 36; *Fifth Annual Report* (New York, 1854), 47. The data in this paragraph is from Billington, *Protestant Crusade*, 265–66.

19. *American and Foreign Christian Union* I (January 1850): 1. Billington, *Protestant Crusade*, 269–70. The quotes in this paragraph are from Smith, "The Cross: Church Symbol and Contest in Nineteenth-Century America," 716–17.

20. Carlton Beals, *Brass-Knuckle Crusade: The Great Know-Nothing Crusade, 1820–1860* (New York: Hastings House Publishers, 1960), 22–23.

21. Ibid. John Higham, *Strangers in the Land: Patterns of American Nativism, 1850–1925* (New Brunswick, N.J.: Rutgers University Press, 1958), 382–85. Final quote in the paragraph in Billington, *Protestant Crusade*, 386.

22. Billington, *Protestant Crusade*, 384–85, 388.

23. Donald L. Kinzer, *An Episode in Anti-Catholicism: The American Protective Association* (Seattle: University of Washington Press, 1964), 12–14, 34–35.

24. John Higham, "The Mind of a Nativist: Henry F. Bowers and the A.P.A.," *American Quarterly* 4 (1952): 16–24; Higham, *Strangers in the Land*, 61, 62, 80–81. Block quote on p. 29. Kinzer, *Episode in Anti-Catholicism*, 36–39.

25. Kinzer, *Episode in Anti-Catholicism*, 178–79, 182–89; Appendix III: "American Protective Association Congressional 'Roll of Honor,'" 259–60; Higham, *Strangers in the Land*, 84–86.

26. On the "original" (Reconstruction era) Klan, the classic work is Stanley F. Horn, *Invisible Empire: The Story of the Ku Klux Klan, 1866–1871* (Montclair, N.J.: Patterson Smith, 1969). An excellent regional history of the "revived" Klan is Robert A. Goldberg's *Hooded Empire: The Ku Klux Klan in Colorado* (Urbana: University of Illinois Press, 1981). My own understanding of the impulses shaping the "revived" Klan was influenced by Leonard J. Moore, "Historical Interpretations of the 1920s Klan: The Traditional View and Recent Interpretations," 17–38, in *The Invisible Empire in the West: Toward a New Appraisal of the Ku Klux Klan of the 1930s*, ed. Shawn Lay (Urbana: University of Illinois Press, 1992). On the role of the film *Birth of a Nation* in valorizing the "new" Klan, see pp. 4–5,

18 in *Invisible Empire*. Higham, *Strangers in the Land*, 286–88; "uppity" on p. 288. For an essentially sociological ("status strain") interpretation of the Klan's role in responding to "cultural strain" (an interpretation that is both problematic in light of significant evidence and simplistic), see David H. Bennett, *The Party of Fear: From Nativist Movements to the New Right in American History* (Chapel Hill: University of North Carolina Press, 1988).

27. On anti-Catholicism as a growing impulse in the revived Klan, see Richard K. Tucker, *The Dragon and the Cross: The Rise and Fall of the Ku Klux Klan in Middle America* (Hamden, Conn.: Archon Books, 1991), 62–66; on Clarke and Tyler see Higham, *Strangers in the Land*, 289. On Clarke's definition of the Klan's mission, see ibid., 291. My understanding of the Fundamentalism of the 1920s is shaped by George Marsden's magisterial study, *Fundamentalism and American Culture: The Shaping of Twentieth-Century Evangelicalism, 1870–1925* (New York: Oxford University Press, 1980). On the "Great Reversal" of 1919, see pp. 85–92 in Marsden.

28. Higham, *Strangers in the Land*, 296–97. Leonard Lanson Cline, "In Darkest Louisiana," *Nation* 116 (1923): 10–11; Rufus L. Duffus, "How the Ku Klux Klan Sells Hate," *World's Work* 46 (1923): 179ff.

29. Higham, *Strangers in the Land*, 298–99. *New York Times*, April 7, 1923; August 17, 1923; August 26, 1923.

30. Michael Williams, *The Shadow of the Pope* (New York: Whittlesey House, 1932), 170–72.

31. Ibid., 178. *New York Times*, June 17, 1928.

32. Ibid., 197, 198, 200–201, 292.

33. Will Herberg, *Protestant, Catholic, Jew: An Essay in American Religious Sociology* (Chicago: University of Chicago Press, 1983 [1955]), 38–39.

34. Ibid., 1–4 (1950s "Religious Revival"); 75ff. ("American Way of Life"); 231 (quote); 264.

35. Roger Finke and Rodney Stark, *The Churching of America, 1776–1990: Winners and Losers in Our Religious Economy* (New Brunswick, N.J.: Rutgers University Press, 1992), chart 4.1 on p. 114; chart 5.4 on p. 171; quote on p. 262.

36. Ibid., 271 ("Future Prospects").

37. "Foreword" in Giuseppe Alberigo, Jean-Pierre Jossua, and Joseph A. Komonchak, eds., *The Reception of Vatican II* (Washington, D.C.: Catholic University of America Press, 1987); Frederick McManus, "Vatican Council II," *Worship* 37 (February 1963): 146–48; Daniel O'Hanlon, S.J., "The Development of Worship at the Second Vatican Council," *Worship* 40 (March 1966): 130–36.

38. Charles R. Morris, *American Catholic: The Saints and Sinners Who Built America's Most Powerful Church* (New York: Times Books, 1997), 323–51; Jay P. Dolan, *The American Catholic Experience: A History from Colonial Times to the Present* (Garden City, N.Y.: Doubleday, 1985), 425–26. See also "Into Uncertain Life" (chapter 7) in my *Catholics and American Culture*, 148–71.

39. George Devine, *Liturgical Renewal: An Agonizing Reappraisal* (New York: Alba House, 1973), 45ff. For a critical appraisal by one of the "Catholic Sixties" participants, see Garry Wills, *Bare Ruined Choirs: Doubt, Prophecy, and Radical Religion* (Garden City, N.Y.: Doubleday, 1971), 2ff; James D. Crichton, *Changes in the Liturgy: Considerations on the Instruction of the Sacred Congregation of Rites for the Proper Implementation of the Constitution on the Sacred Liturgy* (Staten Island, N.Y.: Alba House, 1964), 4ff.

40. "Vernacular Warning: Scandal in Hurried, Undignified Use," *National Catholic Reporter* (November 4, 1965): 3; "The Mood of the Laity: How Are Catholics Reacting to the New Liturgy?" *The Critic* 24 (February–March 1965): 57; Jim Castelli and Joseph Gremillion, eds., *The Emerging Parish: The Notre Dame Study of Catholic Life since Vatican II* (San Francisco: Harper & Row, 1987), 129ff.

Chapter Three / A "New" Anti-Catholic Bias?

1. Andrew Greeley, *An Ugly Little Secret: Anti-Catholicism in North America* (Kansas City, Mo.: Sheed, Andrews & McMeel, 1977). On the disappearance of the "Protestant establishment" in the course of the twentieth century, see William R. Hutchison, ed., *The Travail of the Protestant Establishment in America, 1900–1960* (New York: Cambridge University Press, 1989), "Introduction."

2. The Schlesinger quote in James Martin, "The Last Acceptable Prejudice?" *America* 182 (March 25, 2000): 9; George Weigel, "The New Anti-Catholicism," *Commentary* 93 (June 1992): 25–31. On William Donohue and the Catholic League for Religious and Civil Rights, see William A. Donohue, *The Deepest Bias: Anti-Catholicism in American Life*, one-hour video cassette (New York: Catholic League, 1996); see also *www.catholicleague.org* for links to anti-Catholic web sites. The phrase "culture of disbelief" is from Stephen Carter, *The Culture of Disbelief: How American Law and Politics Trivialize Religious Devotion* (New York: Basic Books, 1993). On the rise of "secularism" in American public culture, see Richard John Neuhaus, *The Naked Public Square: Religion and Democracy in America* (Grand Rapids, Mich.: William B. Eerdmans, 1984).

3. On secularization as the "privatization" of religion, see Martin Marty, *The Modern Schism: Three Paths to the Secular* (New York: Harper & Row, 1969), especially the chapter on the United States entitled "Controlled Secularity"; Peter Berger, *The Sacred Canopy* (Garden City, N.Y.: Doubleday, 1967). On the relation of this "new" anti-Catholicism to the older strain, see Patrick Flaherty, "Anti-Catholicism," *Chicago Tribune*, March 3, 2000; "The Revenge of the Know Nothings," editorial, *Wall Street Journal*, April 1, 2000. The political battle over the appointment of a Catholic chaplain to the U.S. House of Representatives and overt anti-Catholic statements made by Bob Jones University produced a spate of articles and essays; see Jay Nordlinger, "Most Hated U.," *National Review* 52 (July 17, 2000): 40–42; "Anti-Catholicism?" *Commonweal* 127 (April 7, 2000): 6. Martin, "Last Acceptable Prejudice?" 9.

4. Rick Hinshaw, "Anti-Catholicism Today," *The Priest* (February 16, 1000): B11; "Bookseller's Group May Expel Jack Chick," *Christianity Today* (October 23, 1981): 62.

5. "'Catechism' Commentary Accused of Anti-Catholic Bias," *Los Angeles Times*, May 15, 1999; Brian Brown, "Pride and Prejudice," *Wall Street Journal*, July 2, 1999; Bill Steiggs, "Troupe Irks San Francisco Catholics," *New York Times*, March 26, 1999. The "Sisters" also sponsored a "Hunky Jesus" contest on Easter Sunday 1999 and a "Rosary in Time of Nuclear Peril" in 1980.

6. Weigel, "The New Anti-Catholicism," 25. Italics in original.

7. "Anger Over Works Evokes Anti-Catholic Shadow," *New York Times*, October 3, 1999; Martin, "The Last Acceptable Prejudice?" The remarks of Wilder and Mann over the Clarence Thomas nomination in Weigel, "The New Anti-Catholicism," 25. The sacrilege in the cathedral occurred when one ACTUP demonstrator received the host during

communion, broke it, and "hurled it to the floor." *New York Times,* December 11, 1989. Mayor Koch's remark is from *Long Island Newsday,* December 11, 1989. See also the article on the protest in the *New York Post,* December 12, 1989, 26.

8. Jimmy Breslin, "Old Men in Rome Still Don't Get It," *Long Island Newsday,* August 15, 1993. The controversy generated by the catalogue of the show sponsored by the National Endowment for the Humanities is described in Weigel, "The New Anti-Catholicism," 25.

9. Christopher Hitchens quotes from "Mother Teresa and Me," *Vanity Fair,* February 1995, 36; "The Devil and Mother Teresa," *Vanity Fair,* October 2001, 170. Mother Teresa as a "presumable virgin" and "sinister person" from Colman McCarthy, "A Mini-Career in Kicking Mother Teresa," *Washington Post,* February 28, 1995.

10. "Planned Parenthood," AP Worldstream, June 23, 2000. See especially "Political and Social Organizations Dedicated to Anti-Choice Extremism," available online at *www.plannedparenthood.org/politicalarena/far-rightorganizations/organizations.html*

11. Avery Dulles, "Religion and the News Media: A Theologian Reflects," *America* 171 (October 1, 1994): 6–9.

12. Ibid., 7.

13. Weigel, "The New Anti-Catholicism," 30.

14. Ibid., 31.

15. Elizabeth Johnson, "A Theological Case for God-She," in *Commonweal Confronts the Century: Liberal Convictions, Catholic Tradition,* ed. Patrick Jordan and Paul Baumann (New York: Simon & Schuster, 1999), 304. Johnson offers an extended (and often brilliant) discussion of her argument in her prize-winning *She Who Is: The Mystery of God in Feminist Theological Discourse* (New York: Crossroad, 1992).

16. Andrew Sullivan, *Virtually Normal: An Argument about Homosexuality* (New York: Alfred K. Knopf, 1995), 7, 34.

17. Ibid., 35, 36–44.

18. Garry Wills, *Papal Sin: The Structures of Deceit* (New York: Doubleday, 2000).

19. Ibid., 3.

20. Ibid., 5.

21. The articles of Weigel and Donohue (among others), as well as the book by Garry Wills, evince this sense of Catholic "non-fit" in contemporary North American culture. I was first awakened to this perception by Jenny Franchot in *Roads to Rome: The Antebellum Protestant Encounter with Catholicism* (Berkeley: University of California Press, 1994), especially chapters 1 ("Protestant Meditations on Popery," 3–15) and 5 ("Nativism and Its Enslavements," 99–111).

Chapter Four / Do Catholics and Protestants See the World Differently?

1. David Tracy, *The Analogical Imagination: Christian Theology and the Culture of Pluralism* (New York: Crossroad, 1981), 412–13. The title for this chapter has been borrowed from the title of chapter 1 in Andrew Greeley's *The American Catholic: A Social Portrait* (New York: Basic Books, 1977).

2. This and preceding paragraph in ibid., 413.

3. Ibid., 410.

4. Ibid., 414–15.

5. Ibid., 415.

6. Andrew M. Greeley, *The Catholic Myth: The Behavior and Beliefs of American Catholics* (New York: Scribner, 1990), 39. Geertz's definition of religion, which Greeley takes as axiomatic, is: religion is "a system of symbols which acts to establish powerful, pervasive, and long-lasting moods and motivations by formulating conceptions of a general order of existence, and clothing these conceptions with such an aura of factuality that the moods and motivations seem uniquely realistic." Clifford Geertz, "Religion as a Cultural System," in *The Interpretation of Cultures* (New York: Basic Books, 1973), 90.

7. Greeley, *The Catholic Myth*, 44.

8. Ibid., 46–48.

9. Ibid., 48.

10. R. Laurence Moore, *Religious Outsiders and the Making of Americans* (New York: Oxford University Press, 1986), xi.

Chapter Five / Catholic-Protestant Tensions in Postwar America

1. Letter of John Dewey to Melvin Arnold, June 7, 1949, in The Paul Blanshard Papers, Bentley Historical Library, University of Michigan, Ann Arbor, Mich., folder 24, box 1. Dewey's description of Blanshard's book appeared on the dust jacket after its third printing. See John McGreevy, "Thinking on One's Own: Catholicism in the American Intellectual Imagination, 1928–1960," *Journal of American History* 84 (June 1997): 97.

2. Blanshard's own recounting of the Beacon Press publication of the articles from *The Nation* in book form can be found in *Personal and Controversial: An Autobiography of Paul Blanshard* (Boston: Beacon Press, 1973), 192–205. The series of articles that he produced for *The Nation* in 1947 led to a boycott against public libraries receiving that journal, pressed by a number of Catholic bishops in the United States. That "ecclesiastical" boycott was almost immediately perceived as public censorship and led to the "Ad Hoc Committee to Lift the Ban on The Nation," headed by Archibald MacLeish and eliciting the support of not only Hutchins and Mrs. Roosevelt, but also of Leonard Bernstein, Truman Capote, Edward R. Murrow, and Reinhold Niebuhr (ibid., 194). Albert Einstein thanked Blanshard after a Princeton University lecture on the book for his support of democratic values against totalitarianism, and McGeorge Bundy (then at Harvard, but soon to be a member of John Kennedy's "best and brightest" think-tank) termed the publication of *American Freedom and Catholic Power* "a very useful thing" (McGreevy, "Thinking on One's Own," 97).

3. Paul Blanshard, *American Freedom and Catholic Power*, 11th printing (Boston: Beacon Press, 1950 [1949]), 3.

4. Ibid., 43, 44.

5. Dale Francis, *American Freedom and Paul Blanshard* (Notre Dame, Ind.: Ave Maria Press, 1950). James M. O'Neill, *Catholicism and American Freedom* (New York: Harper & Brothers, 1952); see pp. ix–x for O'Neill's discussion of the sequence and motives of publishing his book. Jesuits (members of the Society of Jesus) make formal promises neither to aspire to, nor to accept, hierarchical offices (e.g., offices of church leadership, like that

of bishop) in the church; thus, Blanshard's identification of Murray as the leading voice on church-state issues "in the hierarchy," while undoubtedly amusing to Murray, must also have served to confirm Murray's low opinion of Blanshard's acquaintance with Catholic faith and practice.

6. See Thomas C. Love, "The Problem of Religious Freedom," *Journal of Church and State* 8 (autumn 1965): 475–77, and *John Courtney Murray: Contemporary Church-State Theory* (New York: Doubleday, 1965). *Dignitatis Humanae*, the Vatican II declaration on religious liberty that Murray had the major voice in crafting, can be found in *Vatican Council II: The Conciliar and Post-Conciliar Documents*, ed. Austin Flannery (Northport, N.Y.: Costello Publishing Co., 1980), 799–812. Murray, *We Hold These Truths: Catholic Reflections on the American Proposition* (Kansas City, Mo.: Sheed & Ward, 1960). For Murray's early writings on a "Catholic take" of religious freedom in *Theological Studies* and *America* see "Current Theology: Freedom of Religion," *Theological Studies* (March 6, 1945): 85–113; "Freedom of Religion I: The Ethical Problem," *Theological Studies* (June 1945): 229–86; "Separation of Church and State," *America* 76 (December 1946): 261–63; "Separation of Church and State: True and False Concepts," *America* 76 (February 1947): 541–45; "The Court Upholds Religious Freedom," *America* 76 (March 1947): 628–30; "Religious Liberty: The Concern of All," *America* 77 (February 1948): 513–16.

7. John Courtney Murray, "The Catholic Position: A Reply," in *American Mercury* 69 (September 1940): 274–83. Quote in "Review of *American Freedom and Catholic Power*," *Catholic World* 169 (June 1949): 233.

8. Ibid., 234.

9. John Courtney Murray, "Paul Blanshard and the New Nativism," in *The Month* 191 (1951): 214–25. For an excellent background study of Murray during these years, see J. Leon Hooper, *The Ethics of Discourse: The Social Philosophy of John Courtney Murray* (Washington, D.C.: Georgetown University Press, 1986), esp. 101–3.

10. Murray, "Paul Blanshard and the New Nativism," 216, 220. My understanding of Murray's response to Blanshard has been shaped by Todd Whitmore's fine introduction to a collection of essays on Murray's intellectual heritage in contemporary Catholic theology and political theory: Whitmore, "The Growing End: John Courtney Murray and the Shape of Murray Studies," pp. v–xxiv, in *John Courtney Murray and the Growth of Tradition*, ed. J. Leon Hooper and Todd David Whitmore (Kansas City, Mo.: Sheed & Ward, 1996). As Murray was using the term, a "naturalist" is one who asserts that only the concrete data of "nature" is real and views all claims to realities "beyond nature" (e.g., "God") as at best personal sentiments that should not be part of public discussions. A "monolatrist" is one who worships a single process or method of social organization.

11. Murray, "Paul Blanshard and the New Nativism," 218–20; the last quote in the paragraph is from p. 218.

12. *Personal and Controversial: An Autobiography of Paul Blanshard*, 2–3; 15; 23; 26–27; 33–35; 40–41; 48–49; 52. "P.K." is the common self-identification of "preacher's kids."

13. Ibid., 74, 108.

14. Ibid., 189.

15. Ibid., 191. Blanshard consistently refused (or was unable) to distinguish between Catholic "dogma," "doctrine," "ordinary magisterial teaching," and "standard theological opinion" (*very different* levels of teaching) in his writings — crucial distinctions that Catholic theologians, philosophers, and canonists rely on in discussing their tradition.

This cavalier approach to the complexities of theology tended to make his observations about the "Catholic tradition," despite his self-proclaimed years of study, either amusing, naive, or intentionally malicious to Catholic scholars. For instance, from the standpoint of Catholic theology, there is no such thing as a "Catholic medical *dogma*," as the category of "dogma" (the most important beliefs of Christianity touching on the person and work of Christ, "solemnly proclaimed" and given the highest theological ranking of *de Fide definita* in the *Enchiridion Symbolorum,* the official statement of Catholic belief) could never apply to medical procedures or sexual guidelines. See Richard McBrien, *Catholicism* (San Francisco: Harper & Row, 1994), "Definition of Terms," 64ff.

16. A *Nihil obstat* (from the Latin, "nothing stands in the way") is granted by bishops or other church officials to various kinds of published works in theology and philosophy, guaranteeing that the work has been approved as "free of doctrinal or moral errors." See "Nihil obstat," in the *New Shorter Oxford English Dictionary.*

17. The "Federal Theology" informing this congregationalism drew on an intellectual tradition that stretched from John Calvin and William Ames through John Cotton and Jonathan Edwards to Edwards Amassa Park and William Ellery Channing. Ultimately, this Reformed Christian tradition rested both on a distinctly "primitivist" reading of the New Testament and on what Perry Miller termed an "Augustinian strain of piety." "Federal" theology derives its name from the Greek word *foedus* (covenant). This theology rested on a belief that a "covenant," or agreement, between God and humanity gave legitimacy to revelation (the Bible) and provided a democratic model of how to organize the church (a "covenant" between believers). The seventeenth-century New England churches espousing this theology were collectively termed the "Standing Order," a loose confederation of congregational churches "officially" sponsored by the government. On both the piety and the church order deriving from this theology see Edmund S. Morgan, *Visible Saints: The History of a Puritan Idea* (New York: New York University Press, 1963); Sacvan Bercovitch, *The Puritan Origins of the American Self* (New Haven, Conn.: Yale University Press, 1975). Perhaps the single most influential essay on Puritan federal theology remains Perry Miller, "The Marrow of Puritan Divinity," *Errand into the Wilderness* (Cambridge, Mass.: Harvard University Press, 1956). Miller's description of this "Augustinian strain of piety" can be found in chapter 2 ("The Marrow of Puritan Divinity") in his *The New England Mind: The Seventeenth Century* (Boston: Beacon Press, 1954 [1939]). "Primitivism" refers to a theological impulse in which the "mistakes of history" are simply passed over in favor of creating a timeless (pure) church based on the primitive model of the first century, described in the Acts of the Apostles; see Theodore Dwight Bozemen, *To Live Ancient Lives: The Primitivist Dimension in Puritanism* (Chapel Hill: University of North Carolina Press, 1988).

18. William Perkins and William Ames are generally (if not unreservedly) credited as the intellectual progenitors of what emerged as New England "federal theology": see Janice Knight, *Orthodoxies in Massachusetts: Rereading American Puritanism* (Cambridge, Mass.: Harvard University Press, 1994), esp. 22ff.; 37–39; 52ff. On the distinction between the election sermon tradition and "regular" preaching, see Harry Stout, *The New England Soul: Preaching and Religious Culture in Colonial New England* (New York: Oxford University Press, 1986). For the application of federal theology to both church and state in seventeenth-century New England, see the following primary works published in Alan Heimert and Andrew Delbanco, *The Puritans in America: A Narrative Anthology* (Cambridge, Mass.:

Harvard University Press, 1985): Peter Bulkeley, "The Gospel Covenant," 117–21; John Cotton, "Treatise on the Covenant of Grace," 149–53; John Winthrop, "Defense of an Order of Court," 164–67; 351–69.

19. The famous correspondence between Thomas Jefferson and John Adams on the role of religion in the new republic they were creating evinces an analogous covert reliance on, and overt disdain of, the Calvinist worldview that permeated colonial North America, especially New England. Both took as axiomatic a "voluntary" congregational model of churches that they derived (seemingly unconsciously) from their seventeenth-century British forebears; both likewise understood the hierarchical model of Catholicism to represent a profoundly threatening challenge to republican liberties, although this challenge was usually phrased in eighteenth-century Enlightenment language. See Barry Shain's fine study of Enlightenment/Puritan tensions in the political thought of the founding fathers for a balanced rereading of the social philosophy and communitarian ethic of colonial America: *The Myth of American Individualism: The Protestant Origins of American Political Thought* (Princeton, N.J.: Princeton University Press, 1994), especially 4–18, 48–83. On the Jefferson-Adams correspondence, see 196–98.

20. Blanshard, *American Freedom and Catholic Power*, 5. Italics are in the original.

21. Ibid., 23. On p. 16 Blanshard notes: "The word 'congregation' evokes in the minds of most Americans something democratic in nature, a group of people who meet together as members of some organization to decide something on their own authority. The twelve Congregations which surround the Pope in the government of the Roman Church are not congregations in that sense. They are not committees of Catholic people chosen by members of the local churches in various nations. They are appointed committees of appointed cardinals."

22. Ibid., 23, 39, 44.

23. Ibid., 49. Ernst Troeltsch argued, in one of the classics of the sociology of religion, *The Social Teaching of the Christian Churches*, that Christian history had witnessed three kinds of organizing principles for the church's relation to human culture: the "church," which claimed responsibility for human culture in all of its manifestations; the "sect," which shunned "the world" as evil; and "mysticism," which represented an essentially individualistic, nonsocial appropriation of the gospel. H. Richard Niebuhr pointed out the essentially European nature of Troeltsch's model, arguing that the United States had neither churches nor sects, but rather "denominations," which borrowed the sect's voluntary ecclesiology but nonetheless possessed a "churchly" responsibility for culture. See Ernst Troeltsch, *The Social Teaching of the Christian Churches*, 2 vols. (New York: Harper, 1960); H. Richard Niebuhr, *The Social Sources of Denominationalism* (New York: Meridian Books, 1957).

24. Blanshard, *The Irish and Catholic Power* (Boston: Beacon Press, 1953); *God and Man in Washington* (Boston: Beacon Press, 1960); *Paul Blanshard on Vatican II* (Boston: Beacon Press, 1966), 331.

25. John Courtney Murray, "The Catholic Position: A Reply" (September 1949), in *Bridging the Sacred and the Secular: Selected Writings of John Courtney Murray* (Washington, D.C.: Georgetown University Press, 1994), 296.

26. Hooper, *The Ethics of Discourse*, 101.

27. Donald E. Pelotte, *John Courtney Murray: Theologian in Conflict* (New York: Paulist Press, 1975), 1, 7.

28. Whitmore, "The Growing End," vii. Murray, "Cooperation: Theory and Organization," *Theological Studies* 4 (1943): 271.

29. John Courtney Murray, Review of *American Freedom and Catholic Power* in *Catholic World* (June 1949): 233.

30. Murray, "Paul Blanshard and the New Nativism," 216, 223.

31. Reinhold Niebuhr, "The Children of Light and the Children of Darkness," in *The Essential Reinhold Niebuhr: Selected Essays and Addresses,* ed. Robert McAfee Brown (New Haven, Conn.: Yale University Press, 1986), 160.

32. John Courtney Murray, "Leo XIII on Church and State: The General Structure of the Controversy," *Theological Studies* 14 (1953): 1.

33. Whitmore, "The Growing End," vii–x.

34. John Courtney Murray, *We Hold These Truths,* 48–49.

35. Ibid., 49.

36. On the uncritical eagerness of Catholics to join the U.S. mainstream after 1945, see the introduction, "Oh, The Irony of It All," in my *Catholics and American Culture.* On the "naked public square," see Richard John Neuhaus, *The Naked Public Square: Religion and Democracy in America* (Grand Rapids, Mich.: William B. Eerdmans, 1984).

Chapter Six / The Power of Negative Thinking

1. Peter Braestrup, "Protestant Group Wary on Kennedy: Statement by Peale Group Sees Vatican 'Pressure' on Democratic Nominee," *New York Times,* September 8, 1960. Also on the front page of the *Times* was a separate article by Felix Belair Jr. entitled "Religion as Issue Denounced Again by White House." For a view of the Peale Group from the standpoint of Kennedy's campaign managers, see Theodore C. Sorenson, *Kennedy* (New York: Harper & Row, Publishers, 1965), 188–89.

2. "Protestant Group Wary on Kennedy," *New York Times.*

3. Ibid.

4. Peale quote from "The Power of Negative Thinking," *Time,* September 19, 1960, 21; Nelson Bell quote from "Test of Religion," *Time,* September 26, 1960, 21.

5. "Protestant Group's Statement," *New York Times,* September 8, 1960.

6. Felix Belair Jr., "Religion as Issue Denounced Again by White House," *New York Times,* September 8, 1960. " 'Protestant Underworld' Cited as Source of Attack on Kennedy," *New York Times,* April 11, 1960; "Three Rabbis Assail Electoral Bias," *New York Times,* September 11, 1960.

7. "Peale Quits Organization That Pushed Church Issue," *New York Times,* September 16, 1960; Carol V. R. George, *God's Salesman: Norman Vincent Peale and the Power of Positive Thinking* (New York: Oxford University Press, 1993), 202–3.

8. For the recollection of one of Kennedy's closest advisors on the Houston Speech, see Theodore Sorensen, *Kennedy* (New York: Harper & Row, 1965), 188–89. For an earlier interpretation of the Houston speech, see "A Catholic for President? JFK, Peter Berger, and the 'Secular' Theology of the Houston Speech, 1960" (chapter 6) in my *Catholics and American Culture: Fulton Sheen, Dorothy Day, and the Notre Dame Football Team* (New York: Crossroad, 1999), 128–47. The text of Kennedy's speech in Houston can be found in "On Church and State: Remarks of John F. Kennedy Addressed to the Greater Houston

Ministerial Association," in *The Kennedy Reader*, ed. Jay David (Indianapolis: Bobbs-Merrill, 1967), 363–66.

9. Theodore White, *The Making of the President, 1960*, 2d ed. (New York: Atheneum Publishers, 1969), 260; Massa, *Catholics and American Culture*, 128; Victor Lasky, *JFK: The Man and the Myth* (New York: Macmillan, 1963), 490. This and the following paragraphs utilize material from chapter 6 ("A Catholic for President?") from my *Catholics and American Culture*, 128–48.

10. Kennedy, "On Church and State," in *The Kennedy Reader*, 363, 364.

11. Ibid., 364–65.

12. Ibid., 365.

13. Ibid., 366.

14. Quotes from the Houston speech in this paragraph are from "Remarks on Church and State," in *The Kennedy Reader*, 364–65. Albert Menendez, *John F. Kennedy: Catholic and Humanist* (Buffalo, N.Y.: Prometheus Books, [1978]), 31ff.

15. John F. Kennedy, "The Responsibility of the Press: Address to the American Society of Newspaper Editors, Washington, D.C., April 21, 1960," in *"Let the Word Go Forth": The Speeches, Statements, and Writings of John F. Kennedy*, ed. Theodore Sorensen (New York: Delacorte Press, 1988), 126, 128.

16. Jacqueline Kennedy's remark in Menendez, *John F. Kennedy*, 2. For a secular reading of Kennedy's faith, see Bruce Miroff, *Pragmatic Illusions: The Presidential Politics of John F. Kennedy* (New York: David McKay, 1976), 5–9, 10. Sorensen's recollection is in Sorensen, *Kennedy*, 19.

17. Peter Berger has brilliantly described the privatization of religion. By interpreting "secularization" to mean the privatizing of religious impulses, Berger means that "private religiosity, however 'real' it may be to the individuals who adopt it, cannot any longer fulfill the classical task of religion — that of constructing a common world within which all of social life receives ultimate meaning binding on everyone. Instead, this religiosity is limited to specific enclaves of social life that may be effectively segregated from the secularized sectors of modern society. . . . The world-building potency of religion is thus restricted to the construction of sub-worlds, of fragmented universes of meaning, the plausibility structure of which may in some cases be no larger than the nuclear family." Peter Berger, *The Sacred Canopy: Elements of a Sociological Theory of Religion* (New York: Doubleday, 1967), 133–34.

18. Ruth Peale, the pastor's wife, wrote Kurt Volk on August 19, 1960, about a gathering in Montreux, Switzerland, the day before "with Billy Graham and about 25 church leaders" from the United States. "They were unanimous in feeling that Protestants in America must be aroused in some way." Quoted in George, *God's Salesman*, 198. The title of the chapter in George's book focused on Peale's role in the 1960 campaign is "The Demise of Tribal Politics, 1955–1985," 190–20. The sign to the right of the Fifth Avenue main entrance of the Marble Collegiate Church during the 1960s read, "America's Hometown Church."

19. Murray's collection of essays published in 1960, *We Hold These Truths: Catholic Reflections on the American Proposition*, approached the American constitutional tradition from the standpoint of the "natural law" philosophy of St. Thomas Aquinas, utilizing that Thomistic "read" of natural law quite brilliantly to claim a privileged (Catholic) understanding of such Enlightenment (Lockean) "natural law" documents as the "Declaration of Independence" and the Constitution.

20. James A. Pike, *A Roman Catholic in the White House* (Garden City, N.Y.: Double-day, 1960), 39. Kennedy's remark in *Look* magazine is in "A Catholic in 1960," *Look*, March 3, 1959. "On Questioning Catholic Candidates," *America*, March 7, 1959. *The Nation*'s observation is in Lasky, *JFK*, 326.

21. Sydney Ahlstrom, *A Religious History of the American People* (New Haven, Conn.: Yale University Press, 1972), 740. For the portrayal of Peale's message as "religion mas-querading as pop psychology," see Donald Meyer, *The Positive Thinkers: From Mary Baker Eddy to Oral Roberts*, 2d ed. (New York: Pantheon Books, 1980), chapter 21, "Positive Divine Psychology." For description of his ministry as "a popularizer of the mentalistic self-help tradition," see Richard Weiss, *The American Myth of Success: From Horatio Alger to Norman Vincent Peale* (New York: Basic Books, 1969), 224–27. "Pathological yahoos" is from Michael Kazin, "The Grass-Roots Right: New Histories of U.S. Conservatism in the Twentieth Century," in *American Historical Review* 97 (1992): 97, 136–55.

22. Meyer, *Positive Thinkers*, 259; "a thoroughly Methodist beginning" is the title of chapter 1 in George's *God's Salesman*, 17–45.

23. The obituary for Clifford Peale, Norman's father, dated September 21, 1955, is in the Norman Vincent Peale Manuscript Collection, Bird Library, Syracuse University. On Norman's life in Methodist parsonages, see Norman Vincent Peale, *The True Joy of Positive Living* (New York: Morrow, 1984), 18–35. This and the three following paragraphs are based on George, *God's Salesman*, 19–40.

24. George, *God's Salesman*, 37–38, 39–40; Peale, *The True Joy of Positive Living*, 69.

25. George, *God's Salesman*, 50, 54–55; "Department of Field Work Report, 1924," Boston University School of Theology, Norman Vincent Peale Manuscript Collection, Bird Library, Syracuse University; Peale, *True Joy of Positive Living*, 89.

26. George, *God's Salesman*, 56–57; *History of King's Highway Methodist Episcopal Church*, pamphlet. The Norman Vincent Peale Manuscript Collection, Bird Library, Syracuse University.

27. George, *God's Salesman*, 58–59; Nelson M. Blake, *History of University Avenue Methodist Church* (privately printed, 1970). Advertising for Sunday services from the *Syra-cuse Post Standard* and the Syracuse University *Daily Orange* are in the Norman Vincent Peale Manuscript Collection, Bird Library, Syracuse University.

28. George, *God's Salesman*, 61–62. The Peale quote is from the *Syracuse Post Standard*, September 29, 1931, in the Norman Vincent Peale Manuscript Collection, Bird Library, Syracuse University.

29. George, *God's Salesman*, 68–69.

30. Peale's quote from *The True Joy of Positive Living*, 130. George quote from *God's Salesman*, 69. "Harmonial religion" is the loose inclusive term used to describe a broad spectrum of religious movements — Transcendentalism, Christian Science, etc. — that sought to "harmonize" the individual with the larger universe. On the harmonial religious tradition in the United States, see Sydney Ahlstrom, *A Religious History of the American People* (New Haven, Conn.: Yale University Press, 1972), chapter 60 of part 9, "Harmonial Religion since the Later Nineteenth Century"; and Catherine Albanese, *America, Religions and Religion* (Belmont, Calif.: Wadsworth, 1992), 220–80.

31. Meyer, *The Positive Thinkers*, 264; George, *God's Salesman*, 129. Especially instruc-tive on Peale's own perception of the success and meaning of *Positive Thinking* is his

preface to the 35th Anniversary edition: *The Power of Positive Thinking* (New York: Simon and Schuster, 1994), ix–xv.

32. Peale, *Power of Positive Thinking*, 5, 12.

33. Meyer, *Positive Thinkers*, 278.

34. The exchange over Peale's denouncing Stevenson from the pulpit is in Norman Vincent Peale to William Canfield, letter of September 24, 1956, Norman Vincent Peale Collection, Syracuse University. His understanding of John Wesley's role in sparing England a revolution from a personal interview between Carol George and Peale, February 24, 1981, in Pawling, New York, reported in George, *God's Salesman*, 165.

35. George, *God's Salesman*, 164–81, 193. On Gannett's "Committee," see the pamphlet "Organized Leadership: The Story of the Committee for Constitutional Government," by Peale, printed in 1944. On "Spiritual Mobilization," see James Fifield's sermon, "The Cross vs. the Sickle," published by the First Congregational Church of Los Angeles, August 3, 1947. See also the letter of Peale to Fifield of August 11, 1947, box 216. On the "Christian Freedom Foundation," see the "Report on the Organizational Meeting of the Christian Freedom Foundation, at the Hotel Wellington, New York City, April 17 1950" in box 239. On Hunt's "Facts Forum," see the letter of Peale to H. L. Hunt of December 10, 1951, and of Hunt to Peale of December 14, 1951, and March 13, 1952. All of these documents are in the Norman Vincent Peale Manuscript Collection, Bird Library, Syracuse University. Reported in Carol George, *God's Salesman*, 199.

36. George, *God's Salesman*, 199.

37. "What a Protestant Should Do Today," typescript sermon in the Norman Vincent Peale Manuscript Collection, Bird Library, Syracuse University.

38. Letter of Ruth Peale to Kurt Volk, August 19, 1960. "What a Protestant Should Do Today," typescript sermon, both in the Norman Vincent Peale Manuscript Collection, Bird Library, Syracuse University. Reported in George, *God's Salesman*, 199.

39. The reconstruction of the "Montreux Conference" has a confused (and confusing) history in itself. For various accounts, see Billy Graham, *Just as I Am: The Autobiography of Billy Graham* (San Francisco: Harper, 1997), chapter 21; letter of Mary Creighton (Peale's secretary) to Dr. Daniel Poling, August 24, 1960; letter of Dr. Daniel Poling to Mary Creighton, August 25, 1960; typescript office memo of Mary Creighton, all in the Norman Vincent Peale Manuscript Collection, Bird Library, Syracuse University. On Peale's perception of the Montreux meeting as an "evangelical summit," see Creighton's memo of August 29: "Dr. Peale knew this meeting [at the Mayflower Hotel] was in prospect, as he attended a conference in Switzerland of clergymen and other leaders *brought together by Billy Graham*" (italics my own). George, *God's Salesman*, footnote 35, p. 216.

40. *Time*, September 19, 1960, 21, disclosed the presence of the two reporters.

41. "Fire-breathing" from "The Campaign: The Power of Negative Thinking," *Time*, September 19, 1960, 21–22; "Protestant Groups' Statements," *New York Times*, September 8, 1960.

42. "Statements," *New York Times*, September 8, 1960.

43. "Protestant Group Wary on Kennedy," *New York Times*, September 8, 1960; "The Campaign," *Time*, 21.

44. "Text of Statement on Religious Issue," *New York Times*, September 16, 1960; "Niebuhr and Bennett Say Raising of Religious Issue Spurs Bigotry," John Wicklein, ibid.

See also "Peale Quits Organization That Pushed Church Issue," *New York Times*, September 16, 1960. The *New Republic* likewise chimed in on Peale's part in the events at the Mayflower Hotel: "Protestants in Politics," *New Republic* 143 (September 19, 1960): 3–5.

45. George Duggan, "Peale Disclaims Political Intent," *New York Times*, September 19, 1960. In the same day's edition of the *Times:* "Minister Backed by Congregation"; "Apostle of the Positive: Norman Vincent Peale"; "Text of Peale's Letter to Congregation."

46. Albert Menendez, *John F. Kennedy: Catholic and Humanist* (Buffalo, N.Y.: Prometheus Books, [1978]), 25; Theodore H. White, *The Making of the President, 1960*, 2d ed. (New York: Atheneum Publishers, 1969), 241; Victor Lasky, *JFK: The Man and the Myth* (New York: Macmillan, 1963), 173–79. This and the following paragraphs are based on Massa, *Catholics and American Culture*, 133–34.

47. Lasky, *JFK*, 180–81; See also Appendix B in Lasky: "The Bailey Report," 587–88, 591ff.

48. Lasky, *JFK*, 181–82. Sorensen, *Kennedy*, 83. The editorial is in the *Christian Century*, August 15, 1960, 941. For a Catholic "read" on the import of the Democratic Party's decision in 1956 not to run Kennedy as vice president, see "Senator Kennedy and the Convention," *America*, September 4, 1960, in *The Kennedy Reader*, 359–61.

49. Fletcher Knebel, "A Catholic in 1960," *Look* Magazine, March 3, 1959. Italics in the quote are my own.

50. "Catholic Censure of Kennedy Rises," *New York Times*, March 1, 1959; "Cushing Backs Kennedy on Church-State Replies," New York *Herald Tribune*, March 10, 1959; James Pike, *A Roman Catholic in the White House* (Garden City, N.Y.: Doubleday, 1960), 19ff.

51. Sorensen, *Kennedy*, 112.

52. The "religion issue" was hotly debated throughout February and March 1960, especially in the "liberal" religious press. For a sampling of the latter, see Robert Michaelsen, "Religion and the American Presidency, I," *Christian Century*, February 3, 1960, 133–35. Sorensen, *Kennedy*, 122, 127.

53. Sorensen, *Kennedy*, 137.

54. Ibid., 137, 139.

55. Ibid., 144.

56. Ibid., 146.

57. On the "hard-nosed presidency" of Kennedy, see Bruce Miroff, *Pragmatic Illusions: The Presidential Politics of John F. Kennedy* (New York: David McKay, 1976). On the "naked public square," see Richard John Neuhaus, *The Naked Public Square: Religion and Democracy in America* (Grand Rapids, Mich.: William B. Eerdmans, 1984).

Chapter Seven / The Death Cookie and Other "*Catholic Cartoons*"

1. "Biography of Jack Chick," at *www.chick.com/information/authors/chick.asp*. I gratefully acknowledge the assistance offered on this chapter by Patrick Scanlon of the Catholic League for Civil and Religious Rights and of John Saliba, S.J., of the University of Detroit/Mercy.

2. Jack T. Chick, "Why No Revival?" frame 1 at *www.chick.com/reading/tracts/0008/0008_01.asp*. Frame numbers refer to the progression of frames in the cartoon.

3. Ibid.

4. Ibid.

5. "Biography of Jack Chick" at the Chick Publications home page, *www.chick.com*; "Welcome to Jack's F.A.Q.s: The Most Frequently Asked Questions of Jack T. Chick," at *http://members.tripod.com/monsterwax/chickfaqs.html*. The block quote is from Richard von Busack, "Unearthing Famed Christian Artist Jack T. Chick," at "Comic Book Theology," *www.metroactive.com/papers/metro/04.02.09/comics-9813.html*.

6. Review of "The Imp" by Scott Adams, *www.teleport-city.com/inkings/zines/chick.html*.

7. Jack T. Chick, "The Thing," copyright 1971, frame 7,
    at *www.chick.com/reading/tracts/0066/0066_01.asp*.
    Jack T. Chick, "Alberto. Based on a True Story," copyright 1979,
    at *www.chick.com/reading/comics/0112/0112.asp*.
    Jack T. Chick, *Smokescreens*, copyright 1983, "Introduction,"
    at *www.chick.com/reading/books/153/153intro.asp*.
    Jack T. Chick, *The Godfathers* catalogue ("Alberto Part 3"),
    at *www.chick.com/catalogue/comics/01144.asp*.

8. "A Survey of Chick Publications" online at the Catholic League for Civil and Religious Rights at *www.catholicleague.org/catalyst/1996_catalyst/1096catalyst.htm*.

9. On rock music in church as one of Satan's snares, see Chick's original cartoon tract, "Why No Revival?"

10. Richard von Busack, "Comic Book Theology," at *www.metroactive.com/papers/metro/04.02.98/comics-9813.html*.

11. On the "Roman Catholic Institution," see "Are Roman Catholics Christians?" frames 2 and 6 at *www.chick.com/reading/tracts/0071/0071_01.asp*.

12. Jack T. Chick, "The Beast," copyright 1988, at *www.chick.com/reading/tracts/0007/0007_01.asp*. Jack T. Chick, "Is There Another Christ?" copyright 1983, at *www.chick.com/reading/tracts/0047/0047_01.asp*.

13. Jack T. Chick, "Why Is Mary Crying?" copyright 1987, frames 17, 21 at *www.chick.com/reading/tracts/0040/0040_01.asp*.

14. Ibid., frames 18, 25, 29, and 27.

15. Jack T. Chick, "Last Rites," copyright 1994, frames 8, 10, 14, 15, 16, 30, 31. Italics in quotes are in original. At *www.chick.com/reading/tracts/0082/0082_01.asp*.

16. Jack T. Chick, "The Death Cookie," copyright 1988, quotes from frames 1, 3, and 10. Block quote from frames 11, 14, and 15. At *www.chick.com/reading/tracts/0074/0074_01.asp*. Capitalization in the original.

17. Ibid., frames 5, 9, 11, 15, 19, and 22. Block quote from frames 32, 33, and 34.

18. Ibid., frames 36, 37, and 38.

19. Jack T. Chick, "Are Roman Catholics Christians?" copyright 1985, frame 1, at *www.chick.com/reading/tracts/0071/0071_01.asp*. Capitalization in original.

20. Ibid., frames 1, 2, 3, 4, 17. Block quote from frames 18 and 20. Bold in original. At *www.chick.com/reading/tracts/0071/0071_01.asp*.

21. Ibid., frame 25.

22. "Biography of Jack Chick" at *www.chick.com/information/authors/chick.asp*.

23. Ibid.

24. Ibid.

25. Ibid.

26. Ibid.

27. Ibid.

28. Ibid. The "Biography of Jack Chick" at the Chick website dates its copyright as "1984–2002," thus making it difficult to supply exact chronology or trace historical sequence.

29. Adam Bugler, "Christ Comics," copyright August 21, 2001, *www.freezerbox.com/archive/2001/08/chick.*

30. Ibid. Bugler notes that "Chick stopped granting interviews in the seventies, or so his secretary told me over the phone."

31. Dwayne Walker, "Jack Chick, a Private Man with a Public Message," online at *www.walkertown.com/jack.html.* Part Four: "Meeting the Man!" copyright October 19, 1999. Part Five: "Jack and I Watch Videos." Part Six: "God Told Me to Watch This Movie!"

32. "A Survey of Chick Publications," at *www.catholicleague.org/catalyst/1996_catalyst/1096catalyst.htm,* offering the October 1996 issue of *Catalyst.*

33. Ibid.

34. Aubrey B. Holmes, " 'Christian' Comic Books," *Christian Century,* January 20, 1982, 47.

35. Gary Metz, "Jack Chick's Anti-Catholic *Alberto* Comic Book is Exposed as a Fraud," *Christianity Today* 25 (March 13, 1981): 50.

36. Ibid., 50, 52.

37. Ibid., 1.

38. Holmes, " 'Christian' Comic Books," 47.

39. "Booksellers' Group May Expel Chick," *Christianity Today* 25 (October 23, 1981): 62.

40. Ibid.

41. I take as axiomatic the definition and history of Protestant Fundamentalism offered by George Marsden in *Fundamentalism and American Culture* (New York: Oxford University Press, 1980). Marsden describes the year 1919 as the "Great Reversal," when conservative Protestants once well *inside* the religious mainstream discovered U.S. culture to be moving resolutely in the direction of cultural, intellectual, and religious pluralism. This "betrayal" by a culture in which they were once assured insiders led to their self-imposed cultural exile — at least until the 1980s, when the media rediscovered them as the "New Religious Right." In fact, there was not much "new" about them at all, except for their belated "discovery" by a secular press long accustomed to thinking of conservative religion as a thing of the past.

Chapter Eight / Catholicism and Science

1. Kenneth R. Hardy, "Social Origins of American Scientists and Scholars," *Science* 185 (August 9, 1974): 497. I am indebted to Andrew Greeley's original discussion of this article for bringing up the issues raised by Hardy's study; see Andrew Greeley, *An Ugly Little Secret: Anti-Catholicism in North America* (Kansas City, Mo.: Sheed, Andrews & McMeel,

1977), 10–12. A 1976 study analogous to Greeley's response to Hardy's article, by Abraham D. Lavender and John M. Forsyth, pointed out that Roman Catholics and Protestants in the United States have the same levels of education. See "The Sociological Study of Minority Groups as Reflected by Leading Sociological Journals," *Ethnicity* 3 (December 1976): 388–98.

2. Hardy, "Social Origins," 497–98. Hardy was, in fact, part of a much larger academic discussion regarding the relation of religion and cultural/academic achievement. See Robert K. Merton, *Social Theory and Social Structure* (New York: Free Press, 1968); W. A. Austin, *Predicting Academic Performance in College* (New York: Free Press, 1971); Daniel Patrick Moynahan, *Beyond the Melting Pot* (Cambridge, Mass.: M.I.T. Press, 1970).

3. Hardy, "Social Origins," 497–98. The earlier studies were Harvey Lehman and Paul Witty, "Scientific Eminence and Church Membership," *Scientific Monthly* 33 (1931): 544–49; and Ann Roe, *The Making of a Scientist* (New York: Dodd, Mead, 1952).

4. Robert H. Knapp and Hubert B. Goodrich, *Origins of American Scientists: A Study Made under the Direction of a Committee of the Faculty of Wesleyan University* (Chicago: University of Chicago Press, 1952), p. v in the preface.

5. Ibid., 23–24. Hardy's analysis of *Origins* is in "Social Origins of American Scientists," 498.

6. Ibid., 274–76.

7. Hardy, "Social Origins," 498.

8. Ibid., 502. Hardy's article was widely quoted in other social scientific studies of the "cultural consequences" of Mormon belief, especially with regard to academic achievement, as well as for his broader claims about the relation of specific religious groups to the production of scientists. For an example of how his claims about the relationship of Mormonism to education were later used, see Armand L. Mauss, "Sociological Perspectives on the Mormon Subculture," *Annual Review of Sociology* (1984): 437–53, esp. 450–51; and Merlin B. Brinkerhoff, "Religion and Goal Orientations: Does Denomination Make a Difference?" *Sociological Analysis* 39 (1978): 205–6. For later uses of the "Social Origins" article, see M. Elizabeth Tidball and Vera Kistiakowsky, "Baccalaureate Origins of American Scientists and Scholars," *Science* 193 (August 20, 1976): 647; James R. Shortridge, "Patterns of Religion in the United States," *Geographical Review* 66 (1976): 423; Clark A. Elliott, "Models of the American Scientist: A Look at Collective Biography," *Isis* 73 (1982): 80; Mary Budd Rowe, "Science Education: A Framework for Decision-Makers," *Daedelus* 112 (1983): 123–42.

9. Hardy quote in "Social Origins," 503.

10. Table 7 is on p. 504 of Hardy, "Social Origins."

11. Ibid., 505.

12. Ibid., 503.

13. John Tracy Ellis, "American Catholics and the Intellectual Life," *Thought* 30 (1955): 351. Thomas F. O'Dea, *American Catholic Dilemma: An Inquiry into the Intellectual Life* (New York: Sheed and Ward, 1958), 6. Gustav Weigel, S.J., "American Catholic Intellectualism," *Review of Politics* 19 (1957): 275–307.

14. Weigel, "American Catholic Intellectualism."

15. O'Dea, *American Catholic Dilemma*, 158. In an odd kind of synchronicity, one of O'Dea's most famous works had been published the year before *Dilemma* on the Latter-day Saints (the "Mormons"), the religious group that operated Brigham Young University,

where Hardy taught. See Thomas F. O'Dea, *The Mormons* (Chicago: University of Chicago Press, 1957).

16. Ibid., 158, 159.

17. Andrew Greeley, *Ethnicity, Denomination, and Inequality* (Beverly Hills, Calif.: Sage Publications, 1976), 7.

18. Greeley, *An Ugly Little Secret*, 10. Among the studies published in the two decades before Hardy's article that Greeley suggests illustrate a different position of Catholics in academic life than that offered by Hardy are Daniel J. Bogue, *Population in the United States* (Glencoe, Ill.: Free Press, 1959); Galen L. Bockel, "Income and Religious Affiliation: A Regressive Analysis," *American Journal of Sociology* 74 (May 1969): 632–47; see especially 633–35. Greeley's work on the educational levels of U.S. Catholics includes "Influence of the 'Religious Factor' on Career Plans and Occupational Values of College Graduates," *American Journal of Sociology* 68 (May 1963): 658–71; and "Religion and Academic Career Plans," *American Journal of Sociology* 72 (May 1967): 668–72. Greeley's own "read" of Hardy's article was elucidated in a letter of Greeley to the author, dated June 3, 2002, from the National Opinion Research Center.

19. Greeley, *Ethnicity, Denomination, and Inequality*, 18–19, 21–23. See especially Tables 22 (p. 38), 23 (p. 39), 24 (p. 40), and 25 (p. 41) for the "educational mobility" of Catholics and other U.S. religious groups.

20. Gerhard Lenski, *The Religious Factor: A Sociological Study of Religion's Impact on Politics, Economics, and Family Life* (Garden City, N.Y.: Doubleday, 1961); "religion's impact" and "the relevance" both on p. 6. Andrew Greeley termed Hardy's article an "update" of Lenski's assertion that "Catholicism and intellectual achievement are incompatible." See Andrew Greeley, "The Sociology of American Catholics," *American Sociological Review* 5 (1979): 94.

21. Lenski, *The Religious Factor*, 6–7. Weber's *Protestantische Ethik und der Geist des Kapitalismus* was translated by Talcott Parsons and published in the United States as *The Protestant Ethic and the Spirit of Capitalism* (New York: Scribner, 1948).

22. Lenski, *The Religious Factor*, 77. Seymour M. Lipset and Reinhard Bendix, *Social Mobility in Industrial Society* (Berkeley: University of California Press, 1959).

23. Lenski, *The Religious Factor*, 76, 77 (block quote). Raymond Mack, Raymond Murphy, and Seymour Yellin, "The Protestant Ethic, Level of Aspiration, and Social Mobility," *American Sociological Review* 21 (June 1956): 295–300.

24. Lenski, *The Religious Factor*, 80.

25. Ibid., 80–81.

26. Ibid., 202–3. Knapp and Goodrich's *Origins of American Scientists* is footnoted by Lenski on p. 202. The block quote here is from Lenski, 255.

27. Lenski, *The Religious Factor*, 203.

28. Ibid., 204. Italics are my own.

29. Thomas F. O'Dea, *American Catholic Dilemma: An Inquiry into the Intellectual Life* (New York: Sheed and Ward, 1958), 151.

30. Ibid., 6, 9.

31. Ibid., 83–84, 12.

32. Ibid., 13–14.

33. Ibid., 155–56.

34. Ibid., Italics in the block quote are my own.

35. Ibid., 159–60.
36. Ibid., 160.
37. Ibid., 160, 161.
38. Greeley, *Ethnicity, Denomination, and Inequality,* 7.
39. O'Dea, *American Catholic Dilemma,* 155.

Chapter Nine / "Why Does He Say Those Awful Things about Catholics?"

1. The title for this chapter is taken from a chapter by David Harvey entitled "TV Preacher Jimmy Swaggart: Why Does He Say Those Awful Things about Catholics?" in *The God Pumpers: Religion in the Electronic Age,* ed. Marshall Fishwick and Ray B. Brown (Bowling Green, Ohio: Bowling Green State University Popular Press, 1987), 87; Victor Kelly, "Swaggart Accepts Bishop's Meeting Request," *Baton Rouge Advocate,* June 4, 1984; Ken Woodward, "King of Honky Tonk Heaven," *Newsweek,* May 30, 1983, 89; "Jimmy Swaggart Ministries" as reported in Groupwatch (*www.namebase.org/gw/swaggart.txt*); Janice Peck, *The Gods of Televangelism* (Cresskill, N.J.: Hampton Press, 1993), 118. Jerry Lee Lewis is an early star of the southern "rockabilly" musical tradition, made famous by his number one hit in the 1950s, "Great Balls of Fire." Mickey Gilley, another Swaggart cousin, is a noted country singer whose bar in Texas was made famous in the movie *Urban Cowboy.* On the family history and Swaggart's relationship to both Lewis and Gilley, see Jimmy Swaggart, *To Cross a River* (Plainfield, N.J.: Logos International, 1977), 120–24, 153–62, 171ff.

2. Groupwatch, on their website sponsored by the Interhemispheric Resource Center at *www.namebase.org/gw/swaggart.txt,* offers one set of statistics on Swaggart's TV ministry. I have followed the 1982 Arbitron Ratings reported by Blan Stout in his 1983 Master of Theology thesis at Harvard Divinity School, entitled "Preaching through Television: An Examination of the Preaching of Jimmy Swaggart," Andover Library Archives (1983.4), p. 103. According to Arbitron, Swaggart's telecast was carried by 226 stations nationally, second to the *Old Time Gospel Hour's* 240 stations. Jim and Tammy Fay Bakker's *PTL Club* (which the couple claimed stood for "Praise the Lord" and "People That Love") ranked at the bottom of Arbitron's "Top 10 Religious TV Programs," being watched by 631,000 viewers on 171 stations. Martin Gardner noted that after a series of sex and monetary scandals that drove the Bakkers off the air and Jim Bakker to prison, journalists began saying that "PTL" really stood for "Pass the Loot" and "Pay the Lady." See Martin Gardner, "Giving God a Hand," *New York Review of Books* 34 (August 13, 1987): 17–22, 20.

3. Jimmy Swaggart, "A Letter to My Catholic Friends," *The Evangelist,* January 1983, 5, 6, 7, 9. "Come out from her and be separate" — from the New Testament book of Revelation (18:4) — was originally addressed to first-century Christians endeavoring to flee the coming wrath of Christ's Second Coming by separating themselves from the excesses of their pagan civilization. By the eighteenth century it became the basis for the phrase "Come-outism," a term (and concept) common in North American evangelical Protestantism that advocates that "reborn" Christians leave corrupt churches that don't revive and convert people to form fellowships of "Bible believers." On the biblical usage, see Gregory Beale, *The Book of Revelation: A Commentary on the Greek Text* (Carlisle, U.K.: Paternoster Press, 1999), 823ff. On its meaning in the American religious context,

see Sidney Ahlstrom, *A Religious History of the American People* (New Haven, Conn.: Yale University Press, 1972), 290–94.

4. Swaggart, "Letter to My Catholic Friends," 17. Anne Rowe Seaman, *Swaggart: The Unauthorized Biography of an American Evangelist* (New York: Continuum, 1999), 251–52; Woodward, "King of Honky Tonk," 89; Victor Kelly, "Swaggart Accepts Bishop's Meeting Request," *Baton Rouge Advocate*, June 4, 1983; "Swaggart, Bishop to Talk after Uproar," *New Orleans Times-Picayune*, June 5, 1983.

5. Seaman, *Swaggart*, 252; "Swaggart Accepts Bishop's Meeting Request," *Baton Rouge Advocate*. For rollicking accounts of the media circus surrounding the "Letter" and subsequent Swaggart pronouncements, see Steve Chapple, "Whole Lotta Savin' Goin' On," *Mother Jones*, July–August 1986, 37–45; and "The Koppel Report: Televangelism," ABC News, February 26, 1988, cassette. A defense of Swaggart's actions can be found in Charles R. and Lynda K. Fontaine, *Jimmy Swaggart, To Obey God Rather Than Men* (Crockett, Tex.: Kerusso, 1989).

6. Hunter Lundy, *Let Us Prey: The Public Trial of Jimmy Swaggart* (Columbus, Miss.: Genesis Press, 1999), 55, 75; Seaman, *Swaggart*, 55, 251, 259. Gregorian quote from Kenneth Woodward, "Swaggart's One-Edged Sword," *Newsweek*, January 9, 1984,65. See also J. D. Cardwell, *Mass Media Christianity* (Lanham, Md.: University Press of America, 1984); Randy Fram, "Did Oral Roberts Go Too Far?" *Christianity Today* (January 1987): 43.

7. Lundy, *Let Us Prey*, 55, 75. Block quote from a private interview by Blan Maurice Stout with Jimmy Swaggart, as transcribed in "Preaching through Television," 93–94.

8. Reports on Chile, Costa Rica, Guatemala, and Nicaragua in Groupwatch's report on Jimmy Swaggart Ministries. The quote of Neves from Penny Lernoux, "The Fundamentalist Surge in Latin America," *Christian Century*, January 20, 1988, 51; this article can also be found at *www.religion-online.org/cgi-bin/relsearchd.dll/showarticle?item_id=927*.

9. Lernoux, "Fundamentalist Surge." See also "Catholic Criticizes Churches," *New Orleans Times-Picayune*, November 14, 1984. The latter article quotes Patrick Flores, Catholic bishop of San Antonio, Texas, who accused Protestant "missionaries" like Swaggart of "fomenting religious discord" in Latin America. While Flores noted that "anyone is free to proselytize, it is not necessary to attack the beliefs of others."

10. "Liturgical religious monstrosity" from Woodward, "King of Honky Tonk," 89.

11. Jimmy Lee Swaggart, *Catholicism and Christianity* (Baton Rouge, La.: Jimmy Swaggart Ministries, 1986). The works utilized in this monograph are drawn from a strange mixture of "high level" Catholic theology (Richard McBrien's immense compendium *Catholicism* and papal encyclicals like Pius XII's *Munificentissimus Deus* and Leo XIII's *Providentissimus Deus*) and from anti-Catholic literature aimed at a somewhat different cultural and religious audience. In the latter group are Ralph Woodrow's *Babylon Mystery Religion* (Riverside, Calif.: Ralph Woodrow Evangelistic Association, 1983); Clark Butterfield's *Night Journey from Rome to the New Jerusalem* (P.O. Box 1513, Upland Calif., n.d.), and Bartholomew Brewer's *Pilgrimage from Rome* (Greenville, S.C.: Bob Jones University Press, 1982).

12. Swaggart, *Catholicism and Christianity*, 1, 2–3, viii. Italics in the block quote added; those in the text are Swaggart's own.

13. Ibid., 200, 201.

14. Charles Grandison Finney, *Lectures on Revivals of Religion*, 1835, John Harvard Library, ed. William G. McLoughlin (Cambridge, Mass.: Belknap Press of Harvard University

Press, 1960), Lecture IX, "Means to be Used with Sinners," 140–55; Swaggart, *Catholicism and Christianity*, viii.

15. Gibbs Adams, "Bishop Meets with Swaggart over Article," *New Orleans Times-Picayune*, July 2, 1983.

16. Ibid.

17. Swaggart, *Catholicism and Christianity*, 17, 18. Quotation marks are in original. Swaggart's theology of this individual encounter with Jesus as personal Lord and Savior as the "test" of true conversion can be explored in a number of his sermons printed in *Twenty-five Great Years, Twenty-five Anointed Sermons* (Baton Rouge, La.: Jimmy Swaggart Ministries, 1981): "Four Conditions for Being Included in the Rapture," 8–10. "Ere the Lamp of God Went Out in the Temple of the Lord," 58–64; "The Word, the Will and the Wisdom," 85–90; "The Ministry of the Holy Spirit to the Believer," 295–96; "What Is the Doctrine of Unconditional Eternal Security?" 311–12, 316.

18. Swaggart, *Catholicism and Christianity*, 32, 33.

19. Ibid., 205, 215.

20. "Believers baptism" is the practice of baptizing only adults who, attesting to a conversion experience that they can narrate, makes them "believers" already. "Biblical literalism" is the belief that the Bible is not only inspired by God, but is *literally* true in all of its details (the creation of the world in seven days, etc.). "Premillennialism" is a theological understanding of the "end times" — based on a quite specific and literal reading of the Book of Revelation — in which Christ will physically return to earth for judgment, followed by a thousand-year "reign of the saints," after which believers will be "raptured" into heaven before the last terrible battle of Armageddon. Hunter Lundy, *Let Us Prey: The Public Trial of Jimmy Swaggart* (Columbus, Miss: Genesis Press, 1999), 17. On the Assemblies, see Edith W. Blumhofer, *Restoring the Faith: The Assemblies of God, Pentecostalism, and American Culture* (Urbana: University of Illinois Press, 1993); *Pentecostal Currents in American Protestantism*, ed. Edith W. Blumhofer, Russell Spittler, and Grant Wacker (Urbana: University of Illinois Press, 1999); *Pentecostalism in Context: Essays in Honor of William W. Menzies*, ed. Wansuk Ma and Robert Menzies (Sheffield, Eng.: Sheffield Academic Press, 1997).

21. "Apostolic succession" is the Catholic theological concept that the church's teaching authority — especially as centered on the episcopacy and papacy — rests on a succession of authority going back to the apostles of Jesus. "Transubstantiation" is the term utilized by the future Pope Alexander III before 1153, but classically elaborated by St. Thomas Aquinas, regarding the Catholic understanding of Christ's presence in the bread and wine of the eucharist. According to Thomas, while the "accidents" of the bread and wine (taste, smell, appearance) remain the same before and after the words of consecration ("This is my body"), the "substance" of both is transformed into the body and blood of Jesus Christ, thus assuring the believer that reception of the "accidents" is an intimate encounter with Christ himself. This distinction, at least in its Thomistic form, rests on an Aristotelian understanding of reality in which substance and accidents can be distinguished philosophically. T. A. Sullivan, "Apostolic Succession," *New Catholic Encyclopedia* (Washington, D.C.: Catholic University of America Press, 1967), 1:695–96; C. Villert, "Transubstantiation," *New Catholic Encyclopedia*, 14:259–61.

22. Janice Peck, *The Gods of Televangelism* (Cresskill, N.J.: Hampton Press, Inc., 1993), 106–7.

23. This reading of Swaggart's telecasts accepts as axiomatically true the interpretation crafted by Peck in *The Gods of Televangelism*, 106–7.

24. Ibid., 106.

25. Swaggart's worship service on March 13, 1983 (held "on the road" at Madison Square Garden in New York City) went as follows: a five-minute solo by Swaggart singing "Leaving my Mind"; a three-minute solo by Milo Herrick singing "I'm Going on Home"; a five-minute solo by John Barnes singing "His Touch"; after this a biblical text from 1 Samuel 5:6–10 was displayed on a screen on the stage. Swaggart then read the text from his pulpit, after which he delivered a twenty-five-minute sermon entitled "The Pulling Down of Strongholds," billed as a sermon to Christians on "victory over the flesh." Following the sermon Swaggart delivered a prayer of forty seconds, and then asked everyone to sing "Pass Me Not, Gentle Savior" as he called those who sought to accept Jesus as their savior forward to the platform. Stout, the observer of this service, estimates that hundreds came forward for several minutes while Swaggart offered a prayer. See Blan Stout, "Preaching through Television," 101–10.

26. Peck, *Gods of Televangelism*, 159.

27. Ibid., 161.

28. The Latin *ex opere operato* means "by the working of the work itself." In Catholic theology, this means that sacraments like baptism and the eucharist actually deliver grace apart from the worthiness (or rhetorical abilities) of the priest administering them, as the grace they deliver is a function of the Holy Spirit. Thus, a sinful or abstracted priest pouring water on the head of a slumbering child of lukewarm believers nonetheless delivers the grace of rebirth through the action of the Holy Spirit. P. L. Hanley, "Ex opere operato," *New Catholic Encyclopedia* (Washington, D.C.: Catholic University of America, 1967), 5:700–701.

29. Mircea Eliade, "Roman Catholicism," *The Encyclopedia of Religion* (New York: Macmillan, 1987), 430.

30. Jimmy Lee Swaggart, *To Cross a River*, 13, 14, 19.

31. Ibid., 21, 22, 23.

32. Ibid., 34–35. Quote from Stout, "Preaching through Television," 81. Dwight L. Moody, at the turn of the twentieth century, and Billy Sunday, during the first several decades of the twentieth century, were the most visible and popular revivalists within evangelical Protestantism in the United States. On the North American form of revivalism, see William G. McLoughlin, *Billy Sunday Was His Real Name* (Chicago: University of Chicago Press, 1955); *Modern Revivalism: Charles Grandison Finney to Billy Graham* (New York: Ronald Press, 1950); and *Revivals, Awakenings, and Reform: An Essay on Religion and Social Change in America, 1607–1977* (Chicago: University of Chicago Press, 1978). The last work offers an especially fine overview of the role of evangelical revivalism in the development of U.S. Protestantism in particular, and of North American culture in general. "Best selling gospel artist" from Michael James Guiliano, *Thrice-Born: The Rhetorical Comeback of Jimmy Swaggart* (Macon, Ga.: Mercer University Press, 1999), 15.

33. Swaggart, *To Cross a River*, 122–28; Stout, "Preaching through Television," 5.

34. Swaggart, *To Cross a River*, 124–25; Stout, "Preaching through Television," 8–9.

35. Stout, "Preaching through Television," 10.

36. Swaggart in Stout, "Preaching through Television," 11.

37. Ibid., 12.

38. Ibid.

39. Ibid., 12–13; Guiliano, *Thrice-Born*, 16. See also Saundra Saperstein, "Spreading a $600,000-a-Day Message," *Washington Post*, June 7, 1987.

40. Stout, "Preaching through Television,," 12–13. As the televised programs evolved, Donny Swaggart would appear at the end of the program — after Jimmy had delivered his "scripture message" — and it would be the younger Swaggart who would offer the range of "giving opportunities" to the TV audience, ranging from subscriptions to *The Evangelist* and records to checks to support foreign missionaries.

41. For narrative accounts of Swaggart's meetings with Debra Arlene Murphree in Room 12 of the Travel Inn in New Orleans, see Seaman, *Swaggart*, 11–15; Lundy, *Let Us Prey*, 120–26.

42. Denita Gadson, "Holy Ghost Rally" (Associated Press), at *www.skepticfiles.org/culinfo/congrs.htm*; Jimmy Swaggart, "Pope's Visit: Troubling Times for Catholic Church," published in "Your Opinions/Letters," *New Orleans Times-Picayune*, August 13, 1987.

43. Swaggart, "Pope's Visit."

44. Lawrence Wright, *Saints and Sinners: Walker Railey, Jimmy Swaggart, Madalyn Murray O'Hair, Anton LeVay, Will Campbell, Matthew Fox* (New York: Alfred Knopf, 1993), 80–81; Art Harris and Jason Berry, "Jimmy Swaggart's Secret Sex Life," *Penthouse*, July 1988.

45. Wright, "Jimmy Swaggart: False Messiah," in *Saints and Sinners*.

46. Lundy, *Let Us Prey*, 131.

47. Lundy, *Let Us Prey*, 131, 132; Peck, *Gods of Televangelism*, 118. Lundy observes of this disparity of punishment between the District and national bodies of the Assemblies: "The previous year Jim Bakker had been decertified and turned out of his ministry because he failed to answer charges of sexual misconduct, misappropriation of funds, and alleged homosexual or bisexual activities.... Swaggart, however, who had been undeniably soliciting the favors of a professional whore, was going to step out of the pulpit for only a few months. But he had the Louisiana District Council's blessing. Of course, a $145 million ministry was nothing to dismiss casually; two of the Louisiana District officials were also members of Jimmy Swaggart Ministries' board of directors, and every one of them knew how to read a bottom line" (132).

48. The Arbitron statistics for Swaggart's broadcasts, and the statistics of his fundraising after 1987, are from Peck, *Gods of Televangelism*, 118.

49. Ibid., 162.

Chapter Ten / Betrayal in Boston

1. Andrew Greeley, "'Safe' Men Put Church in Its Crisis," *New York Daily News*, May 7, 2002, op-ed page. "Safe men" in italics is my own. I would like to thank Edward J. Mattimoe, S.J., of St. Patrick's Parish, Huntington, L.I., who provided me with much of the newspaper documentation tracing the clergy abuse scandal in Boston. With his usual prescience, Ned recognized within days of the *Boston Globe's* first article in January 2002 that the story would have profound impact and began clipping stories. In September 2002, he sent four large folders of those clippings to me in Cambridge, Massachusetts; these have proven invaluable in researching and writing this chapter.

2. I have put the adjectives "liberal" and "conservative" in quotes in this paragraph, both because one or both of the individuals so described here might dispute the appropriateness of such designations in describing their respective positions as U.S. Catholics, and because they are slippery as theological designations. I have followed the secular press in so designating them; but while Quindlen has been described as a "liberal" in newspapers and secular journals and Neuhaus is regularly described as a "conservative," I also know that both have pointed out (correctly) that such a use of these essentially political terms is as problematic as it is helpful. My own understanding of the Boston scandals has been shaped by the following superb accounts (especially that of Peter Steinfels) and I gratefully acknowledge their work: Peter Steinfels, "The Church's Sex Abuse Crisis: What's Old, What's New, and What's Needed, and Why," *Commonweal* 129 (April 19, 2002): 13–19; John Meacham, "What Would Jesus Do? Beyond the Priest Scandal," *Newsweek*, May 6, 2002, 22–25; Stephen J. Rossetti, "The Catholic Church and Child Sexual Abuse," *America* 186 (April 22, 2002), also at *www.usccb.org/comm/rossetti.htm*; Garry Wills, "Scandal," *New York Review of Books* 49 (May 23, 2002): 6–9; "Thirty-five Questions and Answers about the Crisis in the Catholic Church," compiled by Ron Brackett and Caryn Baird, *St. Petersburg Times*, April 28, 2002, at *www.sptimes.com*; Carol Eisenberg, "Head U.S. Bishop Admits Church's Sex Abuse Failures," *Long Island Newsday*, June 14, 2002.

3. "Cafeteria Catholics" is the derisive term used by critics of many American Catholics who are perceived to "pick and choose" what teachings of the church they will obey, much like picking out food in a cafeteria line. The block quote is from Greeley, "'Safe Men' Put Church in Its Crisis."

4. "Extraordinary Cloak of Secrecy" is from the front-page story of the *Boston Globe*, January 31, 2002, by the *Globe* staff entitled "Scores of Priests Involved in Sex Abuse Cases." The opening of that article reads: "Under an extraordinary cloak of secrecy, the archdiocese of Boston in the last 10 years has quietly settled child molestation claims against at least 70 priests, according to an investigation by the Globe Spotlight Team."

5. On Herranz, see John L. Allen Jr., "Curia Official Blasts U.S. Media Coverage," *National Catholic Reporter*, May 17, 2002, 7; on Maradiaga, see E. J. Dionne, "What the American Bishops Can Teach Rome," *Boston Globe*, June 11, 2002. For other charges of anti-Catholicism leveled at the press for its coverage of the Boston story, see Sam Dillon, "Role of Bishops Is Now a Focus of Grand Juries," *New York Times*, July 12, 2002; "N.Y. Grand Jury Accuses Church of Cover-Up," *Long Island Newsday*, June 19, 2002; Paul Moses, "Church Scandal Serves as Media 'Rorschach,'" *Long Island Newsday*, May 31, 2002; Garry Wills, "Priests and Boys," *New York Review of Books*, June 13, 2002, 10, 12–13.

6. Carolyn Newberger, quoted in *Betrayal: The Crisis in the Catholic Church*, researched and written by the Investigative Staff of the *Boston Globe* (Boston: Little, Brown, 2002), 152.

7. Among Cardinal Law's most vociferous critics have been Eileen Foley, "Cardinals, Alas, Can't be Ousted," *Toledo Blade*, April 19, 2002; Michael Sean Winters, "Cardinal Sin," *New Republic*, April 15, 2002, and "How to Save the Church: The Betrayal," *New Republic*, May 6, 2002.

8. *Betrayal*, ix; letter of Dr. Robert W. Mullins to Rev. Oates, October 20, 1984, Geoghan court records; photographically reproduced on p. 218 of *Betrayal*. For similar letters about Geoghan's fitness for ministry, see letter of Dr. John H. Brennan to Bishop

Thomas Dailey, January 13, 1981 (p. 208); letter of Bishop Thomas Daily to Dr. Brennan, January 26, 1981 (p. 209); and letter of Dr. John Brennan to Bishop Robert Banks, December 7, 1990 (p. 223), all photographically reproduced in *Betrayal*.

9. "Scores of Priests Involved in Sex Abuse Cases," *Globe* Staff, *Boston Globe*, January 31, 2002.

10. Michael Rezendes and Sacha Pfeiffer, "Cardinal Promoted Alleged Sex Abuser," *Boston Globe*, May 18, 2002; Walter V. Robinson and Sacha Pfeiffer, "Priest Abuse Cases Sealed by Judges," *Boston Globe*, February 16, 2002; Michael Paulson and Kevin Cullen, "More Are Calling for Cardinal to Resign," *Boston Globe*, April 10, 2002.

11. *Betrayal*, xi.

12. "Scores of Priests Involved," *Boston Globe*, January 31, 2002.

13. Ibid. On "what the Cardinal knew, and when he knew it," see Stephen Kurkjian, "Records Show Law Reassigned Pasquin after Settlements," *Boston Globe*, May 5, 2002; Pam Belluck, "Cardinal Law Said His Policy Shielded Priests," *New York Times*, August 14, 2002; Lisa Miller and David France, "Sins of the Fathers," *Newsweek*, March 4, 2002, 43–45; Adam Liptak, "The Whole Truth and Nothing But," *New York Times*, May 12, 2002, Week in Review.

14. "Increasingly enraged part of his flock": in a *Globe*/WBZ-TV poll undertaken in mid-April 2002, 65 percent of self-identified Catholics in Boston said they believed that Cardinal Law should resign; *Betrayal*, 5. Paulson and Cullen, "More Are Calling for Cardinal to Resign," *Boston Globe*, April 10, 2002.

15. Maryetta Dussourd's description in August 24 Deposition, Geoghan court file. Letter of Monsignor John J. Murray, rector of Cardinal O'Connell Seminary, Jamaica Plain, Massachusetts, to the Reverend Thomas J. Riley, rector of St. John's Seminary, Brighton, Massachusetts, July 31, 1954, Geoghan court file. Both of these are quoted in *Betrayal*, 13, 15.

16. Letters between Monsignor Mark H. Keohane and the Reverend Thomas J. Riley are all dated July 1955, from the archdiocesan personnel file in the Geoghan court records, quoted in *Betrayal*, 15–17.

17. Geoghan's statements from St. Luke Institute are in a confidential letter from St. Luke's to the Boston archdiocese in a 1989 report. Geoghan's acknowledgment of sexual arousal in the company of boys is on p. 55 of the deposition given by Dr. Edward Messner, a psychiatrist at Massachusetts General Hospital, taken on December 27, 2001. Geoghan's recollection of abusing four siblings from the same Saugus family are on p. 19 of Geoghan's sentencing report of February 15, 2002, prepared by the Commonwealth of Massachusetts. All of these are in the John Geoghan trial papers published by the *Boston Globe* and reported in *Betrayal*, 17–18.

18. Deposition of the Reverend Thomas W. Moriarity on February 23, 2002, Geoghan court papers, quoted in *Betrayal*, 19.

19. Deposition of Joanne Mueller on August 17, 2000, quoted in *Betrayal*, 19–20.

20. Miceli's court statements are quoted in *Betrayal*, 20–21.

21. Court deposition of Maryetta Dussourd, taken on August 24, 2001, quoted in *Betrayal*, 21.

22. Ibid. Deposition of the Reverend William C. Francis, March 30, 2001, Geoghan court papers. This paragraph closely follows the account offered in *Betrayal*, 22–23. The

"administrator" of a Catholic diocese (in this case an "auxiliary bishop") oversees the day-to-day running of diocesan institutions, but answers finally to the "ordinary" — the chief bishop whom in Boston was Cardinal Medeiros and (after 1984) Bernard Law. For my understanding of the events narrated in this and the next several paragraphs, I have also used Andrew Greeley, "Why? There Were Three Sins," *America*, May 27, 2002, 12–13; Pam Belluck, "Church Erred on Abuses, Boston College Leader Says," *New York Times*, May 16, 2002; Michael Paulson, "Law's Explanation Finds Some Sceptics, Some Believers," *Boston Globe*, May 21, 2002; Walter W. Robinson and Sacha Pfeiffer, "Priest Abuse Cases Sealed by Judges," *Boston Globe*, February 16, 2002.

23. Globe Staff, "Church Allowed Abuse by Priests for Years," *Boston Globe*, January 6, 2002; Thomas Farragher and Matt Carroll, "Delegation of Duty Is Called Faulty," *Boston Globe*, May 10, 2002; Michael Rezendes, "Seventeen More Allege Abuse by Geoghan, File Suit," *Boston Globe*, October 4, 2002; William J. Bennett, "Unfruitful Works of Darkness," *Wall Street Journal*, March 18, 2002; Lisa Gentes, "Cardinal Law Hears Clergy Sex Abuse Concerns from Boston's Catholics," Catholic News Service at *www.cdop.org/catholic_post/post_3_10_02/cns.cfm*; Karl Mauer, "Rev. Joseph Fessio, S.J.: Bishops' Dereliction Made This Spiritual Crisis Possible," Catholic Citizens of Illinois at *http://catholiccitizens.org/press/pressview.asp?c=2049*.

24. Thomas F. Fox, "What They Knew in 1985: Seventeen Years Ago, a Report on Clergy Sex Abuse Warned U.S. Bishops of Trouble Ahead," *National Catholic Reporter*, May 17, 2002, 3. Page 14 of the "Executive Summary" of the report offered to U.S. Catholic Bishops assembled at Collegeville, Minnesota, states: "The necessity for protecting the confidentiality of this document cannot be overemphasized. The document was drafted by retained counsel hired for the specific purpose of communicating to the reader, however, though much of the language is that of the counsel, the document is reflective of the thoughts of clergy and other professionals in different disciplines, professionals who have worked closely with counsel throughout the development of these ideas. An effort has been made to have this document afforded the protection and privilege provided under our law for confidential communications [between legal counsel and client]. That privilege shall not apply should the reader discuss same with anyone other than a recipient of this document." Executive Summary, "The Problem of Sexual Molestation by Roman Catholic Clergy, compiled on June 8 and 9, 1985, by Mr. F. Ray Mouton, J.D., and the Reverend Thomas P. Doyle, O.P.," at *www.thelinkup.com/execsum.html*. Thomas C. Fox, "What They Knew in 1985: Seventeen Years Ago, a Report on Clergy Sex Abuse Warned U.S. Bishops of Trouble Ahead," *National Catholic Reporter*, May 17, 2002, 3, 6. See also Associated Press, "Manchester Union Leader Calls for N.H.'s Bishop's Resignation," May 8, 2002, at *www.boston.com/news/daily/08/abuse_mccormack.htm*.

25. Executive Summary of the 1985 report, 8, 9.

26. Executive Summary, Fox, "What They Knew in 1985"; Steve Twomey, "For Three Who Warned Church, Fears Borne Out," *Washington Post*, June 13, 2002. Transcript of *Meet the Press* for March 31, 2001, with Tim Russert, Ray Flynn, Richard McBrien, John McCloskey, Donald Cozzens, and Thomas Doyle, at *www.msnbc.com/news/731454.asp*.

27. Thomas Doyle, O.P., J.C.D., "A Short History of the Manual," at *www.thelinkup.com/manual.html*; Thomas Doyle, O.P., J.C.D., "Reaction to the *Charter for the Protection of Children and Young People*," at *www.thelinkup.com/reaction-rev.html*; and Thomas Doyle,

O.P., J.C.D., "The Archives and the Secret Archives Required by Canon Law," at *www.thelinkup.com/secretarch.html.*

28. Doyle's recollections of his conversations with Bernard Law from Fox, "What They Knew in 1985," 3.

29. Fox, "What They Knew in 1985," *National Catholic Reporter,* 3; Twomey, "For Three Who Warned Church, Fears Borne Out," *Washington Post.* "The crisis in the Catholic Church lies not with the fraction of priests who molest youngsters, but in an ecclesiastical power structure that harbors pedophiles, conceals other sexual behavior patterns among its clerics, and uses strategies of duplicity and counterattack against the victims" (Jason Berry, author of *Lead Us Not into Temptation,* responding to Cardinal Law's famous pronouncement in 1993: "By all means, we call down God's power on the media, particularly the [Boston] *Globe*"). See Hendrik Hertzberg, "Sins," "Talk of the Town" in *New Yorker,* April 1, 2002.

30. *Betrayal,* 172.

31. Peter Steinfels, "Abused by the Media," *The Tablet,* September 14, 2002, 9–11, 10. "Pedophilia" refers to the sexual molestation of prepubescent children by adults; "ebophilia" refers to the sexual molestation of pubescent or teenage children by adults.

32. *Betrayal,* 174–75. See also Jason Berry, *Lead Us Not into Temptation: Catholic Priests and the Sexual Abuse of Children* (Urbana: University of Illinois Press, 2000), 22ff.; Donald Cozzens, *The Changing Face of the Priesthood* (Collegeville, Minn.: Liturgical Press, 2000).

33. Letter of Dr. John H. Brennan (of Boston Clinical Associates, Inc.), to Bishop Thomas V. Daley, January 13, 1981. Photographically reproduced on p. 208 of *Betrayal.*

34. Letter of Dr. Robert W. Mullins to "The Rev. Oates," October 20, 1984. Photographically reproduced on p. 218 of *Betrayal.*

35. Geoghan's duties in Dorchester are from *Betrayal,* 23.

36. Letter of Margaret Gallant to Humberto Cardinal Medeiros, August 16, 1982, photographically reproduced on pp. 210–13, and transcribed on pp. 214–15 of *Betrayal.*

37. Letter of Humberto Cardinal Medeiros to Mrs. Margaret Gallant, August 20, 1982, photographically reproduced on p. 216 of *Betrayal.*

38. Letter of Humberto Cardinal Medeiros to the Reverend John Geoghan, August 26, 1982, Geoghan court files, quoted on p. 25 of *Betrayal.*

39. Letter of Margaret Gallant to Archbishop Bernard Law, September 6, 1984, quoted on p. 31 of *Betrayal.*

40. Letter of Bernard Cardinal Law to Mrs. Marge (*sic*) Gallant, September 21, 1984, photographically reproduced on p. 217 of *Betrayal.* Law's consultation with Daley, followed by listing Geoghan as "in between assignments," was made public in the document filed on June 8, 2001, that began the *Boston Globe's* investigation. See the final paragraph/note on p. 253 of *Betrayal.* On James Lane, see *Betrayal,* 32.

41. Monsignor Francis Rossiter is credited with having knowledge of the previous allegations against Geoghan at the time of his assignment to St. Julia's, at least according to what the *Globe* called a "confidential church chronology" of Geoghan's career, August 22, 1994. But Rossiter denied that he was informed about Geoghan's troubled past in his own court deposition on April 11, 2001 (pp. 75–81). See the second note at the top of p. 254 in *Betrayal.*

42. Letter of Bishop John M. D'Arcy to Archbishop Bernard Law, December 7, 1984, on the stationery of "Auxiliary Bishop of Boston, Office of the Regional Bishop." Photographically reproduced on p. 219 of *Betrayal*.

43. Evaluation of John J. Geoghan, St. Luke's Institute, April 26, 1989. Accusations against Geoghan at the Waltham Boys & Girls Club are from a Middlesex County Criminal Complaint dated November 22, 1999. Both are noted on p. 254 of *Betrayal*. Letter from the Reverend John J. Geoghan to His Eminence, Bernard Cardinal Law, June 29, 1990, Geoghan court records. Photographically reproduced on p. 222 of *Betrayal*.

44. Letter of Bernard Cardinal Law to the Reverend John J. Geoghan, December 30, 1994. Letter of John J. Geoghan to Monsignor William F. Murphy, November 17, 1995. Letter of Bernard Cardinal Law to the Reverend John J. Geoghan, December 12, 1996. Canonical memo from Monsignor Richard Lennon to the Reverend James McCarthy, May 8, 1998 ("Personal and Confidential"). "Commonwealth of Massachusetts against John J. Geoghan," December 9, 1999, filed in the Middlesex Superior Court. All of these documents are photographically reproduced on pp. 224, 225, 226, 228, 229, and 230–31 (respectively) of *Betrayal*.

45. Rodger Van Allen, "Bishops Should Marry," *Commonweal*, July 12, 2002, 31. On the Paul Shanley case in Boston, see Fox Butterfield and Jenny Honz, "A Priest's Two Faces: Protector, Predator," *New York Times*, May 19, 2002; Nick Madigan, "Sent to California on Sick Leave, Boston Priest Bought Racy Gay Resort," *New York Times*, April 15, 2002; "Priest at Center of Scandal Arrested," *Boston Globe*, May 2, 2002. On the "crisis" of clergy sex abuse in the rest of the country, see Glenn F. Bunting, "Cardinal Mahoney Kept Cleric's Abuse Secret for Sixteen Years," *Los Angeles Times*, May 16, 2002; David Crumm and Patricia Montemurri, "Church Passed Blame in Priest's Abuse," *Detroit Free Press*, May 23, 2002; Elizabeth Fernandez, "Suit Claims Abuse by Burlingame Priest," *San Francisco Examiner*, January 17, 2002; Donna Gehrke-White, "Court: Church Liable in Abuse Cases," *Miami Herald*, March 15, 2002; Laurie Goodstein, "Albany Diocese Settled Abuse Case for Almost $1 Million," *New York Times*, June 27, 2002; David Herszenhorn, "Cardinal Keeps Silent on His Handling of Sex Abuse Allegations," *New York Times*, March 19, 2002; Bruce Nolan and Tara Young, "New Orleans Swept Up in Priest Scandal," *New Orleans Times-Picayune*, May 16, 2002; Jim Schaeffer and David Crumm, "Sixteen Priests Face Inquiry," *Detroit Free Press*, May 10, 2002; Kathleen Shaw, "Suit Claims Priests Ran Sex Ring," *Worcester Telegram*, June 24, 2002; Chris Smith, "Cardinal's Rules," *New York* magazine, May 20, 2002, 27–31; Teresa Watanabe and Richard Winton, "D.A. Demands Mahoney Turn Over Documents on Abuse," *Los Angeles Times*, May 17, 2002. On Michael Rose's book, see "Arguing, Through Repetition, That Liberals Caused Priest Scandal," *Los Angeles Times*, July 29, 2002. One of the best commentaries on the "orgy of blame" was offered by Gail Buckley, "It's Time for Vatican III," *New York Daily News*, May 26, 2002, 48.

46. Newberger, quoted in *Betrayal*, 152.

Acknowledgments

As is always the case with academic works that evolve over time, debts are incurred that must be acknowledged, but cannot truly be repaid: such is assuredly the case with the present work. Harry Nasuti, Jeffrey von Arx, S.J., Nancy Busch, and John Hollwitz (respectively chair of the Theology Department, Dean of the College, Dean of the Graduate School of Arts and Sciences, and Vice President for Academic Affairs, all of Fordham University) supported this work with generous course reductions, as well as a sabbatical year during which the final draft was completed. Harry, Jeff, Nancy, and John are themselves smart scholars as well as nurturing administrators — a rare combination to find in *one* university officer, much less in *four* in the same place! All four made the timely completion of this book possible, and I here publicly acknowledge the debt I owe them.

Vincent Diminuco, S.J., rector of the Fordham Jesuit community, quite generously supplied both the support of the community and *cura personalis* to me during my sabbatical in the best tradition of the Society of Jesus. Dr. William Donohue of the Catholic League for Religious and Civil Rights graciously made the League's considerable resources available to me at the beginning of this project, which took weeks off my initial research. Gwendolin Herder, my perceptive and supportive editor at Crossroad, made cheerful and infallibly correct suggestions about the manuscript in progress: much of what works in the following study is due to her fine editorial eye. To all three I offer my thanks.

What is now chapter 3 of this book was published in *Theological Studies* and was subsequently given in emended form to the Catholic Studies faculty of the College of the Holy Cross in Worcester, Massachusetts, to the Weston Jesuit School of Theology faculty seminar in Cambridge, Massachusetts, and to the faculty seminar of the Jesuit Institute at Boston College. Likewise, what is now chapter 5 was published in the *Harvard Theological Review*. To Michael Fahey, S.J. (editor of *Theological Studies*),

David O'Brien (director of the Catholic Studies faculty at Holy Cross), Roger Haight, S.J. (convener of the Weston faculty colloquium), Dick Blake, S.J. (convener of Boston College's faculty seminar), and to the editors of the *Harvard Theological Review* as well as to the faculty members at their institutions who offered helpful critiques, I acknowledge my debt.

During the Fall 2002 semester I was (quite happily) Visiting Scholar at the Weston Jesuit School of Theology in Cambridge, Massachusetts: Robert Manning, S.J., Randy Sachs, S.J., and John Privett, S.J., offered me generous hospitality and wonderful technical and scholarly support, as well as welcome ears to my musings on research over lunch in the faculty lunch rooms at 3 Phillips Place and 42 Kirkland Street. Likewise, several members of Weston's faculty — John O'Malley, S.J., Jim Keenan, S.J., and Paul Crowley, S.J. — offered welcome insight on several chapters then in progress. I found Weston to be both intellectually stimulating and wonderfully friendly, and I thank everyone there who made my semester both academically fruitful and personally engaging.

Monsignor Dennis Sheehan, pastor of St. Paul's Parish in Cambridge, Massachusetts, head of Catholic Campus Ministry at Harvard University and perceptive observer of all things Catholic in Boston, offered a number of helpful suggestions on what is now chapter 10; likewise, Robert Dorin, S.J., read and critiqued that chapter through a number of revisions. Their thoughtful responses to my attempt to narrate one of the most tragic episodes in the history of North American Catholicism made the result (I hope) both more balanced and more focused, and I acknowledge my debt to their perceptive responses.

Finally, this book is dedicated to two friends and fellow Jesuits who, between them, have supported and challenged me for most of my adult life, Ned Mattimoe and Jerry Reedy. Ned was headmaster of Walsh Jesuit High School in Stowe, Ohio, when I began my teaching career amid high school sophomores; Gerry was the dean of Fordham College who (happily) hired me at that fine place. Both Ned and Gerry are themselves passionate intellectuals, skilled administrators, and first-class classroom presences — as well as dear friends. They were and are, as the dedication attests, the "best of teachers."

Index